The Philosophy of Pl[a]

Play is a vital component of the social life and well-being of both children and adults. This book examines the concept of play and considers a variety of the related philosophical issues. It also includes meta-analyses from a range of philosophers and theorists, as well as an exploration of some key applied ethical considerations.

The main objective of *The Philosophy of Play* is to provide a richer understanding of the concept and nature of play and its relation to human life and values, and to build disciplinary and paradigmatic bridges between scholars of philosophy and scholars of play. Including specific chapters dedicated to children and play, and exploring the work of key thinkers such as Plato, Sartre, Wittgenstein, Gadamer, Deleuze and Nietzsche, this book is invaluable reading for any advanced student, researcher or practitioner with an interest in education, playwork, leisure studies, applied ethics or the philosophy of sport.

Emily Ryall is Senior Lecturer in Philosophy at the University of Gloucestershire, UK. Her main area of expertise is in the philosophy of sport, in addition to an interest in broader ethical and conceptual issues. She is on the editorial board of the *Journal for the Philosophy of Sport* and has published work in peer-reviewed journals and edited collections as well as sole authored books.

Wendy Russell is Senior Lecturer in Play and Playwork at the University of Gloucestershire, UK. She has over 35 years' experience as a playworker, specifically in development, research, education and training. Her research interests focus on play, childhood, space and politics, and she is particularly interested in the dialectics of adult involvement in children's play.

Malcolm MacLean is Associate Dean (Quality and Standards), and teaches in the Faculty of Applied Science at the University of Gloucestershire, UK. His research work explores cultural politics, sport as a form of body and movement culture, and the political economy of knowledge production in contemporary higher education.

The Philosophy of Play

Edited by Emily Ryall, Wendy Russell
and Malcolm MacLean

Routledge
Taylor & Francis Group

LONDON AND NEW YORK

First published 2013
by Routledge
2 Park Square, Milton Park, Abingdon, Oxfordshire OX14 4RN

Simultaneously published in the USA and Canada
by Routledge
711 Third Avenue, New York, NY 10017

First issued in paperback 2014

Routledge is an imprint of the Taylor & Francis Group, an informa business

British Library Cataloguing in Publication Data
A catalogue record for this book is available from the British Library

Library of Congress Cataloging in Publication Data
The philosophy of play / edited by Emily Ryall, Wendy Russell and
Malcolm MacLean.
   pages cm.
   1. Play (Philosophy) 2. Play–Social aspects. I. Ryall, Emily.
   B105.P54P55 2013
   128–dc23   2012043800

ISBN 13: 978-0-415-53835-0 (hbk)
ISBN 13: 978-1-138-83387-6 (pbk)

Typeset in Goudy
by Wearset Ltd, Boldon, Tyne and Wear

To my family and friends who have always enabled me to realise a life worth playing. (Emily)

To my granddaughter Evie who has been the most delightful distraction and is a constant reminder of how to live a life as play. (Wendy)

For Buster, Harold, Stan and Ollie – who taught me it was possible to be serious and playful. (Malcolm)

Contents

Contributors

Núria Sara Miras Boronat is a Postdoctoral Research Fellow at the University of Leipzig (Germany). In 2009 she completed her Ph.D. in Philosophy at the University of Barcelona for a doctoral thesis on 'Wittgenstein and Gadamer: Language, Praxis and Reason'. She has written several essays on pluralism, American pragmatism, philosophy of film and feminism. She is currently working on a project on the history of the philosophy of play in the first decades of the twentieth century. She has also translated science fiction and philosophy books from German into Catalan and Spanish.

Chad Carlson, Ph.D., is Assistant Professor of Kinesiology and Sports Studies at Eastern Illinois University. His philosophical work is on metaphysical and axiological issues of play and games while his history research focuses on amateur basketball in the mid-twentieth century.

Barry Dixon is a Research Facilitator at Cambridge University. He is a recent graduate from Trinity College in Dublin where he completed a Ph.D. on the properties of Platonic dialectic. His current area of research stems from his Ph.D. thesis and is based on deciphering the rules of dialectic in Plato's 'middle' works. He has a keen interest in the hermeneutic philosophy of Hans-Georg Gadamer whose philosophy of 'play' continues to figure in his current research. He has tutored in Classics at University College Dublin, lectured in Philosophy at the National University of Ireland at Galway and worked as a Science Officer at the European Science Foundation in Strasbourg.

David Egan completed his doctoral thesis, which places Wittgenstein and J.L. Austin in dialogue with figures in twentieth-century continental philosophy, at Oxford in 2011. Since that time he has held teaching appointments at Oxford and McMaster University in Hamilton, Ontario. He is a recipient of the 2011 APRA Foundation-Berlin's Multi-Disciplinary Fellowship, and divides his time between academic work and play writing. He is co-editor of *Wittgenstein and Heidegger*, forthcoming from Routledge.

Randolph Feezell is Professor of Philosophy at Creighton University. His research centres on ethics and contemporary philosophy and he serves on the editorial board of *The Journal of Philosophy of Sport*. He is the author of *Sport, Play, and Ethical Reflection* (Illinois University Press, 2006); *Faith, Freedom, and Value: Introductory Philosophical Dialogues* (Westview Press, 1989); *Coaching for Character: Reclaiming the Principles of Sportsmanship* (with Craig Clifford, Human Kinetics, 1997); *How Should I Live?: Philosophical Conversations About Moral Life* (with Curtis Hancock, Paragon House, 1991).

Kevin Flint is Reader in Education at Nottingham Trent University and Chair of the Special Interest Group for Practice Led Research (www.professional-doctorates.org). His interests lie in European – particularly Heideggerian – philosophy which has provided a framework for rethinking the fundamentals of education. He has published work challenging dominant ideas of teaching and learning, on the performance culture in teaching, on technological framing in modern systems of improvement in education, on practice-based inquiry and the pervasive ethic of improvement, and on the development of professional doctorate.

Thomas Hackett was a newspaper and magazine journalist for two decades, writing for *The New Yorker* and *The New York Times Magazine* among many other publications, before seeking a Ph.D. in American Studies at the University of Texas at Austin. He has taught courses on play and on the culture of American sports, and is completing a dissertation on American football. He is the author of *Slaphappy* (Ecco/HarperCollins, 2006) and has written and directed two feature films: *Big Boy* (2011) and *Chloë & Claire at Sixes & Sevens* (2012).

Catherine Homan is a doctoral candidate in Philosophy at Emory University. She holds an MA in Philosophy from Emory University and a BA in Philosophy and German from Creighton University. Her current research interests include philosophical hermeneutics, aesthetics and the intersection of play and ethics. Recent conference presentations include 'Preserving Play in "The Origin of the Work of Art"', Conference at Collegium Phenomenoligicum, Città di Castello, July 2011; and 'Nietzsche's Playful Spectator', Philosophy at Play, University of Gloucestershire, April 2011.

Peter Hopsicker, Ph.D., is Associate Professor of Kinesiology at the Pennsylvania State University, Altoona College. His philosophical work is on the application of the tacit dimension of skilled motor behaviour, and his historical research focuses on Olympic and recreational use of the Adirondack Mountain range.

Stuart Lester is Senior Lecturer in Play and Playwork at the University of Gloucestershire, and an independent play consultant and trainer. Research interests include the nature and value of children's play, everyday playful production of time/space and the conditions under which playfulness thrives. Publications include *Play, Naturally* (with Martin Maudsley, National Children's Bureau, 2007), *Play for a Change. Play, Policy and Practice: A Review of Contemporary Perspectives* (NCB and Play England, 2008), and *Children's*

Right to Play: An Examination of the Importance of Play in the Lives of Children Worldwide (Bernard van Leer Foundation, 2010) [both with Wendy Russell]. He has also contributed to a number of play publications.

Malcolm MacLean studied anthropology and history with a Ph.D. from the University of Queensland, and is Associate Dean (Quality & Standards) at the University of Gloucestershire, where he teaches in the Faculty of Applied Science. He has previously taught history in New Zealand, and worked as a policy analyst and historian in the New Zealand Ministry of Justice. His primary research and teaching interests are cultural politics, sport as a form of body and movement culture, and the political economy of knowledge production in contemporary higher education. He has a particular interest in colonial and post-colonial settings. His publications deal with sports-related anti-apartheid protests, as well as in the cultural politics of settlement colonies and associated discourses of indigeneity associated with sport, body and movement cultures. Malcolm is actively involved in international sports studies networks and was Chair of the British Society of Sports History.

Maria Øksnes, Ph.D., is Associate Professor of Pedagogy at the Norwegian University of Science and Technology, Program for Teacher Education, Norway. She is fully trained as a pre-school teacher and her professional work has included work in early childhood education and care, after-school day-care services and teacher education. Her research interests relate to play, leisure, childhood, children, youth, dialogue, improvisation and resistance. She is inspired by the ideas of such thinkers as Michel Foucault, Hans-Georg Gadamer and Mikhail Bakhtin. She has published several articles and chapters on these topics. In 2010 she published her first book.

Rebecca Pitt successfully defended her thesis *Jean-Paul Sartre and the Question of Emancipation* in April 2012. She studied philosophy at the University of Essex and currently works at the Institute of Educational Technology, The Open University (UK). Her interests include feminism, Marxism, sexuality, phenomenology, critical theory, contemporary French philosophy and widening participation in philosophy.

Wendy Russell is Senior Lecturer in Play and Playwork at the University of Gloucestershire and a consultant on children's play and playwork. She has worked in the UK playwork sector for over 35 years, first as a playworker on adventure playgrounds, then in play development, research, and education and training. Her freelance work includes designing and delivering courses from entry to postgraduate level, and working on development, strategic, evaluation and research projects for local authorities, the private sector, and local, national and international voluntary organisations. Recent publications, co-authored with Stuart Lester, include *Play for a Change* (NCB, 2008) and *Children's Right to Play* (Bernard van Leer Foundation, 2010).

Emily Ryall is Senior Lecturer in Philosophy at the University of Gloucester-shire. Her main interests lie in the philosophy of sport and she has written and published on a number of topics in this area. She is author of *Critical Thinking for Sports Students* (Sage, 2010) and a forthcoming text, *The Philosophy of Sport* (Bloomsbury). She is also vice-chair of the British Philosophy of Sport Association and serves on the executive committee for the International Association for the Philosophy of Sport. She still manages to play rugby, despite the limitations imposed by her body.

Monica Vilhauer is Assistant Professor of Philosophy and Coordinator of the Gender and Women's Studies Concentration at Roanoke College. She earned her MA and Ph.D. in Philosophy at the New School for Social Research in New York. Her primary interests are in ethics, social-political philosophy, feminist philosophy, Ancient philosophy, and nineteenth- and twentieth-century European philosophy. She is author of *Gadamer's Ethics of Play: Hermeneutics and the Other* (Lexington Books, 2010), and is currently working on a new book project on Plato and desire.

John Wall is Professor and Chair of Religion, with a joint appointment in Childhood Studies, at Rutgers University, Camden. He is also Chair of the Childhood Studies and Religion Group at the American Academy of Religion. He is a theoretical ethicist who writes on moral life's relation to language, culture, religion and age. His books include *Ethics in Light of Childhood* (Georgetown, 2010), *Moral Creativity* (Oxford, 2005), and the co-edited volumes *Children and Armed Conflict* (Palgrave, 2011), *Marriage, Health, and the Professions* (Eerdmans, 2002), and *Paul Ricoeur and Contemporary Moral Thought* (Routledge, 2002). He is currently working on two further monographs: *Being and Making* and *Childhood and Democracy*.

David Webster is Senior Lecturer in Religion, Philosophy and Ethics. His main research interests are in Buddhist studies, the philosophy of desire, and issues of ageing, sickness and death in philosophy and religion. He is the author of *Dispirited: How Contemporary Spirituality Makes Us Stupid, Selfish and Unhappy* (Zero Books, 2012) and *The Philosophy of Desire in the Buddhist Pali Canon* (RoutledgeCurzon, 2005).

Acknowledgements

We would like to express our deep gratitude to colleagues who helped us organise the inaugural Philosophy at Play conference in April 2011 from which this book originated: Hilary Smith, Francis Barton, Kate Gordon, Leonie Labistour and Karen Benjamin. Thanks also to the University of Gloucestershire for supporting and hosting the conference, in particular Jane Cantwell and Mike Cogger. We would also like to say a very big thank you to those who have contributed to this book, and whose goodwill, good humour and good timekeeping have made our jobs much easier than they would otherwise have been.

Emily Ryall, Wendy Russell and Malcolm MacLean,
October 2012

Introduction

Who said that the philosopher is someone who watches the audience and not the stage at the *café chantant?*

This is what Umberto Eco has his protagonist – the thoroughly unlikeable Simone Simonini – ask in a contemplative aside in his 2010 novel, *The Prague Cemetery* (p. 162). In doing so he reiterates a view of philosophy both as socially grounded, grappling with the material world, and also as a second-level form of analysis exploring the hows and whys of those social and material aspects of life rather than, necessarily, the whats of more empiricist forms of knowledge. Simonini's aside has a more nuanced meaning, however. He asks his question in the context of his time spent meandering through Parisian *passages* where his focus is not on the shopping but on those he calls *suiveurs*, the men who watch the 'factory girls' who promenade. Simonini's image of Paris is one where *suiveurs* indulge 'factory girls' and life is understood watching the audience at the *café chantant*. This is the indulgence of the banal, the ordinary and the all-too-often-understood-as-meaningless. This is not a stereotypical and over-parodied image of the philosopher contemplating the meaning of Truth or Being from a chair in the corner of the senior common-room, but is Eco's more social view of the philosopher among the popular – a view also seen in essays such as those in *Travels in Hyper-reality* or *Five Moral Pieces*.

To discuss the philosophy of play is, in some senses, to take a step further than this version of the ordinary, the popular or the trivial to consider a ubiquitous phenomenon that is often seen as beyond reason. It is not work, which offends the sensibilities of industrial moralities; furthermore it is widely seen as the activity of children or at least childlike, which places it either in the context of learning or diversion, meaning that it is paradoxically justified (for children) and condemned (for children and adults) in instrumentalist terms. Both of these approaches place play beyond the norms that determine those things that are important, meaning that even when play is admitted to the legitimate realm of study it is often as the *object* of study, the subjects being those who play while on a path to somewhere else (be that adulthood or a state of being that is relieved of the stress caused by life in the modern world). When play becomes the *subject* of study, however, it takes on a new hue that allows it to be seen as an element of the everyday, the ordinary, the mundane and the taken-for-granted, or what, following Henri Lefebvre (1991: 86), we may consider to be 'the simple moments and the highest moments of life'. It is in this sense of the ordinary that the philosophical investigation of the richness and diversity of lived experience may be opened up, allowing, as Stephen Jay Gould (1987: 23) noted, the 'close observation of individual differences [that] can be as powerful a method in science as the quantification of predictable behaviour in a zillion identical atoms'. In this context, there is a risk that this approach may imply support for the assumption that a defining and necessary characteristic of play is that it is freely chosen, yet as some of the contributions that follow show, neither this assumption nor the necessity of free choice is valid; it is a contradiction that runs through play praxis, a tension between players and their play.

It was in the light of these kinds of issues that we became part of a group wanting to explore a variety of philosophical issues in play, leading to hosting a conference in April 2011 that saw a vibrant dialogue between philosophers who play and players who philosophise, comprising academics, play sector workers, policy advocates, analysts and others. As a sample of work from that dialogue, this collection includes meta-analyses of play from a range of philosophical approaches as well as an exploration of some key applied ethical issues. Its main objective is to provide a richer understanding of the concept and nature of play, and its relation to human life and value. It also aims to provide scholars and practitioners working in the spheres of play, leisure, sport, education, childhood studies and related disciplines with a deeper understanding of philosophical thinking and to open dialogue across these disciplines.

We make no claims for this collection being anywhere near the last word, but see it rather as dipping the toe in the ocean of philosophical play and playful philosophy in the hope that it may stimulate more work in the field. The themes and approaches of the papers received for the conference and subsequently those included in this collection demonstrate the way in which the subject of play may be considered from metaphysical, epistemological, ontological and ethical perspectives. They also draw from a range of philosophic traditions with contributions from Western ancient, analytic and continental standpoints, and which utilise the work of renowned philosophers such as Plato, Wittgenstein, Gadamer, Nietzsche, Sartre and Deleuze. By way of introduction to the papers included here, this Introduction offers an overview of what Western philosophy has had to say about play before outlining each of the contributions herein and considering the questions they pose.

In his seminal work on play in modern philosophical discourse, Mihai Spariosu (1989) contends that the history of Western philosophising on play may be understood alongside and in relation to the history of Western mentality, and that this has oscillated between a pre-rational and a rational pole, with cultural paradigm shifts occurring alongside periods of crisis in established values. The conventions of analytical and continental philosophy might be seen in this light, in which case it may come as little surprise that the continental philosophers, what Spariosu terms 'artist-metaphysicians', have had more to say about the nature and value of play's pre-rational elements, whereas analytical philosophy has sought to subordinate the emotional and unconstrained excesses of pre-rational play to its civilising role in rational ethics and epistemology.

In archaic, pre-Socratic, pre-rational Greece, play was the prerogative of violent, unpredictable gods who used people as their playthings. The primary pre-rational play concept is *agon*, the violent play of the forces of Nature (or gods) and the immediate competition of war, seen as the foundation of aristocratic virtues such as courage, endurance and physical strength. In its rational form, competition becomes mediated through symbolic sports and games with rules. Closely linked to *agon* is what Spariosu terms 'chance-necessity', sometimes referred to as *alea* (Caillois 1961) or *chaos* (Sutton-Smith 1997): the unpredictability of the *kosmos* and the struggle to survive against the whims of the gods and/or natural forces. In its rational form, this becomes rule-bound games of chance and risk-taking. In both *agon* and *alea/chaos*, might wins out in pre-rational forms, whereas justice and ideas of fair play regulate rational forms. *Mimesis* refers to what we now know, in rational play discourse, as performance and representations of life through various forms of art, literature or play. Spariosu suggests that pre-rational *mimesis* was less a representation of life and more an imitative performance intended to 'presence' something, in the sense of invoking or calling forth. This calling forth is generally to do with emotions: through ritualistic rhythms, music and other performance techniques, the audience identifies with the player and can experience the emotions being invoked. This idea still exists today in the arts, from the catharsis of tragedy through to the vitality of emotions aroused in horror films or comedies. An extension of the ideas of *mimesis* is the concept of play as an *as if* activity or way of being. In pre-rational *mimesis* this is through ritualistic simulation; in its rational form it is the play of reason as a part of creative cognitive processes in problems of knowledge and truth as seen in the work of Plato, Kant and Schiller. Spariosu's final play concept is play as freedom. In its pre-rational guise, this is linked to the unconstrained play of forces in *agon* and *alea-chaos*: the sense of freedom is closely linked to displays of power. In its rational form, freedom is both contained within social conventions (play as carnival, or specific situations where normal rules no longer apply) and is also seen as a release from everyday responsibilities – the dualism of play and work.

Ancient Greece and early Rome, seen as the dawn of Western thought, were predominantly pre-rational, whereas Hellenistic Greece and Imperial Rome were for the most part rational (Spariosu 1989). As an illustration, Plato's rational epistemology sees playing as the route to learning, not only for children but for philosophers too: philosophy *as* play. This is the rationalisation of *as if*, the interrelatedness rather than bifurcation of seriousness and play: playfulness is at the basis of Socratic dialogue and dialectic (Ardley 1967).

Such ideas re-emerge towards the end of the Age of Reason and into the period of German Idealism, although in forms reflective of their Enlightenment context. For Kant, 'mere play', such as in the competitive *agon* of metaphysicians, does not have a place in the necessary thoroughness of serious philosophy; however, a rational, rigorous and orderly form of *as if* thinking is used as a bridge between pure empiricism (in terms of understanding that which cannot be experienced) and the inevitable delusions of pure reason. This is a cautious endorsement of a particular form of playing aimed at higher order activity. Indeed, Kant (2006: 74) warns that overindulgence in play may lead to laziness, bad habits and a dulling of mental capacities.

Schiller (2006) develops Kant's ideas on the relationship between play and aesthetics, and suggests that what he calls the 'play drive' can mediate between natural, physical drives and logic, between animal sensuous experiences and rational, moral behaviour, to create both aesthetic and human potential. This is, again, a rationalisation of both *as if* and *mimesis* play forms, and although it extends Kant's original ideas beyond the cognitive into the sensual and prac-tical, it is still reason that dominates. Thus when play advocates quote Schiller as saying 'Man plays only when he is in the full sense of the word a human being, and he is only fully a human being when he plays' (letter XV, 9), this is only telling the rational half of the story. For, as Schiller develops his iterative argument in his *Letters on the Aesthetical Education of Man*, it becomes clear that he is not talking about all forms of play but a particular transcendental rather than physical form:

> [M]an is serious only with the agreeable, with the good, and with the perfect, but he plays with beauty. In saying this we must not indeed think of the plays that are in vogue in real life, and which commonly refer only to his material state.
>
> (letter XV, 7)

Laxton (2011) shows how Schiller's differentiation of 'good' and 'bad' play (together with his discussion on beautiful and vulgar art) reveals the elitist assumptions of his project for humanity. Rational forms of play are to be exalted, while pre-rational forms are to be constrained as mere play, a class-based theme that arguably persists today in the concepts of high and low (or indeed adult and child) culture.

If Plato, Kant and Schiller provide examples of the rationalising of play, then Nietzsche can offer a paradigmatic foundation for the return to pre-rational phi-losophising on play and power. For Nietzsche the world is at play, and this divine game is the chaotic, arbitrary, agonistic and violent play of the forces of the world and the Will to Power. He retains the aesthetic perspective of Kant and Schiller, but returns it to its original meaning of sensations (as the opposite of thought) rather than beauty, thereby inverting 'the Platonic-Kantian hier-archy of metaphysical values: the play of the senses and the imagination gains priority over the play of understanding and reason' (Spariosu 1989: 75). Logic, science and progress are, for Nietzsche, built on ideals of harmony and beauty – Apollonian ideals – that have become static and reified. Rather than being understood as universal truth, knowledge may be found in the constant dynamic *agon* between Apollo and Dionysus, the god of frenzy, intoxication and ultimately rhapsodic oneness with others and the world (Laxton 2011; Spariosu 1998).Through this return to pre-rational concepts and principles, Nietzsche lays the foundation for postmodernism and the ideas of many of the continental philosophers explored in the following chapters.

This collection provides a philosophical analysis of play that begins from abstract considerations of the concept itself and ends by shedding light on the value and meaning that play has in daily human life. Randolph Feezell begins this journey with a consideration of metaphysical accounts of play, since it is through understanding the nature of play that we are in a better position to recognise its significance. Beginning with Bernard Suits' analysis of play, Feezell considers five different conceptions of the term and concludes by defending a non-reductive and pluralist account. This pluralist approach is complemented in Chapter 2 by John Wall, who provides an ontological understanding of play from the perspective of the child. His 'childist' approach maintains that human playfulness is not reducible to irrationality, spontaneity, or use for work but rather is an avenue to create meaning in life. In Chapter 3, and expanding on Feezell's starting point, Emily Ryall examines Suits' analytic definition of play in more detail and assesses the critical responses it has received. Drawing upon the early work of Wittgenstein, she attempts to provide a defence of Suits' account of play from these criticisms. The work of Wittgenstein is also employed by David Egan in Chapter 4 when he argues against Rush Rhees' rejection of Wittgenstein's metaphor of 'language-game'. While Rhees believed that the metaphor was limited in its usefulness, Egan maintains that Wittgenstein's fluid understanding of the distinction between games and non-game play demonstrates how his conception of language as open-ended play enables new possibilities in moral debate and discussion. This relationship between language and game-playing is further explored by Barry Dixon in Chapter 5, when he demonstrates how Plato's philosophical method of dialectic, as presented in his *Gorgias*, provides key 'rules' as to how to engage in dialogue in a Platonically appropriate way. Dixon utilises the work of Gadamer in order to illuminate these rules, and Gadamer's conception of play is further drawn upon in Chapters 6 and 7 by Monica Vilhauer and Núria Sara Miras Boronat. In a theme that runs throughout this book in demonstrating the value of play to human life, Vilhauer argues that Gadamer's conception of play as the process of all understanding enables a greater understanding of others and opens up ethical possibilities. She argues that successful communication ('dialogue-play') requires an openness to the Other and to other truth claims as well as a readiness to challenge old prejudices and thereby be transformed. The work of Gadamer and Wittgenstein is further illustrated in Boronat's playful account of a fictional encounter between them that provides an informative and historical description of their contrasting lives and characters.

The work of other key philosophical figures is applied to the aesthetics and phenomenology of play in the ensuing chapters, with authors drawing upon Nietzsche, Sartre, Burke and Deleuze. In Chapter 8, Catherine Homan considers how Nietzsche's work sheds light on the role of play in artistic creation and artistic life from the perspective of the spectator. Stemming from Nietzsche's assertion that life requires both play and art, Homan argues that considering the spectator as player enables the 'will to power as art' that allows us to exercise our freedom. In Chapter 9, Rebecca Pitt provides a contrasting account of freedom through a largely unacknowledged analysis of play in the work of Jean-Paul Sartre, as given in two pages of his notable work, *Being and Nothingness*. Pitt argues that Sartre's critique and radicalisation of play has the potential to develop or challenge other definitions of play and reveals his work as a critique of, rather than statement about, our existence. This existential analysis is complemented by Thomas Hackett's consideration of the sublime in Chapter 10. Hackett utilises the work of Edmund Burke to argue that play is the realm of life best suited to dealing with our existential apprehensions, and presents us with self-affirming and self-realising occasions. Concluding these aesthetic and phenomenological enquiries, Stuart Lester (Chapter 11) provides an ostensive demonstration of Deleuzian theory in order to show that play is an avenue that opens up new possibilities, different ways of both being and becoming, and 'unheard of futures'.

The final chapters develop further these aspects or dimensions of play from applied or empirical perspectives. Through a synthesis of her empirical work with Mikhail Bakhtin's description of carnival, Maria Øksnes (Chapter 12) returns us to some of the ideas given in Wall's chapter, illustrating through her observations the ways in which children's perspectives on play might be understood as a sophisticated subversion of adult rules rather than the dominant adult expectations of its contribution to learning and development. Following this, Kevin Flint (Chapter 13) considers the place of play in today's information age by drawing upon the work of Derrida. Complementing some of the ideas in Lester's chapter, Flint argues that play may be seen as grounds for critical bricolage by enabling possibilities of the desire to make strange, to disturb and to destabilise everyday familiar ideas providing an alternative against the programmable, bivalent, digital information of today's world. In Chapter 14, Wendy Russell focuses on the paradoxical world of the playworker, whose role is to create space for children to play. Using Lefebvre's conception of the production of space, she explores the coexistence of planning assumptions, spatial practices and moments of playful disturbances of adult ordering of time and space. The relationship between adult and child in play is further explored by Peter Hopsicker and Chad Carlson (Chapter 15) in their consideration of parenthood, in which they assess some of the ethical questions that arise during an episode of parent–child pretend play. Finally, in Chapter 16 David Webster explores masculinity and the notion of 'kidult' in adult (classified 18+) video games. While many of these games appear to expose a masculinity of aggression and violence, Webster asks whether they might be an ally in delivering another kind of man, for another kind of world.

In the spirit of this collection as opening up debates and discussions, we are left wondering where this set of papers takes us in terms of what play does for philosophy and what philosophy does for play. At the heart of this is the ongoing issue of the effects on both of making play the *subject* of philosophical inquiry and practice. Central to this focus on play as subject are the ethical and inherently political questions raised by the recurrent presence of the Other in many of these papers; that is, the openness of play in and at play with the Other. Within dominant modes for discussing play, the most obvious and pressing forms of analyses of this alterity lie in the issues raised by John Wall's childism. This case suggests not just an ethical argument for hearing and prioritising children's voices in play but for making sense of play in terms of children's ontologies and epistemologies. This case makes profound demands on play studies in that it requires not just a methodological shift to hear children's voices in their own terms – as Maria Øksnes takes us towards – but also shifts in worldview to recognise the existence and legitimacy of the meaning-making that comes from children's standpoints. In this demand for a childist understanding of play, play studies has much to learn from the debates that surround feminist standpoint epistemology.

Limiting these alterity-based enquiries to childhood risks maintaining a narrow view of play as an object only of childhood. The tension here is two-fold; in the first the continuing association of play with childhood or childlike activities denies the possibility of other Others, notably adult play; yet a consequence of the dominance of rationalism and the derogation of the *agon* and *alea–chaos* dialectic is the false association of play with non-work. While not wanting to fall into the trap of equating middle adulthood with non-play, the condition of retired people as being in a state of non-work suggests rich potential for exploring many possibilities for adult play. Many of the settings for adult play are obvious, as David Webster notes in gaming and as Peter Hopsicker and Chad Carlson discuss when adults enter a child's world of play, and also in retirement homes, for instance, which regularly develop activities that are play-like for residents. Other sites of adult play are less obvious, and might include the extent to which political activists' engagements with and ways of doing politics become or resemble play, at either an individual phenomenological level or as political strategy and tactics. In the latter case, this may be seen in the activism associated with forms of situationism, from the notion of the beach beneath the street to the satirical interventions in the UK of Chris Morris in the *Brass Eye* television series, and the more recent *The Revolution Will Be Televised* series. In a similar manner, and drawing on Gadamer, the presence of play in festival and ritual suggests important areas for philosophical exploration of adult play (Grondin 2001).

The second tension related to the problem of conceiving play as only-of-children may be seen when play is held to be a disposition rather than an activity. The notions of 'play as a way to' and play as an articulation of Otherness are themes that run through much of this collection. Monica Villhauer's Gadamer-based call for playfulness as a mode of dialogue with Otherness, for instance, or Catherine Homans' exploration of the playful spectator in Nietzsche, suggest other ways to open up the philosophical exploration of play. Drawing, for instance, on Emmanuel Levinas' notion of the irreducible alterity of the Other points to a line of enquiry that goes beyond a sense of respect for 'difference' to a more profound critique that opens up a form of transcultural play space (to extend the Andamanese ethnography of David Tomas (1996)) that may be seen as a third space of anOtherness; neither self nor the Other but a new space (an other Other) of dialogic meeting-in-play that retains difference, transcends *différance* (see Flint's chapter) and offers opportunities for new ontological and epistemological modes that incorporate but do not subsume multiple forms of being Other. That is to say, drawing on Levinas' ethics of alterity may allow explorations of play as means not to transcend difference through tolerance, but to set difference aside through meeting in the now.

The strand of work drawing on alterity, in either its binary or more fluid post-modern forms, suggests further questions linked to its dialectical partner, mimesis. Many discussions of mimesis in play studies draw on a form of nostalgic discourse of loss, which as the anthropologist Michael Taussig suggests, may be seen as a theory of primitive magic highlighting an isolated 'world that we have lost' (Taussig 1993: 59), where the copy takes its power from the original. Yet the notions of play we see in Emily Ryall's and Randolph Feezell's chapters suggest that play's fundamental being relies on this sense of openness – that is, that openness, not just to a sense of Other but in some more fundamental way, is at the essence of play. When this openness is linked to the Sartrean notion of conversion which Pitt discusses or the Lefebvrean idea of disalienation in Wendy Russell's chapter, then play as open and free may be seen not in nostalgic terms as a mimetic copy of an original but as a mimetic anticipation of a non-alienated freedom – staying with Pitt and Russell's broad Marxist framework, as an experience of freedom that allows the individual player to overcome their estrangement from the species to enact a form of 'species-being' (Marx 1975). Taussig would suggest that this element of mimesis is a sort of 'invisible world' that it is in dialectical tension with alterity.

Conceptualising mimetic play in this sense – as neither nostalgic nor primitive magic but as mimetic anticipation – extends the point proposed by several contributors of play's autotelicity. It is this autotelic character of play that comes through many of these chapters most powerfully. It is at the centre of play-as-subject and remains the most problematic aspect of the notion of play as freely chosen. It points to a profound challenge for philosophical enquiries into play that need to address, in explicit terms, its ontological aspects: that is, to explore the question of play-as-being and of being-as-play not as the individualist freedom of the self to choose to play but as play as a form of collective association where, drawing on Deleuze (see Lester's chapter), play repeats but also defers suggesting repetition that is different from that which went before. It is in this sense that many of the chapters suggest that play may have some form of profound transformative potential.

It is the potential for transformation that suggests the final two areas where there may be productive philosophical enquiry into play. The first requires a shift from some of the current approaches to discussions of play by moving from a focus on modes of play to conditions for play. Although this issue is raised

most forcefully by Kevin Flint and David Webster in their focus on the technological form of the world and social circumstances of play, and by Stuart Lester
in his discussion of postmodern playgrounds, this question of conditions for play
pervades the applied aspects of almost all the chapters.

The final aspect of further enquiry in this context draws together several of
these themes derived from the invisible ('as if') world proposed by mimetic
activity and extends the principle of autotelicity to examine the extent to
which play both crafts other ways of being and manages a tension between
technē and *phronesis*. Play may be seen as both artifice (technē) and the making
of knowledge in general (phronesis), by 'truthfully' creating through the invisible world proposed by mimesis. Posing the question of play as technē, as craft,
allows for an interpretation of play as the space of the (Aristotelean) development of virtues over time, and as such further isolates play from the practice
only of children. Given, however, that many of the contributions, in their
emphasis, for instance, on autotelicity, propose play as a form of critique of
techno-rationalism, this technē–phronesis dialectic may also suggest a contradiction between positivism with its claims to truth, certainty and rational
empirical epistemologies and the uncertainty and vagueness of playfulness.
Technē's other pairing, with *poiesis*, also points towards mimesis where this
autotelicity anticipates an autopoiesis, an ontology in and of itself both being
and becoming – an invisible world proposed by play in an agonistic dialectical
relationship with techno-rationalism that takes us back to species-being or disalienation: play's liberatory potential.

In closing, we return to our opening metaphor: this collection dips its toe
into the ocean of philosophical play and playful philosophy, and in doing so
indicates the expansiveness of that body of water. Our concluding questions,
based in repeated readings of these essays and the discussions they have
prompted between us, are some of the ways in which we believe it may be fruitful to explore the limits and extent of our philosophical understanding of play,
our limited engagement with the range of playful activities and ways of being,
doing, thinking and experiencing that world. These are some of the ways in
which we believe we can collectively make sense of the challenges that
exploring play (a banal, ordinary, mundane and taken-for-granted phenomenon) poses to our world as it is currently mapped – but they are far from the
only ways. These challenges suggest that here, indeed, be monsters, and that
these monsters, like Maurice Sendak's Max's, are ones that are good to know as
well as being good to do and good to think.

Bibliography

Ardley, G. (1967) 'The Role of Play in the Philosophy of Plato'. *Philosophy*, 42: 226–244.
Caillois, R. ([1961] 2001) *Man, Play and Games*, trans. Meyer Barash. Urbana and
    Chicago: University of Illinois Press.
Eco, U. (1986) *Travels in Hyper-reality*. London: Picador.
Eco, U. (2002) *Five Moral Pieces*. London: Vintage.

Eco, U. (2010) *The Prague Cemetery*. London: Harvill Seecker.

Gould, S.J. (1987) 'Animals and Us'. *New York Review of Books*, 25 June.

Grondin, J. (2001) 'Play, Festival, and Ritual in Gadamer: On the theme of the immemorial in his later works', in L.K. Schmidt (ed.) *Language and Lingusiticality in Gadamer's Hermeneutics*. Lanham, MD: Lexington Books.

Kant, I. (2006) *Anthropology from a Pragmatic Point of View*, ed. R.B. Louden. Cambridge: Cambridge University Press.

Laxton, S. (2011) 'From Judgment to Process: The Modern Ludic Field', in D.J. Getsy (ed.) *From Judgment to Process: The Modern Ludic Field*. University Park: Pennsylvania State University Press.

Lefebvre, H. (1947/1991) *Critique of Everyday Life, Vol 1: Introduction*. London: Verso.

Leiter, B. and Rosen, M. (eds) (2007) *Oxford Handbook of Continental Philosophy*. Oxford: Oxford University Press.

Levy, N. (2003) 'Analytic and Continental Philosophy: Explaining the differences'. *Metaphysics*, 34: 284–304.

Marx, K. (1975) 'Economic and Philosophical Manuscripts, 1844', in *Early Writings*. London: Penguin.

Nietzsche, F.W. (1911) *Ecce Homo*, trans. A.M. Ludovici. New York: Macmillan.

Schiller, F. ([1795] 2006) *The Project Gutenberg EBook of The Aesthetical Essays, EBook #6798*. Online. Available at: www.gutenberg.org/files/6798/6798-h/6798-h.htm> (accessed 8 June 2012).

Spariosu, M.I. (1989) *Dionysus Reborn: Play and the Aesthetic Dimension on Modern Philosophical and Scientific Discourse*. New York: Cornell University Press.

Sutton-Smith, B. (1997) *The Ambiguity of Play*. Cambridge. MA: Harvard University Press.

Taussig, M. (1993) *Mimesis and Alterity: A Particular History of the Senses*. London: Routledge.

Tomas, D. (1996) *Transcultural Space and Transcultural Beings*. Boulder, CO: Westview Press.

1   A pluralist conception of play[1]

Randolph Feezell

The philosophical and scientific literature on play is extensive, and the approaches to the study, description and explanation of play are diverse. In this chapter I intend to provide an overview of approaches to play. My interest is in describing the most fundamental categories in terms of which play is characterized, explained and evaluated. Insofar as these categories attempt to describe what kind of reality we are talking about when we make claims about play, I hope to clarify the metaphysics of play. Once this categorical scheme is made clear, we will be in a better position to evaluate the task of definition, claims about the relation of sport and play, and assertions about the significance of play. First, I place the discussion in the context of Bernard Suits' account of play and some other recent approaches to play. Next, I distinguish the following approaches to play: (1) play as behaviour or activity; (2) play as motive, attitude or state of mind; (3) play as form or structure; (4) play as meaningful experience; and (5) play as an ontologically distinctive phenomenon. There is a natural progression in the way the analysis unfolds. In the final section I argue that my analysis generates a pluralist, non-reductive account of play.

The question of play

It may appear that there is very little new under the sun for a philosopher to say about play. This is in striking contrast to the growing science of play. In various scientific fields there are lively and ongoing debates about the evolutionary and neuroscientific bases of play, occasioning numerous research programmes and new theories about what's going on when animals and children, in particular, engage in playful behaviour. Scientists seem not to be as worried about the kinds of questions that worry philosophers, yet such questions cannot be ignored, except by stipulation. What is play? Can it be defined? How is it recognized? Is it good? Why is it good? How is play related to other significant cultural activities, such as art or religion? And, for our purposes, what is the relation between sport and play?

I have been impressed recently by the differences between more simplified accounts of play and the enormous diversity of play phenomena that are mentioned and studied outside of the philosophy of sport by scholars in various fields. While some philosophical discussions have focused on the canonical texts written by Johan Huizinga (1955) and Roger Caillois (2001), and have generated relatively broad notions of play involving a variety of characteristics, others have been suspicious of the supposed scope of play. Yet when some scientifically informed scholars have been forced to offer a definition or a philosophical account of play, they inevitably turn to Huizinga and offer at least a variation on a theme described in *Homo Ludens*.

Bernard Suits, eminent philosopher of sport and 'paidiatrician', has produced an account of play that some philosophical scholars of sport have largely taken for granted (1988a, 1988b, 1988c, 2004, 2005). His 'words on play' have been taken to be the final words, so to speak. It is against the background of his provocative early essay on play (as well as some later comments) that I wish to reconsider some issues concerning the unity and diversity of play, its relation to sport and its value.

In his essay 'Words on Play', Suits combines his interest in pursuing the traditional philosophical task of definition with his suspicion about claims concerning the scope of play phenomena. Why look for a definition of play? Why attempt to overcome Wittgensteinian objections to such a task? Suits responds: 'chiefly because a definition is a kind of restriction or limitation, and I believe that, ever since Huizinga began to find play under nearly every rock in the social landscape, quite a bit too much has been made of the notion' (1988c: 17).

Early on Suits offers three claims that are particularly relevant for this discussion. First, he agrees with the common view that play involves activities that are ends in themselves or desired for their own sake. All play is autotelic, as opposed to instrumental. Autotelicity is a necessary condition of play, but he denies that all autotelic activities are instances of play. 'In other words, I regard autotelicity as necessary but not sufficient for an adequate definition of play' (1988c: 19). Next, he denies that there is a logical relation between playing and playing games. Despite the fact that we speak of 'playing' games, he considers such usages to indicate merely that we are participating in a game; we may or may not be playing. For example, when we speak of playing a musical instrument we are indicating performance, not necessarily play. Sometimes game-playing is playing, but it may not be because of the autotelicity requirement. This leads Suits to say the following (which many take to be obvious – I don't):

> That one has to be playing in order to be playing a game seems equally implausible. When professional athletes are performing in assigned games for wages, although they are certainly playing games, we are not at all inclined to conclude from that fact that they are without qualification playing. For we think of professional athletes as working when they play their games and as playing when they go home from work to romp with their children.
>
> (Suits 1988c: 20)

Third, Suits recognizes that his account of play (which I will mention in a moment) is at odds with a variety of common usages, yet he insists that such figurative or metaphorical usages are nonetheless valuable. If we combine an account that places a boundary on the concept of play and an awareness of the vast array of ordinary usages of the word, we identify a helpful avenue of enquiry, 'since an explanation of how they are figurative requires a sorting out of the respects in which the thing at issue is, and the respects in which it is not, play or a game' (1988c: 22).

For Suits the sorting is relatively simple because we merely have to relate autotelicity (a genus) to the way in which we use resources in certain activities (a specific difference). For example, little Johnny is rebuked for playing with his food, a resource normally used for nutrition. Here is Suits' definition of play: 'X is playing if and only if x has made a temporary reallocation to autotelic activities of resources primarily committed to instrumental activities' (1988c: 22). According to Suits, when we temporarily reallocate any resource to intrinsically valued activities, including time or energy, we are playing.

For now, let us turn from Suits' words on play to some other recent words, written by, respectively, Colin McGinn, a very fine philosopher, Diane Ackerman, a very fine essayist and poet, and Stuart Brown, a very fine (I presume) medical doctor, psychiatrist and clinical researcher. First is a comment from McGinn, in a book about sport and a discussion of his attempt to improve his tennis game.

> Certainly, tennis, like other sports, is a form of play.... Play is a vital part of any full life, and a person who never plays is worse than a 'dull boy': he or she lacks imagination, humour and a proper sense of value. Only the bleakest and most life-denying Puritanism could warrant deleting all play from human life.... Play is part of what makes human life worthwhile, and we should seek to get as much out of it as we can.
>
> (McGinn 2008: 100–102)

In a beautiful book-length meditation on 'deep play', the most deeply absorbing and 'ecstatic' form of play, Diane Ackerman writes:

> The spirit of deep play is central to the life of each person, and also to society, inspiring the visual, musical, and verbal arts; exploration and discovery; war; law; and other elements of culture we've come to cherish (or dread).
>
> This book is not a conclusion but an exploration. It invites you to look closely at the human saga, and consider how much of it revolves around play.... Indeed, it's our passion for deep play that makes us the puzzling and at times resplendent beings we are.
>
> (Ackerman 1999: 26)

Finally, Stuart Brown, founder of the National Institute on Play, expresses thoughts based on forty years of conducting play studies and taking over 6,000 'play histories' of all kinds of people.

I have found that remembering what play is all about and making it part of our daily lives are probably the most important factors in being a fulfilled human being.

(Brown 2009: 6)

I don't think it is too much to say that play can save your life. It certainly has salvaged mine. Life without play is a grinding, mechanical existence organized around doing things necessary for survival. Play is the stick that stirs the drink. It is the basis of all art, games, books, sports, movies, fashion, fun, and wonder – in short, the basis of what we think of as civilization. Play is the vital essence of life. It is what makes life lively.

(Brown 2009: 11–12)

The world needs play because it enables each person to live a good life.

(Brown 2009: 201)

The contrast between Suits' attitude and approach and these enthusiastic claims about the value of play is noteworthy. When Suits considers play, he thinks there is much less there than meets the eye. He offers a tidy conceptual analysis which attempts to deflate the Huizingian notion that there is 'play under nearly every rock in the social landscape'. On the other hand, these contemporary 'playologists' (if I may coin a term) do see the pervasive influence and importance of play in human life. Huizinga was right, they tell us. Play is under a lot of rocks. Diane Ackerman makes the influence of Huizinga explicit. 'From time to time, this book becomes a fantasia on a theme by Huizinga, in which I play with some of his ideas, amplify them, follow their shadows and nuances' (1999: 18). Brown gets no further than Chapter 2 before he brings his own 'foundational definition' into relation with Huizinga's famous discussion (2009: 16–21). While McGinn does not explicitly mention Huizinga, his comments about entering a magical world with its own rules and goals, play and seriousness, freedom, and ridding ourselves of ordinary existence are well-known elements in Huizinga's analysis (2008: 100–102). One problem with Suits' approach is this. Should we accept his definition, we would have no idea, based on his account, why so much has been made of making a 'temporary reallocation to autotelic activities of resources primarily committed to instrumental activities'. We are left in the dark about the common forms and experiences of activities that typically involve such reallocation and why our neo-Huizingians value it so highly. Now contrast Suits' definition with Huizinga's frequently cited words on play summarizing his account. (This will be a useful reference for the following discussion.)

Summing up the formal characteristics of play we might call it a free activity standing quite consciously outside 'ordinary' life as being 'not serious,' but at the same time absorbing the player intensely and utterly. It is an activity connected with no material interest, and no profit can be gained by it. It proceeds within its own proper boundaries of time and space according to fixed rules and in an orderly manner. It promotes the formation of social groupings which tend to surround themselves with secrecy and to stress their difference from the common world by disguise or other means.

(Huizinga 1955: 13)

... play is a voluntary activity or occupation executed within certain fixed limits of time and place, according to rules freely accepted but absolutely binding, having its aim in itself and accompanied by a feeling of tension, joy and the consciousness that it is 'different' from 'ordinary life.'

(Huizinga 1955: 26)

It is evident from this brief overview of claims about play that there are different approaches to the study, description and evaluation of play. Undoubtedly there is a startling diversity of phenomena associated with play. A noted scholar of play, Brian Sutton-Smith, refers to the 'ambiguity of play' in his important book, but he is most interested in what he calls 'the ideological underpinnings of play theories' (1997: 3). My focus will be on the attempt to understand the diversity of play phenomena rather than the diversity of play scholarship and what he calls the 'rhetorics' or rhetorical underpinnings of different theories of play (1997: 1–17).

Approaches to play

1 Play as behaviour or activity

Diane Ackerman begins her book by saying, 'Everyone understands play'. In one sense this is not quite right, because there is considerable controversy about the question of definition. We can, however, wield the concept and recognize paradigm cases of play. That is because play is initially categorized as a kind of behaviour. It's something we can see or observe. It has been and continues to be extensively studied by scientists who are interested in both animal and human play. My son picks up our dog's chew toy and she immediately perks up, exhibits the 'play bow', paws outstretched on the floor with her rump raised in the air, and wants the toy to be thrown, after which she sprints to the toy, then coyly brings it back, waiting for it to be tossed again. Chimps exhibit a 'play face', analogous to the look of the joyous, smiling faces of children playing in the playground, running, jumping, skipping – spontaneous, improvisational, vigorous, unrestrained. Scientists tell us that play is prominent throughout the animal kingdom, not just in mammals. We are told that 'animal play researchers have established specific criteria that define play behaviour', and that 'most species have ten to 100 distinct play signals that they use to solicit play or to reassure one another during play-fighting that it's still all just fun' (Marantz 2008: 3). In more primitive forms, play is pure movement and motion, for no apparent reason. When animals are playing in the wild, they are not looking for food nor being attentive to threats from the environment. When children are playing, they are not living under the constraints of material needs or desires. They are 'just playing', freely and exuberantly. They appear to be enjoying themselves immensely, like the two juvenile grizzly bears in the Alaskan wilderness observed by Stuart Brown and Bob Fagen, an expert on animal play behaviour. Brown asks why the bears are playing. Fagen replies, 'Because it's fun.' Brown says, 'No, Bob, I mean from a scientific point of view' (Brown 2009: 27–29).

The exchange between the two is interesting because it both separates and connects the notions of animal behaviour and human activity, or play as behaviour and play as activity. Play behaviour in animals is 'apparently purposeless', as biologists claim.[2] When animals are playing they are not, apparently, engaged in any kind of instrumental activity associated with their survival needs. Their play may be 'fun', as the animal behaviour scientist claims, but there must be something biologically deeper going on. Because of the prevalence of play in animals there is the presumption that there must be some adaptive advantage associated with play behaviour. This generates scientific theories about the biological usefulness of 'apparently' biologically useless behaviour. When pushed, Fagen says, 'In a world continuously presenting unique challenges and ambiguity, play prepares these bears for an evolving planet' (Brown 2009: 15–16). Other scientists have added to or revised the play-as-preparation hypothesis, arguing that play contributes to neural development (the growth of the cerebellum and the development of the brain's frontal cortex) and more flexible and responsive brains.[3]

When we turn to human play, especially the play of children, we can ask the same sorts of questions about such behaviour. Play is unproductive insofar as it is not obviously pursued for the sake of satisfying material needs. It seems as wasteful and superfluous as animal play, a useless squandering of energy. We're animals, of course, so play can be studied from the standpoint of understanding the paradox of behaviour that is both apparently useless yet has some adaptive advantages. But behaviour may now be thought of as action, which human beings may explicitly and self-consciously choose to engage in at least at some point in development. It is still preconscious and preverbal in certain contexts and to a certain developmental stage, as Brown says (2009: 15–16), and extremely varied, but now it may be approached in terms of its unique phenomenology, which is described as extending from children to adults. The concept of 'apparent purposelessness' in animal behaviour leaves open the issue of play's biological usefulness and allows the scientist to speculate about animal psychology. The bears certainly appeared to be having fun. For human play, the concept of 'apparent purposelessness' leads naturally to the issue of what it means to choose an action for its own sake, or what it means to desire an activity as an end rather than as a means to some further end. It leads inevitably to considering psychological elements that are involved in playing; that is, engaging in intrinsically valued activities.

2 Play as motive, attitude or state of mind

For some philosophers of sport, like Bernard Suits (as we have seen) and Klaus Meier, it's a bit of a truism to say that play essentially involves an attitudinal component. The key to play is autotelicity, engaging in activities for their own sake or as ends in themselves. This involves the question of the de facto motives, reasons or purposes involved when activities are undertaken. According to Suits, play requires that an activity is valued for itself. Klaus Meier holds that 'autotelicity is both a necessary and sufficient trait' (1988: 50) for play.[4] As he says, 'I wish to provide a definition based on the orientation, demeanor, or stance of the participants' (ibid.). Play requires intrinsic reasons, and if our reason (exclusive? predominant?) for doing whatever we choose to do is intrinsic to the activity, it is play. 'Consequently, if games or sports are pursued voluntarily and for intrinsic reasons, they are play forms; if they are pursued involuntarily or engaged in predominantly for extrinsic rewards, they are not play forms' (p. 50). Angela Schneider echoes these views when she claims that judging an activity to be play 'is determined not by the nature of the activity itself... but rather by the attitude of the player toward the activity' (2001: 156). As she says, 'Playing is not a type of activity, but rather a mode of performing any activity' (ibid.: 158). These comments distinguish play as an attitude (or having an essential attitudinal component), and classifying an activity as play depends on the context within which it is performed in specific circumstances, rather than its structure.

This way of approaching play raises the issue of the relation between claims about play as an activity and play as attitudinal. Stuart Brown describes cases of golfers he has seen playing Pebble Beach who, instead of enjoying the experience of playing on one of the most famous and spectacular golf-courses in the world, transform what should be a highlight of their golfing experiences into misery and unhappiness. Brown denies that they are playing. 'They are self-critical, competitive, perfectionistic, and preoccupied with the last double bogey. These emotions don't allow them to feel the playful, out-of-time, in-the-zone, doing-it-for-its-own-sake sensation that accompanies joyful playfulness' (2009: 59). From our tennis matches to our pick-up basketball games, most of us have encountered the tortured player whose misery and unhappiness infects all those with whom he is playing. This leads Brown to say the following: 'Sometimes running is play, and sometimes it is not. What is the difference between the two? It really depends on the emotions experienced by the runner. Play is a state of mind, rather than an activity' (ibid.: 60).

This emphasis on the attitudinal component of play may be misleading. It may lead to confusion between an activity and an attitude. To say that play 'is a state of mind', as Brown does, doesn't really make sense if we interpret the claim literally. Play is an activity which may or may not require a certain kind of attitude, but the attitude isn't the activity itself. Would it make sense to say that we are playing when in fact we're doing nothing, perhaps paralysed in a drug-induced but affirmative haze of consciousness, glad to be experiencing paralysis for its own sake? (Assume no 'play of ideas' going on in the mind of the person.) If a person were hooked up to an experience machine (in Robert Nozick's famous thought experiment), electrodes attached to his brain, giving him mental states ('experiences') while he is floating like a blob in a tank, it would make no sense to say that the person could be playing. (Let us say he is being fed the joyful experience of winning the US Open in golf.) It would make more sense to say that the person has playful attitudes, or the 'state of mind' associated with play. The miserable golfers are doing something – they are playing golf, unhappily and without any joy. Better to say, as Suits, Meier and Schneider do, that play is an activity that requires a certain kind of attitude, or is defined in terms of the attitude we take towards the activity; that is, an activity engaged in as an end in itself or for intrinsic reasons.

Despite the fact that many philosophers of sport take this position to be obvious, some puzzling questions arise. If autotelicity is sufficient for play, as Meier insists, does this mean that we could, in principle, transform any activity into play? Would Sisyphus' interminable rock-rolling be magically transformed into play if the Gods injected a magic potion into his veins that caused him to identify with his pointless toil? How about an apolitical functionary who spends his free time volunteering at Auschwitz, enjoying the unpaid activity of marching the Jews to the gas chambers? Fun? Is he playing? We may say that these activities are play for these individuals, but, at the least, it strikes us that these are not the kinds of activities that are either commonly or even appropriately categorized as play, as they would have to be if autotelicity were sufficient for play. This raises the question of whether certain kinds of formal requirements might be, if not necessary, at least typical and causally relevant for appropriateness. It would be helpful to be able to say more about the form or structure of activities for which it would be appropriate to have intrinsic reasons to perform them. Recall Colin McGinn's comment: that tennis, like other sports, is a form of play. If I understand his claim, he holds that tennis, as such, is play, or sports, as such, are play activities. Suits finds these claims to be ridiculous. He says, 'I have never – anywhere – made, or even entertained the ridiculous assertions that some games or sports as such are play or that some as such are not' (2004: 9–10). It is not clear to me why it is ridiculous to assert that play activities may have formal or structural requirements. It is also unclear what sort of argument is offered for the view that autotelicity is necessary and sufficient for play, other than the claim that it is just obvious in paradigm cases. If the argument is ultimately a phenomenological one, the phenomena require a more nuanced and thicker description.

This line of argument leads to questions about mixed motives. Suits also seems to think it's obvious that when professional athletes are playing games, they aren't really engaged in play because they are being paid. They are working, not playing. As we will see, they are engaged in activities that have a certain structure, but if play requires autotelicity, professional game-playing is instrumental, not autotelic. Furthermore, Suits offers the provocative thesis that Olympic athletes, 'amateurs' in some sense, aren't playing when participating in

Olympic events, because they are acting under a compulsion to win the gold medal rather than being motivated to engage in their Olympic athletic activities simply for the sake of participation. Pick-up games are autotelic; highly competitive Olympic events are not. Suits says, 'I am suggesting that acting under such a compulsion, rather than the desire to win simply because winning defines the activity one is undertaking, is what turns a game that could be play into something that is not play' (1988b: 36).[5]

The problem is that when we engage in certain activities we may have a variety of motives. Even if autotelicity is necessary for play, it's not clear why an activity that has some external end couldn't also be desired for its own sake. Suppose I love to throw a rubber ball against a wall and catch it with my bare hands. I then develop some rules. I throw at certain angles, at certain spots, with certain velocities, and I see if I can catch the ball before it bounces a specified number of times within a defined space. I establish a point system. I love playing wall ball! I tell my good friend how much fun I have playing wall ball and he joins me. We develop our skills, play tense and competitive games, and deeply enjoy our encounters. Our friends hear about wall ball and want to watch, but we decide to make them pay for the pleasure of being spectators. Now we're professional wall ballers. We're admired. We establish a league. More people want to watch. According to Suits and many others, it makes no sense to ask whether wall ball, as such, is a playful activity, since it depends on participants' attitudes. Was wall ball transformed into 'work' as soon as I was paid? Suppose that I was extremely happy to be paid for playing wall ball, grateful that I could play my game for money, hopeful that I could continue to play, and that I never lost my love for the game. In fact, my attitudes could be quite complex. My desires could be characterized as conditional or hypothetical. I am happy to be paid for playing wall ball, but I would play even if I didn't get paid.

Consider another example, somewhat closer to home. My job is to teach and engage in philosophy. As an undergraduate I received no compensation for this. As a graduate student I received a stipend to study and teach. At one point, philosophy became my job, my work, yet doing philosophy is, in an important sense, something I do for the immense satisfaction it gives me. It's valued as an end, despite the fact that the activity can also be characterized instrumentally. It's something I would continue to do whether or not I am paid to do it. My motives are mixed; my attitudes are complex.[6]

Play is attitudinally more complex than Suits and others seem to think. Consider another aspect of this complexity. Wall ball, like other games, is strictly conventional. It's made up. Its rules are imaginative constructions which are the conditions for a certain kind of activity to occur; that is, conditions for playing wall ball. It's not work, art, science, religion, poetry, war, or anything else. As Huizinga says, 'it's not "ordinary" or "real" life. It is rather a stepping out of "real" life into a temporary sphere of activity with a disposition all of its own' (1955: 8). He's talking about play. I'm talking about wall ball as a form of play. Huizinga continues by giving the example of the young child playing 'trains', pretending that chairs are something other than 'real life' and urging Daddy to act accordingly. He says, 'This 'only pretending' quality of play betrays a consciousness of the inferiority of play compared with "seriousness," a feeling that seems to be something as primary as play itself' (ibid.: 8). Here I would speak of a distinctive attitude towards playful activities. They aren't 'serious', but, of course, they can be wholly absorbing and engaged in quite seriously. I have called such an attitude 'serious nonseriousness'.[7] Even professional athletes are sometimes pushed in times of crisis to admit the 'nonserious' character of their activity. A young Major League Baseball pitcher is killed in a car crash. One of his team mates comments sadly, 'This is real life, not baseball.' The attitude taken by the professional baseball player is essentially related to the form or structure of the activity, as if such an attitude is appropriate because baseball, as such, isn't 'real life'. Play is structurally nonserious.

One other element of attitudinal complexity is important. When the scientist is asked why the bears play, he says, 'because it's fun'. We may not be sure about bear phenomenology, but when we consider the play of children and adults, when we think of our youthful and grown-up play, it's natural to speak of fun, joy, enjoyment, or satisfaction. Brown says his miserable golfers didn't feel the 'playful, out-of-time, in-the-zone, doing-it-for-its-own-sake sensation that accompanies joyful playfulness'. The pleasure of play, however, isn't like the pleasure of sensations in which we take delight – the pleasurable sounds, tastes, smells and feel of ordinary experiences, for example, the pleasurable sensation of orgasm. Fred Feldman's recent defence of hedonism makes explicit what has been implicit in important historical accounts of the values and kinds of pleasure, including Epicurus' account of the good life. Feldman distinguishes sensory pleasure and attitudinal pleasure. Sensory pleasures are feelings; that is, pleasurable sensations. Attitudinal pleasures need not be felt. 'A person takes attitudinal pleasure in some state of affairs if he enjoys it, is pleased by it, is glad that it is happening, is delighted by it' (2004: 56). Feldman gives the example of a person being pleased by the fact that there are no wars going on in the world. I may be pleased by Barack Obama being elected President or I may enjoy the company of a good friend. Attitudinal pleasures are intentional and they need not have the 'feel' of sensations. 'We know we have them not by sensation, but in the same way (whatever it may be) that we know when we believe something, or hope for it, or fear that it might happen' (ibid.). (These are propositional attitudes.)

For many, sport is a rich source of attitudinal pleasure. It was for me and it continues to be. It is also clear that there is a close relationship between enjoying an activity and desiring to engage in it for its own sake. If we add that certain kinds of activities are such that their form or structure occasions an attitudinal recognition of being set apart from 'real life', then we have arrived at a more complex attitudinal account of play, whose elements may have an equal claim in locating or categorizing an activity as play. Why shouldn't we take the attitudinal recognition of the conventional nature of certain kinds of activities as sufficient for play? But now more needs to be said about the formal or structural elements in play activities. Whatever other motives or attitudes a person may have, if an activity is enjoyed, attitudinally recognized as not 'real life', and is intrinsically attractive, regardless of other motives, then there are good reasons to categorize it as play – independent of whether a person is also being paid to perform the activity.

3 Play as form or structure

The emphasis on form or structure redirects our attention to features of the activity itself rather than to the subjectivity of the player. It also makes way for an approach that emphasizes relational elements or the interplay between sub-jectivity and features of the activity. The emphasis on form or structure – here, lack of form or structure – first appeared in the description of animal behaviour and children's play as improvisational and spontaneous rather than mechanical and determined. Suits distinguishes between primitive play – the baby splashing water in the bath-tub – and sophisticated play, which involves rules and the development of skills (1988b: 30). Kenneth Schmitz categorizes play in terms of a continuum from the least formal to the most formal types: frolic, make-believe, sporting skills and games (1988: 30–32). Play need not be formal, but it often is. It is especially the game-like elements of formal play that are relevant when considering whether it is reasonable to claim that sports or games as such are play – despite the fact that Suits and others may believe that such assertions are 'ridiculous'. This is because it is plausible to claim, as Suits does, that 'the elements of sport are essentially – although perhaps not totally – the same as elements of game' (1988a: 39).

Suits' insightful and familiar account of the elements of playing games pro-vides the basis for an emphasis on play as activity having a certain form or struc-ture, and the claim that sport as such is activity having this structure. First, games are means–ends activities; they have a structure in which means are related to ends in a specified manner. There are goals that may be described independently of the respective games, such as a golf ball coming to rest in a cup, a basketball going through a hoop, a soccer ball entering a netted goal, or a football being carried beyond a certain point. But these goals may be brought about in a variety of ways. I may place the golf ball in the cup with my hand, climb a ladder to put the basketball through a hoop, and so on. Games are developed when means are limited by specific rules that prescribe and proscribe the ways in which goals may be brought about, transforming prelusory goals (pre-game goals) into lusory ends (ends intrinsic to the game), one of which is to win the game by achieving certain lusory goals. Since the means specified by the rules always eliminate the most efficient way to achieve a pre-lusory goal, games are quite unlike real life, in which efficiency is often the hallmark of rationality. Hence, because of their structure games do require an attitude that allows for the injection of gratuitous difficulty into life simply for the sake of the occurrence of the activity itself. Suits summarizes the elements of playing games in the following definition.

To play a game is to attempt to achieve a specific state of affairs (pre-lusory goal), using only means permitted by rules (lusory means), where the rules prohibit use of more efficient in favor of less efficient means (constitutive rules), and where such rules are accepted just because they make possible such activity (lusory attitude). I also offer the following only approximately accurate, but more pithy, version of the above definition: Playing a game is the voluntary attempt to overcome unnecessary obstacles.

(Suits 1988a: 43)

To say, as Huizinga does, that play isn't 'ordinary' or 'real life' or to claim, as Roger Caillois does, that play is both 'separate' and 'unproductive' is to acknowledge a formal or structural feature of play.[8] Formal play, by its very nature, is not instrumental, in the sense in which instrumentality is understood in everyday life. To say that play is 'superfluous', as Huizinga does, or to claim that playing games involves gratuitous difficulty or the overcoming of unnecessary obstacles, affirms the difference between a world of play, with its own meanings – its own requirements and delimitations of space or time – and ordinary life. To say that games aren't 'serious' is to equivocate, unless it is clear that nonseriousness may be either a claim about the structure of the activity or the attitude of the player. Caillois says, 'The confused and intricate laws of ordinary life are replaced in this fixed space and for this given time, by precise, arbitrary, unexceptionable rules that must be accepted as such and that govern the correct playing of the game' (2001: 7). When the professional baseball player speaks of death as a part of 'real life' compared with baseball (not 'real life') he is recognizing the difference between ordinary means–ends activities in life and the structure of formal play; that is, the playing of games. Some play is improvisational and joyous; other forms of play express our attraction to gratuitous difficulty and the value we place on overcoming obstacles, even unnecessary ones. Furthermore, many complex forms of play may well involve both: bursts of speed, creative physical movements and spontaneity within the limits of the rules of the game or activity.[9]

Suits ends one of his influential essays on sport, play and game by referring to a *New Yorker* cartoon in which an angry golfer is saying something to his partner: 'The caption reads, "Stop saying it's just a game! Goddamit, it's not just a game!" And he is quite right. For him, golf is not play, and so it is not, therefore just a game' (1988b: 36). I would say that Suits' comment misleadingly reduces play to activity defined merely in terms of an attitude, ignores the formal aspects of the game of golf that are relevant in determining its character as play, and diminishes the experiential complexity of the activity, which may also be relevant in our judgements about play. For me, the cartoon suggests that the golfer has a rather shallow appreciation of the playful possibilities that are available in the experience of playing golf – at least in this particular example. How are such possibilities described?

4 Play as meaningful experience

When we conceive of play as a certain kind of attitude that can be intentionally directed towards any kind of activity (object), or we think of play activity itself as having a certain form or structure, it is as if we are focusing on two poles or aspects of experience that are importantly related or whose interplay constitutes a richer account of play phenomena. For many descriptions of the features of play it is less misleading to speak of the lived experience of the player interacting with her environment or becoming experientially involved with something other than herself. When different aspects of play experience are described, at least some of these features are at the same time both formal elements of the activity and psychological features of the agent. To say that play is 'uncertain', as Caillois does, describes both the course of undetermined events and the experience of the tension of not knowing what will happen or who will win. For these approaches, a dualism that abstractly separates subject and object is phenomenologically inadequate, although some features may seem to focus more on one aspect of playful involvement than another. In the following, I will mention various characteristics of play without taking the time to offer an extended analysis of each feature – which would require considerable space. My procedure illustrates the difference between a focus on attitude or state of mind, which subjectivizes play, and experiential properties that are occasioned by involvements which require an account of that with which one is involved or which cannot be reduced simply to states of mind. After mentioning various characteristics, I will refer to some lists of properties, including Huizinga's (as we have seen) and Caillois', to make the discussion more manageable.

First, here are some features of play that have been emphasized and analysed in the expansive literature on the subject. Play is activity characterized by freedom, separateness, nonseriousness, illusion, unreality, delimitation of space and time, isolation, purposelessness, order, make-believe, a play world, superfluousness, suspension of the ordinary, internal or intrinsic meaning, inherent attraction, unalienated participation, internal purposiveness, serious nonseriousness, diminished consciousness of self, unselfing, absorption, responsive openness, attunement, experience of difficulty, overcoming obstacles, risk-taking, finitude, narrative structure, unity, contingency, possibility, uncertainty, spontaneity, improvisation – and fun. I'm sure I have not exhausted the possibilities!

Recall Huizinga's summary definition in which each part is significant and analysed at some length. Huizinga insists that all 'play means something' (1955: 1), and 'We shall try to take play as the player himself takes it: in its primary significance' (p. 4). When we attend to the experience of play, parsimonious descriptions are impossible owing to the experiential richness of these activities. The freedom of play is both attitudinal, in which a player deeply enjoys engaging in such activities, and experiential, in which involvement with a wholly conventional playworld separates a player from the cares of ordinary life. The experience of 'secludedness', 'isolation' or even 'tension' is the experience of structure and it is attitudinally significant. 'Experience' describes the abundant unity of meaningful activity (movement) and valuable intentional attitudes. Likewise, Caillois' list of the essential properties of play is best interpreted as an attempt to describe the essential experiences involved in the playing of games. Play is free (not obligatory); separate (limited in space and time); uncertain (outcomes aren't determined in advance and are due to players' innovations); unproductive (no new goods are created); governed by rules (conventional suspension of ordinary norms); and make-believe (an awareness of the unreality of the playworld) (2001: 9–10).

Although Stuart Brown claims at one point in his interesting recent book that play is a 'state of mind', when he initially and tentatively offers a 'foundational definition' of play, in large part for heuristic reasons, the properties he mentions richly combine claims about movement, attitude, structure and experience. Here are the properties he lists, along with a brief description of each.[10]

a   Apparently purposeless (done for its own sake)
b   Voluntary ('not obligatory or required by duty')
c   Inherent attraction ('It's fun. It makes you feel good.... It's a cure for boredom.')
d   Freedom from time ('When we are fully engaged in play, we lose a sense of the passage of time.')
e   Diminished consciousness of self ('We stop worrying about whether we look good or awkward, smart or stupid.... We are fully in the moment, in the zone.')
f   Improvisational potential ('We aren't locked into a rigid way of doing things. We are open to serendipity, to change.... The result is that we stumble upon new behaviours, thoughts, strategies, movements, or ways of being.')
g   Continuation desire ('We desire to keep doing it, and the pleasure of the experience drives the desire. We find ways to keep it going.... And when it is over, we want to do it again.')

Parts of Brown's list of properties are quite familiar after having considered briefly the seminal accounts of play found in Huizinga and Caillois. Some of the properties add additional or even new insights when we consider the experiential richness of play. The absorption described by Huizinga becomes 'diminished consciousness of the self' as players are fully involved in the activity of cycling, windsurfing, tennis, etc. Improvisational potential connects the frolic of animals and children to the openness and free play of possibilities in rule-governed play. The category of improvisation describes the phenomenology of movement, a certain kind of kinesthetic freedom. Continuation desire is connected to attitudinal pleasure and the structure of repetition emphasized by Huizinga. 'In this faculty of repetition lies one of the most essential qualities of play' (1955: 10). Games begin, are played out, even end, only to be repeated by players who want to continue playing, over and over again. When Brown speaks of freedom from time, the language is experiential rather than structural. Time is experienced differently because the time internal to the game – due to the way in which the game is temporally articulated according to rules – is often quite different from ordinary clock time. Play time starts and stops, speeds up and slows down, extends limitlessly, or is extinguished. Or, when we are absorbed in the activity, 'in the moment', we lose our sense of the flow of time even when the activity itself isn't articulated in terms of innings, periods, quarters, etc.

A final approach to play deserves to be mentioned because the notion of play as a meaningful experience, which unifies the different approaches to play as activity, attitude and form, may be a derivative notion, dependent on an ontologically distinctive account of play that makes experiential accounts metaphorical rather than literal.

5 Play as an ontologically distinctive phenomenon

In *Truth and Method*, Hans-Georg Gadamer is not primarily interested in the concept of play. He is centrally concerned with the question of truth and understanding in the human sciences. He attempts to give an account of hermeneutical consciousness that describes the proper role of the historicity of existence in human understanding. Gadamer's discussion of play is merely a moment in his attempt to provide an analysis of aesthetic experience, an analysis which itself is a part of his monumental account of an experience of truth that cannot be reduced to scientific methods of understanding. Gadamer says, 'the experience of the work of art includes understanding, and thus represents a hermeneutical phenomenon – but not at all in the sense of a scientific method' (1995: 100). His account of play is, however, significant.

Gadamer claims that play has its own mode of being and that play cannot be explained simply in terms of the subjectivity of the player. 'Play has its own essence, independent of the consciousness of those who play' (ibid.: 102). Gadamer argues that play is analogous to the way in which a work of art is fulfilled in the aesthetic experience of a spectator and is the real 'subject' of the experience. Play requires a player with a certain attitude in order to come into being, but play isn't reducible to the player's attitude: 'play merely reaches presentation (*Darstellung*) through the players' (ibid.: 103). For Gadamer, when we attend to apparently metaphorical usages of 'play', as when we speak of the play of light, waves or natural forces, 'what is intended is to-and-fro movement that is not tied to any goal which would bring it to an end' (ibid.: 103). It is a mistake, however, to think that these usages are figurative while our references to human or animal play are literal. The subject of play is play itself, not the subjectivity of the player. 'Play clearly represents an order in which the to-and-fro movement of play follows of itself. It is part of play that the movement is not only without goal or purpose, but also without effort' (ibid.: 104–105). The experience of freedom from the strains of ordinary life is the result of play playing itself through the player. 'The structure of play absorbs the player into itself, and thus frees him from the burden of taking the initiative, which constitutes the actual strain of existence' (ibid.:105). For Gadamer, the mode of being of play is a 'pure self-representation'. Nature, in its unceasing, purposeless movement, renewing itself in 'constant repetition', also exemplifies the being of mobility as self-representation. 'Thus in this sphere it becomes finally meaningless to distinguish between literal and metaphorical usage' (p. 105).

If Gadamer's approach seems unduly opaque and metaphysically obscure, consider the claim that his approach to play helps clarify the 'playful character of the contest' (p. 105). For those who deny that contests or competitive games can be play, he reminds us that 'through the contest arises the tense to-and-fro movement from which the victor emerges, and thus the whole becomes a game' (ibid.: 105). Gadamer's ontological approach clarifies the ordinary view that players (or spectators for that matter) can develop a love or respect for 'the game' as an independent phenomenon which is, in a sense, larger than the players, just as aesthetic appreciation or aesthetic experience recognizes the autonomy of a work of art standing over against the aesthetic consciousness as a demanding and authoritative presence.[11] The game or the work of art constitutes a reality in itself. 'In cases where human subjectivity is what is playing, the primacy of the game over the players engaged in it is experienced by the players themselves in a special way' (ibid.: 106). Gadamer's comment reflects the development of our discussion of the metaphysics of play, in which the subjective approach to play is chastened by references to form or structure. Gadamer's remarks ring true, both phenomenologically and ontologically, when he comments that the 'attraction of a game, the fascination it exerts, consists precisely in the fact that the game masters the players' (ibid.). The player gives herself over to the game, or, if there is some dispute about speaking of a 'game' in terms of the development of certain sporting skills, the player is taken up by her enjoyable experience of confronting gratuitous difficulties (or unnecessary obstacles). When the game is played, the 'real subject of the game... is not the player, but instead the game itself. What holds the player in its spell, draws him into play, and keeps him there is the game itself' (ibid.). Attitudes are intentionally related to the nature of the task required for playing the game. 'One can say that performing a task successfully 'presents it' (*stellt sie dar*)' (ibid.: 108). Hence, we again arrive at the notion that playing games (or overcoming unnecessary obstacles), insofar as they are purposeless – that is, ends in themselves – shows that: 'Play is really limited to presenting itself. Thus its mode of being is self-presentation' (ibid.). Gadamer summarizes his approach to play. 'We have seen that play does not have its being in the player's consciousness or attitude, but on the contrary play draws him into its dominion and fills him with its spirit. The player experiences the game as a reality that surpasses him' (ibid.: 109). Gadamer affirms the supposedly 'ridiculous' notion that sport, as such, conceived broadly as game-playing (in Suits' own sense) is play, ontologically interpreted as presenting itself in the tasks defined by the 'make-believe goals of the game', in Gadamer's words (ibid.: 108). Gadamer's account of play returns us to the first approach or moment in our discussion, when play is taken to be behaviour or action, some observable natural phenomena characterized much as

Gadamer describes, spontaneous and purposeless 'to-and-fro' movement. The scientist then explains the phenomena biologically or in terms of neural development, the social scientist or humanist explains it in human terms, and we are led, dialectically, down a path that leads to Gadamer's interpretation of the original phenomena, in which play is 'decentred' and taken to be ontologically distinctive, manifested in and through natural events, animals, children and adults.[12]

Now we are in a position to bring these approaches together in order to offer some conclusions about the nature of play, its relation to sport, and its value and role in a good human life.

Play, pluralism and good lives

We began our discussion by attending to some of Bernard Suits' 'words on play'. Suits, always playfully provocative, voiced suspicions about attempts 'to find play under nearly every rock in the social landscape', expressed doubts about those who make so much of the notion, offered his own attempt to place strict boundaries on the concept, and acknowledged that figurative uses of the word 'play' force us to explain the relevant similarities and differences involved when we speak of the 'play of light', the 'playful dog', 'child's play', 'playing a game' and 'playing professional sports'. The upshot of our examination of approaches to play is evident. It is no wonder that play is found under nearly every rock in the social landscape, given the multiplicity of possible approaches and the legitimacy of each to tell us something important, even if incomplete, about the concept of play. Each approach picks out relevant properties generated by taking a certain descriptive or explanatory perspective on play phenomena. Each may claim to be a total account of play only by ignoring the legitimacy of other perspectives. Because of the plurality of the ways in which we can approach play, each should be taken to be a significant contribution to a nonreductive account of play.

The new prophets of play, Brown, Ackerman and others, attempt to rouse us out of the doldrums of ordinary existence by awakening (or reawakening) in us moments of joy, exuberance, creativity, spontaneity, freedom, optimism, fun – often associated with activities that are usually a part of early life but somehow become lost along the way. In attempting to enliven us to the possibilities of playful experience, they connect play to a notion of a good human life. Recall the initial comments by McGinn, Brown and Ackerman. McGinn's comments on play are secondary; they arise in an intellectual memoir that is robust and confessional about the role of sports and games in his life, from childhood and adolescence through adulthood: marbles, trampolining, diving, pole vaulting, table tennis, bowling, pinball, fishing, squash, running, video games, lifting weights, skiing, kayaking, windsurfing, and tennis. Of course sport is play, he tells us. Brown and Ackerman are most interested in play, not sport, yet each assume in some of their comments that sporting activities are playful activities. Sport should be placed in the context of play and living well – joyously, freely, creatively. They call us to the possible enchantment of moments in our lives, when we are captivated by the absorbing activities that enable us to transcend everyday life, to 'suspend the ordinary', as Kenneth Schmitz described the 'essence' of play.[13]

So, is sport an expression of play? Should we understand sport in terms of the concept of play? As far as I can tell, there are two primary reasons given for resisting the relationship, one of which we have already examined. Both avenues of criticism claim that sport may be infected by desires that are incompatible with play. Many claim, as Suits does, that play for pay isn't really play, that professional sport is instrumental rather than autotelic. As we have seen, this view falls prey to the problem of mixed motives and the reduction of play to attitudinal considerations, ignoring the relevance of other properties, both structural and experiential. Activities may be characterized in complex ways and the rejection of professional sport as play on attitudinal grounds hides the ways in which such activities have play-like properties. Moreover, even if Suits and others are right about the dissociation of professional sport and play, in numerous instances in which people play sports, the activities embody many properties that are associated with play: freedom, separateness, absorption, purposelessness, etc.

The other avenue of criticism stresses the role of the desire to win in sports, rather than the extent to which sporting activities may be infected by elements that make sports one's work or profession. Suits also argued that the compulsion to win, even for supposed amateurs like Olympic athletes, is incompatible with the notion that play must be engaged in as an end in itself. The stronger version of this criticism comes from Alfie Kohn, who insists that any desire to win, not simply an overarching compulsion, disqualifies an activity from being play. For Kohn, play and competition are incompatible. Since sport, by its very nature, involves competition, sport and play are incompatible. Because play involves the familiar idea of choosing an activity for its own sake, play can have 'no goal other than itself' (1992: 81). Competition is rule-governed, often extrinsically motivated (by the desire for social approval), and is goal-oriented (a product orientation), rather than being a 'process orientation'. Therefore, because sport is competitive, 'sports never really qualified as play in the first place. Although it is not generally acknowledged, most definitions of play do seem to exclude competitive activities' (ibid.: 82). Kohn is undoubtedly correct to emphasize the dangers of competition, and the metaphor he uses is apt: 'Clearly competition and play tug in two different directions. If you are trying to win, you are not engaged in true play' (ibid.: 83). Yet there is more insight in his view when he resorts to metaphor than when he engages in essentialist pronouncements. There is no essence of play. If we recognize the multiplicity of relevant considerations involved when we attempt to understand play phenomena, we should resist Kohn's view that play can be neither competitive nor rule-governed. To say that play cannot be rule-governed seems to reduce playful activities to frolic. However, there are more or less formal modes of play which many have pointed out. Rules may be formulated to create noncompetitive games (leap-frog) or games in which there is an internal goal (winning) sought by participants if they intend to engage in the activity. To say that play cannot be 'goal-oriented' either reduces it to frolic or equivocates on the notion of the 'goal' of the activity in question. Certainly playing a game, attempting to overcome unnecessary obstacles, or freely confronting gratuitous difficulty, may be engaged in for the sake of the activity, even if the activity has an internal end that cannot be shared by the victor and the vanquished. Furthermore, overcoming obstacles within the game means that sport, construed as game-playing or skills development, is 'goal-oriented'. The process itself has internal products. The process may or may not also have extrinsic motives but those considerations must be placed along with others that count for or against our judgement about the way to categorize certain activities.

In the end, if we are reminded of the multiple approaches to play and the varieties of usages, both literal and figurative, that are involved when we refer to the concept of play, we are left with a framework within which to sort out relevant similarities and differences when we speak in terms related to play. I don't think that a pluralist account of play leaves things too open-ended; nor do I think that there are no constraints on what we call play. No doubt such an account does leave things more messy than Suits' essentialism suggests, but that is because of the complexity of the phenomena and the nature of the concept of play. Given what we have said about the variety of approaches to play, the fecundity of play phenomena, and the connection between play and a good human life, we should reinforce, whenever it is appropriate, the notion that sport is found in the neighbourhood of play. In addition, we should do this in order to encourage the enchanting possibilities of sport, play, and life itself. When we find that sport has strayed from its natural home, we must encourage the wayward child to come back from the world.

Notes

1 This article was originally published in the *Journal of the Philosophy of Sport*, 2010, 37, 147–165.
2 This is the first property of play mentioned by Brown (2009: 17), and it is also mentioned in the *New York Times* article by Marantz (2008: 3).
3 See Brown's (2009) discussion (esp. pp. 30–42, 47–73), and Marantz (2008).
4 I refer to the article as it appeared in *Philosophy of Sport*, edited by Holowchak.
5 I refer to the article as it appeared in *Philosophy of Sport*, edited by Holowchak.
6 Daniel Dombrowski (2009: 26) offers a similar argument:

> Nonetheless, I would like to offer a preliminary example to indicate some of the complex factors involved in judgments regarding amateur and professional. Unlike Socrates (Apology 19E), I am a professional philosopher in the sense that I get paid to teach philosophy and to read and write as a philosopher. I do not get paid a great deal, but certainly enough to live well. But at the same time I am an amateur in the sense that I love what I do and wake up every morning with a Bergsonian élan vital and a bounce in my step as I go to 'work.' I would philosophize even if I were not paid to do so; indeed, for many years I (along with many others) willingly studied philosophy without pay. Hence, my being a professional

philosopher does not strike me as being at odds with philosophizing 'for its own sake.' It is unclear to me why something analogous could not obtain for paid athletes who love their sport.

7 See Feezell (2004). I offer this description at various points in the book. See esp. ch. 4, 'Play and the Absurd', and ch. 5, 'Sport and the View from Nowhere'.
8 See Huizinga's definition, previously quoted, and Roger Callois (2001: ch. 1).
9 See Caillois' analysis of 'paidia' and 'ludus' (2001: 13, 27–35). Rules are inseparable from play as soon as the latter becomes institutionalized. From this moment on they become part of its nature. They transform it into an instrument of fecund and decisive culture. But a basic freedom is central to play in order to stimulate distraction and fantasy. This liberty is its indispensable motive power and is basic to the most complex and carefully organized forms of play. Such a primary power of improvisation and joy, which I call 'paidia', is allied to the taste for gratuitous difficulty that I propose to call 'ludus', in order to encompass the various games to which, without exaggeration, a civilizing quality may be attributed. In fact, they reflect the moral and intellectual values of a culture, as well as contribute to their refinement and development (p. 27).
10 See Brown (2009: 17–18) for the list of properties and any direct quotations.
11 See Mikel Dufrenne (1973) for an account of aesthetic experience which emphasizes the autonomy and demanding character of the aesthetic object, that is, the work of art as perceived. Dufrenne characterizes the being of the aesthetic object as an 'in-itself': 'it means that the object does not rely upon me in order to exist and that there is a fullness of the object which remains inaccessible to me' (p. 221).
12 See Drew Hyland (1984: 79–115) for an informative treatment of a 'decentred' approach to play, including a discussion of Gadamer, Fink, Derrida, Foucault and Nietzsche.
13 See Kenneth Schmitz (1988): 'The essence of play comes into existence through the decision to play. Such a constitutive decision cannot be compelled and is essentially free. Through it arises the suspension of the ordinary concerns of the everyday world' (p. 32). Of course, the pluralism generated by the analysis in the paper suggests that there is no 'essence' of play.

Bibliography

Ackerman, D. (1999) *Deep Play*. New York: Vintage Books.
Brown, S. with C. Vaughn. (2009) *Play: How it Shapes the Brain, Opens the Imagination, and Invigorates the Soul*. New York: Penguin Books.
Caillois, R. (2001) *Man, Play and Games*, trans. M. Barash. New York: The Free Press of Glencoe (1961). Reprinted (2001) Urbana, IL: University of Illinois Press.
Dombrowski, D. (2009) *Contemporary Athletics and Ancient Greek Ideals*. Chicago, IL: The University of Chicago Press.
Dufrenne, M. (1973) *The Phenomenology of Aesthetic Experience*, trans. E.S. Casey. Evanston, IL: Northwestern University Press.
Feezell, R. (2004) *Sport, Play, and Ethical Reflection*. Urbana, IL: University of Illinois Press.
Feldman, F. (2004) *Pleasure and the Good Life: Concerning the Nature, Varieties, and Plausibility of Hedonism*. Oxford: Clarendon Press.
Gadamer, H.G. (1995) *Truth and Method* (second, revised edn, trans. revisions J. Weinsheimer and D.G. Marshall). New York: Continuum.
Huizinga, J. (1955) *Homo Ludens: A Study of the Play-Element in Culture*. Boston, MA: Beacon Press.

Hyland, D. (1984) *The Question of Play*. Lanham, MD: University Press of America.

Kohn, A. (1992) *No Contest: The Case against Competition* (revised edn). Boston, MA: Houghton Mifflin.

Marantz, R. (2008) 'Taking Play Seriously'. *New York Times Magazine*, 17 February.

McGinn, C. (2008) *Sport*. Stockfield: Acumen.

Meier, K. (1988) 'Triad Trickery: Playing with Sports and Games'. *Journal of the Philosophy of Sport*, 15: 11–30. Also in *Philosophy of Sport*, ed. M. Holowchak (2002). Upper Saddle River, NJ: Prentice-Hall, pp. 38–54.

Schmitz, K. (1988) 'Sport and Play: Suspension of the Ordinary'. In *Philosophic Inquiry in Sport*, ed. W.J. Morgan and K.V. Meier. Champaign, IL: Human Kinetics, pp. 29–38.

Schneider, A. (2001) 'Fruits, Apples, and Category Mistakes: On Sport, Game, and Play'. *Journal of the Philosophy of Sport*, 27 (2): 151–159.

Suits, B. (1988a) 'The Elements of Sport'. In *Philosopic Inquiry in Sport*, ed. W.J. Morgan and K.V. Meier. Champaign, IL: Human Kinetics, pp. 34–48.

Suits, B. (1988b) 'Tricky Triad: Games, Play, and Sport'. *Journal of the Philosophy of Sport*, 15: 1–9. Also in *Philosophy of Sport: Critical Readings, Crucial Issues*, ed. Holowchak (2002) Upper Saddle River, NJ: Prentice-Hall, pp. 29–37.

Suits, B. (1988c) 'Words on Play'. In *Philosophic Inquiry in Sport*, ed. W.J. Morgan and K.V. Meier. Champaign, IL: Human Kinetics, pp. 17–38.

Suits, B. (2004) 'Venn and the Art of Category Maintenance'. *Journal of the Philosophy of Sport*, 31(1): 1–14.

Suits, B. (2005) *The Grasshopper: Games, Life and Utopia*. Peterborough, Ontario: Broadview Press.

Sutton-Smith, B. (1997) *The Ambiguity of Play*. Cambridge, MA: Harvard University Press.

2 All the world's a stage

Childhood and the play of being

John Wall

Play may be considered as a particular kind of activity, distinct, say, from work. Or it may be considered as a fundamental element of human being; that is, as expressed in some way in *any* particular activity. While these two senses of play are obviously related, it is this latter sense that I wish to focus on here. Call it an 'ontological' examination of play as a mode of *ontos* or 'being'. Such an exploration is not historically new; indeed, it has a long history and, as we will see, has intensified over the past century particularly in phenomenological philosophy.

My own contribution is to explore the ontology of play in light of the play experiences of children. You would expect to be able to learn a great deal about play from the one-third of humanity who are under the age of eighteen. In fact, contemporary philosophies of play tend to be based narrowly (if without always acknowledging it) on the experiences only of adults. Using an approach that I call 'childism', which I will say more about below, I wish to look not at how conceptions of play may be applied to children, but instead at how the experiences of children may be applied to conceptions of play. If philosophy is on some level about questioning assumptions, then considering the often marginalized perspectives of the young should be one of its most important practices.

In what follows, I first outline what I mean by childism, then examine three broad ways in which childhood has had an impact on philosophies of play throughout Western history, and finally use postmodern resources to develop a more fully childist and hence more fully human understanding of play. My chapter title, 'All the world's a stage', comes from the melancholy Jaques in William Shakespeare's play *As You Like It*. It is a sigh of lament at life's meaninglessness (Shakespeare 1951: 266). Can the experiences of children suggest, on the contrary, that the play of existence is precisely what makes life meaningful?

Childism

First, then, 'childism'. By this I mean something analogous, though not identical, to recent forms of feminism, womanism, environmentalism, queer theory and so on (Wall 2010). Children are a historically disenfranchised group whose experiences should both deconstruct and reconstruct inherited social norms. But since children's experiences are not the same as those of other groups, the methods and conclusions may be different.

Childism may be said to represent a 'third wave' of childhood studies, if I may borrow a feminist metaphor that is not in fact used in childhood studies itself. Just as 'first wave' feminism arose over a century ago with efforts by women to gain greater public voices, so also first wave childhood studies arose in the 1980s with efforts to study and include children's voices and agency. Of course, children have been objects of academic study as long as there has been scholarship, from the ancient Greek academy to twentieth-century developmental psychology. But the distinctive field that began to call itself 'childhood studies' (or sometimes 'the social sciences of childhood') – first among sociologists, anthropologists, and historians, and then across a wide range of disciplines – seeks to recognize children as not just pre-adults or adults-in-development, but as culturally diverse social actors in and of themselves. As Allison James and Alan Prout put it, 'children must be seen as actively involved in the construction of their own social lives, the lives of those around them and of the societies in which they live' (James and Prout 1997: 4). For example, a child soldier in Sierra Leone is not just a passive victim or someone arrested in development, but an agent who makes his or her own choices in the context of particular social and cultural constructs.

A 'second wave' of childhood studies may be identified with increasing efforts since the late 1990s to include children themselves as research and societal participants. Just as women made new inroads into work, culture, politics and academics starting in the 1960s, so also are children now beginning to be included as contributors towards scholarly research and conferences, children's parliaments, policy making, and other areas from which they were previously excluded (Percy-Smith and Thomas 2010). Children should not just be adult objects but also social and scholarly subjects. As Pia Haudrup Christensen puts it, childhood studies should adopt a 'dialogical approach' involving 'a shift toward engaging with children's own cultures of communication' (Christensen 2004: 174).

These 'waves' of childhood studies are significant achievements. However, as 'third wave' feminists began to recognize in the 1990s, when it comes to gender, even agency and participation face the limits of systematically structured oppression. The very playing field of a society – the very 'frame' of social understanding – has already been defined by historically dominant groups. While third wave feminism is multifaceted, thinkers such as Luce Irigaray, Judith Butler and Leslie Heywood make two important arguments for our purposes (Butler 1990; Heywood and Drake 1997; Irigaray 1993). First, there is no single normative femininity; instead it is globally, culturally, sexually, racially, religiously, and in many other ways diverse. Second, the goal of feminist research and activism is not merely to gain equality with men, but, more radically, to reconfigure historical power structures in response to issues of gender.

My view is that a similar third wave is needed when it comes to childhood. This I would call 'childism' proper. The goal here would be a political one: not only to understand children's agency and to welcome children's voices and participation but, in addition, and more radically, to deconstruct the ways in which agency and participation across societies assume a basis in experiences of adulthood, and then to reconstruct their global meanings in response to the particular experiences of children. Philosophy would then engage in self-critique in terms of not only gender, culture and ethnicity, but also age.

The best example of how this approach is already under way is in the area of children's citizenship, where scholars are now asking what it might mean, for example, for a seven-year-old growing up in poverty in the South Bronx of New York City to be treated as a full citizen; and concluding that citizenship itself would have to be reimagined, not as an expression of independence or autonomy, but as one of interdependence and learning (Jans 2004; Lister 2008; Moosa-Mitha 2005). In my own work, I have argued for a new methodology for childhood studies that may be described as a 'hermeneutical ellipse': an interpretive circle that never assumes a single centre of understanding, but is endlessly decentred in response to second centres of difference (Wall 2006).

Three philosophies of play

From this perspective, the philosophy of play turns out to have a lively if problematic history. One surprise is that Western philosophers have often learned a great deal from children. That is, arguments about human being, ethics, politics, aesthetics, epistemology and so on have sometimes been profoundly shaped by consideration of children's distinctive experiences. At the same time, these efforts to humanize children have also paradoxically led to various forms of children's dehumanization – and hence the dehumanization of humanity. I would like to suggest here that there are three basic ontologies of play that have persisted over Western philosophy (there are analogies in Eastern philosophies too, though I cannot examine them here), and that each has both its benefits and its drawbacks.

The top-down approach

One approach may be labelled 'top-down'. On this view, play describes human nature's childhood starting point as one of unruliness, passion and disorder. This original state of being requires rationality or divine law to be imposed upon it from above. Philosophical thinking and social practices exist to discipline and civilize humanity's original playfulness towards some higher order of being.

The most influential such thinker is Plato, who argues at length in The Republic and Laws that children are 'the craftiest, most mischievous, and unruliest of brutes', so that 'we should seek to use games [and play in general] as a means of directing children's tastes and inclinations toward the station they are themselves to fill when an adult'. Plato's famous censorship of the story-tellers is precisely because the play of imagination only encourages children and childlike adults to love changing appearances of truth instead of unchanging truth itself

(Plato 1961a: 1379, 1243; 1961b: 624). Another example is the fourth-century Christian theologian Augustine, who uses children's play to prove his central concept of 'original sin', games and amusements demonstrating pleasure in worldly creations rather than the true happiness of rest in the world's eternal Creator (Augustine 1961).

In a different way again, the Enlightenment philosopher Immanuel Kant argues that children's play exhibits humanity's fundamental subjection to desire and impulse, which may be overcome only by the self-discipline of learning to exercise autonomous reason. According to Kant's last published work, *Education*, children's 'very lively imagination ... does not need to be expanded or made more intense ... [but] needs rather to be curbed and brought under rule'; and 'playing with and caressing the child ... makes him self-willed and deceitful' (Kant 1960: 78, 50, 52–53). While such views may seem old-fashioned, they in fact remain very much alive today, both in popular movements for social discipline and order, and in philosophical arguments such as Alasdair MacIntyre's communitarian claim that children's love of games encourages individualism and needs to be redirected towards higher communal virtues (MacIntyre 1984: 188).

Such ontologies of play are both useful and problematic. What is useful is that children show that all human play involves real existential struggle: struggle with one's nature, passions, relations and very being. As in William Golding's *Lord of the Flies*, children's play is not automatically good but potentially destructive and violent. What is problematic, however, is that such approaches obscure the senses in which play may be socially creative. They discourage experimenting with desires and imagination in ways that might open up new meaning and relations. There is even something self-contradictory in asserting that human being starts out utterly disordered but should be able to pursue order as its higher goal.

The bottom-up approach

An opposed historical understanding of play may be called 'bottom-up'. This approach views play as the expression of humanity's basic goodness and wisdom, its natural or sacred spontaneity and simplicity. Play is an expression of human authenticity and should be nurtured from the ground up as a way of resisting the corrupting habits of the world. Metaphors here tend to involve plants rather than animals: the tender shoots of inborn innocence needing to be cultivated to survive and grow strong in the world.

There are again many examples. The Jewish Bible's Genesis story of Creation may be interpreted to affirm humanity's original playful innocence prior to its fall. In the New Testament, Jesus tells his disciples that 'unless you change and become like children, you will never enter the kingdom of heaven' (Matthew 18:3; see similar sayings in Mark 9:37 and Luke 9:48). Several early church theologians argue that adults should 'imitate' the playfulness of children so that they can become, as Clement of Alexandria puts it, 'simple, and infants, and guileless, … and lovers of the horns of unicorns', and unconcerned with mere worldly ambitions (Browning and Bunge 2009: 104).

A similar view is also evident in the eighteenth-century Romantic philosopher Jean-Jacques Rousseau, whose *Emile* and *Social Contract* depict children as 'noble savages' whose playfulness is the groundwork of morality and democratic liberty. 'Cultivate and water the young plant before it dies', Rousseau says; 'its fruits will one day be your delights'; and 'all of childhood is or ought to be only games and frolicsome play' (Rousseau 1979: 38, 125, 153). The founder of modern Protestantism, Friedrich Schleiermacher, claims that humanity's true 'gift' from God is its inborn playful openness and love (Schleiermacher 1959, 1990, 1991, 1999). Such a view also animates many of the late nineteenth- and early twentieth-century philosophers of play such as in Friedrich Fröbel (1891), Karl Groos (1912), Luther Gulick (1920), Johan Huizinga (1955) and Roger Caillois (2001). Huizinga, for example, argues in *Homo Ludens* ('playful humanity') that, as seen in children, 'the first main characteristic of play [is] that it is free, is in fact freedom' (Huizinga 1955: 8). Similarly, today's play theorist Stuart Brown claims that 'when we play *right*, all areas of our lives go better. When we ignore play, we start having problems. When someone doesn't keep an element of play in their life, their core being will not be light' (Brown 2009: 202).

Such ontologies of play have their strengths and drawbacks too. The main strength is that children's play is highly valued. Children's apparently fuller capacities for imagination, pretend, and invention are models of authentic human existence. They should be preserved in adult life and institutions. The drawback, however, is that play and childhood thereby risk being over-sentimentalized: placed upon an ethereal pedestal where children's actual lives are stripped of human struggle and complexity. As other historical 'minorities' have discovered, being a model of purity also means being sequestered into a separate sphere where this purity can be guarded. It obscures the actual complexity of children's play experiences.

The developmental approach

Finally, a third possibility arising from history can be termed 'horizontal' or 'developmental'. The developmental view is that play is neither wayward nor pure but rather a neutral instrument to be used for humanity's gradual improvement. Play is a means for individuals, societies, and history to make progress over time. Here the metaphors tend to consist, not of animals or plants, but of raw materials: blank pages, uncut jewels, lumps of wax, and the like that can be written upon or moulded.

Such a view is also far from new. Aristotle claims that children do not come into the world *ir*-rational but rather *pre*-rational, in a state of unformed natural potential. Children's play ought to be used for teaching them to find pleasure in virtuous rather than vicious habits (and in three successively more rational seven-year stages) (Aristotle 1947: 348 and 361; 1995: 294–96). A similar argument is made by the medieval Christian theologian Thomas Aquinas (1948:

II-II, Q. 10, a. 12, and III, Supplement, Q. 43, a. 2) and the medieval Jewish theologian Moses Maimonides (1904: chap. 54).

In modernity, John Locke argues in both *An Essay Concerning Understanding* and *Some Thoughts Concerning Education* that children start out life 'as white Paper, or Wax, to be moulded and fashioned as one pleases', so that 'all the Plays and Diversions of Children should be directed toward good and useful Habits, or else they will introduce ill ones' (Locke 1989: 265 and 192). Locke also argues that children's development is the basis of empirical science and democracy, since both rely on the human potential to play with new experiences over time. Today, developmental psychologists following Jean Piaget (1972) tend to understand children's play as important to becoming cognitively and morally adult. Brian Sutton-Smith interprets children's play in a similarly functional way as the basis of evolutionary development, in which play's 'function is to reinforce the organism's variability in the face of rigidifications of successful adaptation' (Sutton-Smith 1997: 231; see also Burghardt 2005, Cotter 2004, and Greenberg 2004).

The chief advantage of developmentalism, for our purposes, is that it connects childhood to adulthood along a shared play continuum. Children's play is neither to be overcome nor preserved but rather formed in new ways over time. The disadvantage, however, is that play is interpreted chiefly through the lens of the fully developed beings that children, by definition, *are not yet*. It is understood functionally as a means toward a future state of adulthood. This criticism is made by those in the field of childhood studies who view developmental psychology as having neglected children's own agency. More generally, play is not just a means to an end but a meaningful activity in and of itself.

Play as creativity

This historical typology is obviously too simple. It merely identifies persistent tendencies that continue to shape understanding today, even if they can also be combined in various ways. But it does demonstrate that efforts to include children's play in philosophy can be deeply paradoxical. The question posed to us by this history is whether we can learn from children's play without in the process obscuring childhood itself. Can we at least press these various insights toward new understandings of a deeper play reality? While I cannot presume to overcome my own adultism either, I do believe that play can be understood in a broader and more complexly childist way.

An example

I would like to start with a somewhat counter-intuitive example, one that may not seem like children's play but in fact helps us imagine more of play's ontological complexity. If play is an element of human being per se, then it should be found throughout the range of human activities and in many different forms. The following is merely one telling illustration.

Ying Ying Fry was born in Hunan province in China and adopted by a middle class family in the United States. She is one of millions of infant girls who were abandoned by their birth families because of China's one-child policy, designed to spur economic growth. It was likely a painful decision for her birth mother to leave her newborn outside a police station, and it was undoubtedly difficult for Fry herself to lose the only relationships she knew. The smells, sounds, and relationships into which she was born suddenly disappeared and were replaced by the new environment of a large government-run orphanage.

Fry herself tells this story of her infancy when she is eight years old in her book for children and adults titled *Kids Like Me in China*, which she wrote shortly after revisiting her old orphanage with her adoptive parents. While Fry does not directly remember her infancy, she describes what it must have been like in powerful ways: 'To get people to have small families, the [Chinese] government made some rules, and they're really strict about them. But the babies didn't do anything wrong! Why do they have to lose their first families? I don't think those rules are fair to babies' (Fry 2001: 2–3).

As both a newborn and an eight-year old, Fry must constantly 'play' with her own experiences and meaning in the world. As her infancy shows, she is shaped by untold layers of relationships, communities, policies, and histories. She is partly who she is because of her birth parents, her biological ancestors, the Chinese government, global economic systems, international adoption agencies, her adoptive parents in the United States, their own ancestors, their larger cultures and societies, and so on beyond any conclusive reckoning. At the same time, however, none of these conditions merely shape Fry passively. She also actively creates senses of meaning out of them for herself. As both a baby and an eight-year-old, she invests her complex and powerful surroundings with her own responses, ideas, and aspirations. She is both 'played by' and 'plays with' her worlds of meaning. She exists, in short, within an endless hermeneutical ellipse: a world that shapes the meaning of her experiences even as she in turn reshapes this meaning in new ways for herself.

This ontological experience that starts in childhood is not particularly well explained by history. Fry is certainly in part the plaything of unruly nature, but this does not mean that she cannot also play with her natural desires and feelings on her own terms. Likewise, while she clearly does play in the sense of acting freely and spontaneously, this does not mean she is somehow wholly pure or separate from the world, or relieved of painful struggle and imposing contexts. And while it can be said that she uses play to develop toward healthy adulthood, *to her* play is not just a means but also an end in itself. It is how she constructs meaning in each new experienced present. On any of the three traditional views, Fry's experiences of play are misunderstood.

Phenomenological underpinnings

A more complex sense of play can begin to be fleshed out using insights from postmodern phenomenology. There are two reasons for this. First, while phenomenological philosophers rarely in fact say anything about children, they do have new things to say about human being as 'play'. And second, what is new here is an effort to describe play in terms of concrete phenomena or *experiences*. Phenomenologists reject the Cartesian dualism underpinning modernity in which human being is divided into subjectivity and objectivity, inner reason and outer nature. They argue instead that human being is 'being-in-the-world': the experience of interactively belonging to relations, societies, and cultures. In other words, human being can be described as an experience of play in the world.

Interestingly, the three most influential phenomenologies of play mirror the three perspectives described above from history, even as they bend them in more interactive directions. Martin Heidegger and Hans-Georg Gadamer, for example, turn a basically top-down view of play into a description of human being's dynamic belonging to history. For Heidegger, play is 'the historical movement of Being,' the way that 'Being "toys with" man. The role of man [*sic*] is to "play along with" the play ... and man is caught up in that play' (Heidegger 1957: 206, quoted in Caputo 1970: 34). Or as Gadamer puts it, play is the movement of 'historical consciousness' that, in a somewhat 'tragic' way, is less 'something a person does' than something that 'absorbs the player into itself' (Gadamer 1989: 104–105 and 110). In contrast, Jacques Derrida argues for a more bottom-up ontology of play in which historical being is subjected to constant deconstruction or undoing. According to Derrida's more comic view, human being finds meaning only in 'the play of differences,' the presence of absences, the mischievous and disruptive 'movement of play that "produces" ... differences' of meaning in the first place (Derrida 1996: 441, 449, and 459). Finally, something akin to a developmental perspective (though this is a bit more of a stretch) is found in Richard Kearney's suggestion that play is the endless imagination of life's unfolding 'possibilities' (Kearney 2002). To be human is to play with continually new possibilities for meaning and thereby constructing over time a 'narrative identity woven from [one's] own histories and those of others' (Kearney 2003: 188).

While useful, what is strange about these philosophies of play is that, unlike throughout history, they entirely ignore the play of children. Against their own call for attention to differences of experience, they assume the rather narrow play perspective of adulthood. As the example of Fry suggests, each only touches on part of the proverbial elephant. She 'plays' with her world of meaning by all at once *being played by* her historical conditions, *playing with* their endless deconstruction, and *playing out* her own emerging narrative possibilities.

A revised phenomenology of play – revised along childist lines – would describe human being as playful in a more fully elliptical sense. To play is endlessly to recreate over time one's already created worlds of meaning. It is to participate, from birth to death, in the great ongoing drama of humanity's recreation of the meaning of its existence. If play is to include children, it must be understood as the capacity for decentering or stretching out one's historically given horizons of meaning according to one's own changing and particular lived experiences. As the chorus in Sophocles' *Antigone* declares: 'Many are the wonders, none is more wonderful than man.... He faces nothing that is to come without contrivance' (Sophocles 1991: lines 369–374). From humble acts of eating and conversation to powerful works of art and science, humanity plays with the meaning of its own being by constantly deconstructing and reconstructing it anew. This poetics of play or world-creativity is what it means to be human.

The play of philosophy

If play is this ontological capacity for world-creativity, then it has a range of implications for scholarship and policy. I would like here to briefly sketch three implications specifically for the field of philosophy.

First, play is not only a legitimate object of philosophical study, but also a way of describing what it means to think philosophically in the first place. Play is not unlike other experiences such as anxiety and love: it has particular characteristic expressions but also deeper ontological significance. The word 'play' in English already points in this direction, referring either to specific activities such as recreation, music, and theatre, or to a quality of experience itself such as expressiveness, spontaneity and engagement (the word's Germanic root *plegan* suggests self-engagement or risk). While philosophers are not normally thought of as either childlike or playful, in fact the practice of philosophizing comes down to reconstructing deep historical constructs of meaning. It is innovative in the profoundest sense. Philosophy is not just a professional occupation but also an activity of being human. And from this point of view, it is practiced by all human beings from birth to death. To think philosophically is to 'play with' the most basic meaning of being human.

Second, philosophy thereby finds an opening into questions of cultural diversity. Some argue that play is so culturally and historically specific as to defy generalization (Chudacoff 2007: xiii; Göncü 1999: 4; and Lancy 2007). Others claim in contrast that play lies at the very root of cultural expression itself (most famously Huizinga's assertion that play is the agonistic force behind the formation of civilizations) (Huizinga 1955: 4, 8, 10, 13, 75, 156, 173; see also Malaby 2009: 211). I would argue that both perspectives are right. Each is an expression of the more ontologically basic capacity to play with meaning. For children and adults alike, the ability to innovate and imagine new worlds is the grounds for the possibility of *both* culture as such *and* cultures' endless diversities. Culture is both universal and irreducibly differentiated because it represents human being as play.

Finally, the philosophy of play, so understood, has significance not only for ontology but also for ethics and politics. As I and others have argued, children are full moral beings who exercise empathy, seek justice and take responsibility for others around them (Bluebond-Langner 1996; Gordon-Smith 2009; Matthews 1994; Thorne 1993; Wall 2010). A childist account of play can help in formulating a more dynamic and child-inclusive ethics. From birth to death, the most fundamental obligation of human beings is to play amidst differences of experience in order to create more broadly expansive human relations. If human being is play, then being ethical is not reducible to merely accepting a higher order, expressing inner freedoms, or progressing in social rationality. It means responding ever more creatively over time to humanity's endless differences of experience. It means playing with relations to one another by reconstructing historical assumptions, imagining one another's different experiences, and endlessly striving to create more diversely inclusive worlds. While the Convention on the Rights of the Child affirms children's right to play (in Article 31), in a broader sense it is everyone's human right to play a part in the formation of their societies (Wall 2010: 113–138).

Conclusion

Whatever its particular consequences, the philosophy of play makes a vital contribution to understanding human being. Central to this contribution is its ability to deconstruct philosophy's historically limited adultist horizons and reconstruct them through childist critique. Not only has play functioned as an important lens through which philosophers have thought about human nature, but it has much still to learn from the complex play experiences of those who are newest to the world. Philosophy should play with these historically suppressed experiences. What it will learn is that play is not just an irrational, spontaneous or useful activity, but rather the grounds for the human possibility for meaning. If all the world is play, this does not mean that therefore life is pointless. On the contrary, it means that life is open to meaning's creation. Philosophy is not only *about* play. Philosophy *is* play.

Bibliography

Aquinas (1948) *Summa Theologica*, trans. Fathers of the English Dominican Province. New York: Benziger Brothers.
Aristotle (1947) *Nicomachean Ethics*, trans. W.D. Ross, in R. McKeon (ed.), *Introduction to Aristotle* (2nd edn revised and enlarged). Chicago, IL: The University of Chicago Press, pp. 346–581.
Aristotle (1995) *Politics*. New York: Oxford University Press.
Augustine (1961) *Confessions*, trans. R. S. Pine-Coffin. New York: Penguin Books.
Bluebond-Langner, M. (1996) *In the Shadow of Illness: Parents and Siblings of the Chronically Ill Child*. Princeton, NJ: Princeton University Press.
Brown, S. (2009) *Play: How It Shapes the Brain, Opens the Imagination, and Invigorates the Soul*. New York: Avery.
Browning, D. and M. Bunge (eds) (2009) *Children and Childhood in World Religions*. New Brunswick, NJ: Rutgers University Press.
Burghardt, G.M. (2005) *The Genesis of Animal Play: Testing the Limits*. Cambridge, MA: The MIT Press.
Butler, J. (1990) *Gender Trouble: Feminism and the Subversion of Identity*. New York: Routledge.

Caillois, R. (2001) *Man, Play and Games*, trans. M. Barash. Urbana, IL: University of Illinois Press.

Caputo, J.D. (1970) 'Being, Ground, and Play in Heidegger'. *Man and World*, 3(1): 26–48.

Christensen, P.H. (2004) 'Children's Participation in Ethnographic Research: Issues of Power and Representation'. *Children and Society*, 18:165–176.

Chudacoff, H. (2007) *Children at Play: An American History*. New York: New York University Press.

Cotter, M. (2004) 'A Closer Look at the Ontological Role of Play', in R.L. Clemens and L. Fiorento, *The Child's Right to Play: A Global Approach*. Westport, CT: Praeger, pp. 329–341.

Derrida, J. (1996) 'Différance', trans. D.B. Allison, in R. Kearney and M. Rainwater (eds) *The Continental Philosophy Reader*. New York: Routledge, pp. 441–464.

Fröbel, F. (1891) *The Education of Man*, trans. W.N. Hailmann. New York: D. Appleton and Company.

Fry, Y.Y. with Katzkin, A. (2001) *Kids Like Me in China*. St Paul, MN: Yeong & Yeong Book Company.

Gadamer, H-G. (1989) *Truth and Method* (2nd revised edn), trans. J. Weinsheimer and D.G. Marshall. New York: Crossroad.

Göncü, A. (ed.) (1999) *Children's Engagement in the World: Sociocultural Perspectives*. New York: Cambridge University Press.

Gordon-Smith, P. (2009) 'The Morality of Young Children in their Early Years Setting'. *Childhoods Today* Special Issue.

Greenberg, N. (2004) 'The Beast at Play: The Neuroethology of Creativity', in R.L. Clemens and L. Fiorento (eds), *The Child's Right to Play: A Global Approach*. Westport, CT: Praeger, pp. 309–327.

Groos, K. (1912) *The Play of Man*, trans. E.L. Baldwin. New York: D. Appleton and Company.

Gulick, L. (1920) *A Philosophy of Play*. New York: Charles Scribner's Sons.

Heidegger, M. (1957) *Der Satz vom Grund*. Pfullingen: Verlag Günter Neske.

Heywood, L. and Drake, J. (1997) *Third Wave Agenda: Being Feminist, Doing Feminism*. Minneapolis, MN: University of Minnesota Press.

Huizinga, J. (1955) *Homo Ludens: A Study of the Play Element of Culture*. Boston, MA: Beacon Press.

Irigaray, L. (1993) *An Ethics of Sexual Difference*. Ithaca, NY: Cornell University Press.

James, A. and Prout, A. (1997) 'Introduction', in A. James and A. Prout (eds), *Constructing and Reconstructing Childhood* (second edn). New York: RoutledgeFalmer.

Jans, M. (2004) 'Children as Citizens: Towards a Contemporary Notion of Child Participation'. *Childhood*, 11(1): 27–44.

Kant, I. (1960) *Education*, trans. A. Churton. Ann Arbor, MI: The University of Michigan Press.

Kearney, R. (2002) *On Stories*. New York: Routledge.

Kearney, R. (2003) *Strangers, Gods, and Monsters: Interpreting Otherness*. New York: Routledge.

Lancy, D. (2007) 'Accounting for Variability in Mother–Child Play'. *American Anthropologist*, 109(2): 273–284.

Lister, R. (2008) 'Why Citizenship: Where, When and How Children?' *Theoretical Inquiries in Law*, 8(2): 693–718.

Locke, J. (1989) *Some Thoughts concerning Education*, ed. J.W. and J.S. Yolton. Oxford: Clarendon Press.

MacIntyre, A. (1984) *After Virtue* (2nd edn). Notre Dame, IN: University of Notre Dame Press.

Maimonides, M. (1904) *A Guide for the Perplexed*, trans. M. Friedländer. New York: E.P. Dutton.

Malaby, T. (2009) 'Anthropology and Play: The Contours of Playful Experience'. *New Literary History*, 40(1): 205–218.

Matthews, G. (1994) *The Philosophy of Childhood*. Cambridge, MA: Harvard University Press.

Moosa-Mitha, M. (2005) 'A Difference-Centred Alternative to Theorization of Children's Citizenship Rights'. *Citizenship Studies*, 9(4): 369–388.

Percy-Smith, B. and Thomas, N. (eds) (2010) *A Handbook of Children and Young People's Participation: Perspectives from Theory and Practice*. New York: Routledge.

Piaget, J. (1972) *The Psychology of the Child*. New York: Basic Books.

Plato (1961a) *Laws*, in E. Hamilton and H. Cairns (eds), *The Collected Dialogues of Plato*. Princeton, NJ: Princeton University Press.

Plato (1961b) *Republic*, in E. Hamilton and H. Cairns (eds), *The Collected Dialogues of Plato*. Princeton, NJ: Princeton University Press.

Rousseau, J.-J. (1979) *Emile, or On Education*, trans. A. Bloom. New York: Basic Books.

Schleiermacher, F. (1959) *Aphorisms on Pedagogy*, in *Ausgewählte pädagogische Schriften*. Paderborn: F. Schöningh.

Schleiermacher, F. (1990) *Christmas Eve: Dialogues on the Incarnation*. Lewiston, NY: Edwin Mellon.

Schleiermacher, F. (1991) *The Christian Household: A Sermonic Treatise*. Lewiston, NY: Edwin Mellen.

Schleiermacher, F. (1999) *The Christian Faith*. Edinburgh: T & T Clark.

Shakespeare, W. (1951) *As You Like It*, in P. Alexander (ed.), *The Complete Works of Shakespeare*. London: Collins.

Sophocles (1991) *Antigone* in *Sophocles I* (2nd edn), trans. D. Grene. Chicago, IL: The University of Chicago Press.

Sutton-Smith, B. (1997) *The Ambiguity of Play*. Cambridge, MA: Harvard University Press.

Thorne, B. (1993) *Gender Play: Girls and Boys in School*. New Brunswick: Rutgers University Press.

Wall, J. (2006) 'Childhood Studies, Hermeneutics, and Theological Ethics'. *Journal of Religion*, 86(4): 523–548.

Wall, J. (2010) *Ethics in Light of Childhood*. Washington, DC: Georgetown University Press.

3 Playing with words

Further comment on Suits' definition

Emily Ryall

In 1977, as a development from his previous consideration of 'game-playing', Bernard Suits constructed a definition of 'play'. In direct response to (the later) Wittgenstein, Suits was of the view that it was possible to define these terms and he attempted to demonstrate this in practice; most notably through his seminal work, *The Grasshopper: Games, Life and Utopia* (1978). Despite receiving criticism from several positions about his definitions of both 'game' and 'play', Suits defended their precision and continued to offer ripostes against such attacks until his death in 2007. The purpose of this chapter is to consider Suits' definition of 'play' in the light of subsequent criticisms (Bäck 2008; Morgan 2008; Royce, 2011; Schmid 2011) and will conclude by offering a defence of Suits and his conception of play from one of the most unlikely places: from (the early) Wittgenstein, the author whose ideas he was inspired to challenge.

In *The Grasshopper*, Suits wished to respond to Wittgenstein's claim that the term 'game' cannot be defined, for in *Philosophical Investigations* (2001b) Wittgenstein maintained that a word must be understood in accordance with its use in language rather than defined with reference to necessary and sufficient conditions. Wittgenstein concluded that in attempting to define 'games', all that can be found are a series of family resemblances, not a set of necessary and sufficient conditions:

> Don't say: 'There must be something common, or they would not be called 'games' [1] – but look and see whether there is anything common to all. – For if you look at them you will not see something that is common to all, but similarities, relationships, and a whole series of them at that.
>
> (Wittgenstein 2001b: §66)

Suits' response was to chastise Wittgenstein for not looking hard enough. Thomas Hurka noted, in the Preface to the second edition, that Suits' book is a 'precisely placed boot in Wittgenstein's balls' (Suits 2005: 11). Indeed, Suits appears to demonstrate Wittgenstein's misjudgement by formulating a precise, analytic definition of the term 'game', a short one that states, 'game playing is the voluntary attempt to overcome unnecessary obstacles' (Suits 2005: 55), and a longer one which includes a detailed description of his four necessary and sufficient criteria of *goal*, *means*, *rules* and *lusory attitude*.

Following his definition of 'game-playing' (which he first proposed in 1966), Suits returned to consider the more foundational notion of 'play' upon which 'game-playing' seems to depend. He began by criticising Johan Huizinga's conclusion that 'all is play' (Huizinga 1970: 239), although he did accept Huizinga's assertion that one of the fundamental aspects of play is that it is a voluntary activity done for its own sake and not for any instrumental purpose (autotelicity). Nevertheless, Suits argued that in calling all autotelic activity 'play' one manages to side-step a definition, since it would include both a cat chasing its tail and Aristotle contemplating the existence of God. Both are autotelic activities yet it would be absurd to say that both are instances of play. Suits concluded that *autotelic activity* and *play* cannot therefore be synonymous. Autotelicity may be a necessary condition for play, Suits argued, but not a sufficient one. He proposed that an additional criterion is required which must be concerned with the notion of 'seriousness', something which Huizinga had also considered. Yet it is not so straightforward to say that one must be involved in a non-serious autotelic activity to be playing; for, as Suits acknowledged, many instances of play, namely game-playing, are taken very seriously. To overcome this issue Suits proposed that 'play' and 'game-playing' are not logically dependent. On this, Suits says,

> In contending that playing and playing games are logically independent, I mean that, even though game-playing very often is playing, one cannot conclude that because x is an instance of playing that x is therefore an instance of game-playing, and also that one cannot conclude that because y is an instance of game-playing that it is therefore an instance of playing.
>
> (Suits 1977: 120)

Suits reaches his conclusion by arguing that games and play are two different types of categories; 'play' is a relative term that can only be understood in a context against things that are not play, while 'game' is a non-relative term. The analogy he uses is between the relative terms 'light' and 'dark', and the non-relative term the colour 'blue'. Asking, 'what is the opposite of blue?' is as nonsensical as attempting to understand the term 'light' without reference to something darker.[2] Play therefore can only be understood in relation to things that are not play (work, for instance), whereas games can be understood in isolation. As such, two people could be involved in the same game: one which is playing, the other which is not. Suits maintains that when we denote that someone is playing, we issue a relative statement – we are tacitly saying that they are not treating whatever they are playing with (and this may be an object or the environment, or even time itself) in the way in which it should be treated, i.e. with the required level of seriousness. A game, however, may be taken seriously or not seriously.[3] In conceptualising play as a relative term, Suits argues that its relativity stems from an allocation of resources. Play, he argues, is a reallocation of resources from an instrumental to an intrinsic use; for instance, the use of a chair as a spaceship, or the use of a sweatshirt as a goalpost.

From this consideration, emerges Suits' definition of play:

> [A] temporary reallocation to autotelic activities of resources primarily committed to instrumental purposes.
>
> (Suits 1977: 124)

However, in recent years all aspects of this definition have been challenged, including the notion of autotelicity itself. The criticisms of those such as Bäck (2008), Morgan (2008), Royce (2011) and Schmid (2011) are persuasive to the extent that together they demonstrate the inadequacies of Suits' definition. Despite this, the purpose of this chapter is to show that Suits arguably does provide a comprehensive account of play in his *Grasshopper*, albeit through more subtle means than given in his analytic definition.

I will begin by outlining the criticisms of Suits' definition to illustrate in which ways it may be considered deficient. The first is concerned with his notion of 'reallocated resource' (e.g. the reallocation of a stick as a sword, or a pig's bladder as a football). Suits (1977: 121) himself recognised that there seemed to be an initial problem which stemmed from his notion of reallocation of resource, in that we can be playing without playing with anything in particular (for instance, when Jonny goes outside to play). Thus he overcomes this problem by including time as a resource. Yet, as Morgan (2008) notes, time is a necessary factor in *all* instances of play and therefore can always be the resource which is to be reallocated, thus making the criterion of 'reallocation' redundant.

Moreover, as Morgan rightly identifies, Suits' requirement of a reallocated resource produces a peculiar, and unpalatable, consequence. Since a baseball bat, for example, is *instrumentally* designed to hit baseballs, it is under Suits' definition, not an instance of playing. However, attempting to shove a baseball bat up your nose is, since that is not its primary instrumental purpose. Consequently, as Morgan notes, in the former example one would not be playing; in the latter one would be. This appears counter-intuitive, but it was a consequence that Suits accepted (1977: 124). This being the case, as Morgan contends, what Suits says in 'Words on Play' and what he actually argues are two different things: Suits says that games and play are logically independent but he actually argues that they are logically incompatible. According to Suits' definition, 'game-playing' can never be an instance of 'playing' because the resources are purposely designed for that game and not reallocated. This, as Schmid (2011) notes, is also the case for professional players who, according to Suits, can never play their sport. This seems an odd conclusion indeed. To return to Wittgenstein and the ideas expressed in his *Philosophical Investigations* (2001b), we end with a definition of a word that seems directly opposed to how it is usually used in our language. Suits' response may well be that we are being confused by our language; people can play (i.e. participate in) their sport but to say they are playing with or at their sport is to say they are not taking it seriously.

To help Suits overcome this problem, Morgan focuses on the distinction between objectively *instrumentally* valuable activities and objectively *intrinsically* valuable activities. Both are objectively valued by either being agent-neutral or agent-relative. That is, they are not valuable simply because of someone's subjective preference regardless of any of the features or characteristics of the thing-in-itself. Morgan's preferred conceptualisation of an objectively valuable activity is that for something to be agent-neutral the value must be contained within the object and not from a valuer's perspective, and for something to be agent-relative its value is conferred intersubjectively and thereby inherent within social practices.

In order to apply this to Suits' definition, Morgan returns to two of Suits' criteria for game-playing: *means* and *ends*. The means, by definition, are instrumental, since they lead to particular ends (winning or achieving a specific state of affairs; for instance, putting a golf ball into a cup). What is distinctive to games in comparison with other activities is that the ends cannot be separated from the means. The end of getting a ball into a cup only makes sense as the game of golf when it is done using particular means; starting at a designated point several hundred yards away, using long-headed sticks to move the ball, and avoiding man-made obstacles of sand and water. In contrast, the ends in instrumentally valued activities can be separated from the means. I value my car because it enables me to get to work, but if someone invented a teleport machine that meant I could get out of bed half an hour later, I would use that instead. Furthermore, the ends of games are trivial and arbitrarily chosen. There is no intrinsic value in getting a ball into a cup; rather it is the instrumental means that provides it with value.

Morgan maintains that this is how Suits can remedy the flaw in his definition whereby an instance of game-playing is logically incompatible with an instance of play. As the means and the ends are inseparable in game-playing, and a game requires the use of inefficient means, there is no need for further allocation of instrumental resource. In a game, as resources have already been reallocated, they, therefore, can be instances of play.

In response to Morgan, Royce (2011) argues that reconceptualising the reallocation of resources is unnecessary and it could be quite conceivable that when one is playing (i.e. being involved in) a game, it is not and never will be, an instance of 'play'. The difference between these positions (Suits' and Royce's to that of Morgan's) appears to stem from a differing emphasis on the notion of seriousness and non-seriousness (or triviality). Both Suits and Royce maintain that to play is to treat an activity with an attitude that recognises that it is not of ultimate value and that there are other activities that are of greater importance, whereas Morgan (and Schmid) take a more Wittgensteinian approach, and focus on the way in which the term 'play' is generally used in relation to games and sport. This issue of ultimate value is one that will be discussed further in response to Suits' conception of utopia.

Royce highlights two further problems with Suits' definition: first, with the concept of temporality. How, Royce asks, do we know whether a resource has been temporarily reallocated? Is this a relative or non-relative term? If the former, then relative to what? If the latter, then some further criterion is required. Since it seems unnecessary to answer these questions in relation to an understanding of play, Royce concludes that the term 'temporary' is superfluous to the definition. Royce's second criticism is again concerned with the terms 'reallocation' and 'primarily committed'. In particular, the criteria by which a primary commitment of a resource is to be determined. Is it, for instance, dictated by importance (subjective value) or design? To illustrate this problem, let us imagine that Jessica created an artefact to be used as an advertising tool (say, for a promotional photo-shoot) but it fulfilled the exact specifications of an implement to be used for a particular sport. If the photo-shoot is cancelled and Jessica decides to use it instead for her match that weekend, does that mean that she 'reallocated' her resource and, furthermore, does that mean that Jessica is 'playing' (by using the 'reallocated' implement), whereas Lewis (who is using a specifically 'game-designed' implement) is not 'playing'? Royce notes that this highlights the absurdity of the reallocation criterion. Furthermore, a resource *by definition* must have an instrumental purpose; otherwise it would not be a resource. Therefore, Royce concludes that it is not possible for there to be a 'reallocation away from an instrumental purpose to some other sort of *purpose*' (Royce 2011: 99).

Royce's concern with Suits' 'primary commitment' of a resource focuses on the way in which we determine value. This, Royce argues, is a further empirical problem with Suits' definition, which he labels the 'divided-priority' problem. The problem stems from a mistaken conceptualisation of human priorities that is founded on a particular historical notion of primitive man, and the more recent idealisation of the protestant work ethic. Royce maintains that it may be correct to apply Suits' definition to previous examples of human societies, but that does not make it necessarily true to human lives today. With welfare systems, and the abundance of food, clothing and leisure time, human priorities are no longer dictated towards survival. Indeed, the 'primary commitment' of most (Western) lives is not those things that enable survival but those things Suits had in mind that were contained within his definition of 'play'. Survival – in terms of the meeting of basic human needs – is no longer, according to Royce, a relevant issue and therefore the primary commitment of a resource, such as time, can be the means used to play.

So far, criticisms of Suits' definition have concentrated on the additional criteria that seem fundamental to the central one of *autotelicity*. However, Schmid (2011) maintains that this too is an unnecessary criterion. Schmid accepts Suits' conception of play as a relative term but argues that when we make the distinction between play and work we are making a value judgement, and it is this on which a definition of play should be focused.[4] One of the most fundamental aspects of play is that it is a voluntary activity, and its voluntariness dictates that we are assigning it a preference over other things. Schmid argues that one would *always* rather play than work. Work, by definition, is something that is a means to an end that allows us to pursue other, more desirable activities, for example, play. So far, this seems to be congruent with Suits' definition. Schmid, however, argues that Suits' conceptualisation of this (in terms of his notion of 'autotelicity') is off-focus. Providing an analytic definition of autotelicity is challenging, as Suits recognises when he accepts that autotelicity and play are not synonymous. Schmid contends that Suits is inconsistent in his definition; sometimes he argues that autotelic activities are ends in themselves; at other times they are intrinsically valuable, yet others require motivational reasons (which could be intrinsic or extrinsic; for example, pure enjoyment, or a means to an end (which may change over time)). As Schmid rightly argues, it is difficult to defend an objective, metaphysical account of autotelicity, since the concept must require an acknowledgement of states of mind and attitudes – things are of value *to* humans (be it intrinsically or instrumentally) because they hold particular mental states towards them. Yet, Schmid's psychological account of play maintains that the concept of value cannot simply be understood via emotional responses or reactions but must also consider the reasons provided by agents for valuing that particular activity. Reasons are not the same as feelings but provide a reflective account about intention and motivation behind the activity. This, according to Schmid, is a better way of understanding the nature of play and overcomes the problem with autotelicity. As Schmid notes, reasons and motivations for participating in an activity are fluid and can change even during the activity itself; for instance, a boy feeling joy while playing football indicates a value motivated by an intrinsic reason. When he hears his dad shouting on the sidelines he then becomes conscious of playing for his dad's pride which changes his motivation to an extrinsic one. Schmid accepts that we tend to value intrinsically motivated activities over extrinsically motivated ones (and therefore a definition of play should include reference to intrinsic reasons and emotions such as fun, joy, pleasure and satisfaction), but argues that these cannot be objectively, subjectively, or even intersubjectively fixed as those such as Morgan imply.

Furthermore, Schmid criticises Suits for attempting to exclude aesthetic appreciation and religious contemplation from his definition by arguing that they are not truly autotelic. Suits maintains that we value such things because they are thought to be 'good *for* us, and not solely because they are thought to be good in themselves' (Suits 1977: 128–129). Yet, as Schmid notes, if one is unable to conceive of those two activities as being autotelic it is far harder to consider that sport or games fit these criteria. Suits seems to suggest that only participating in sport and games for random – as opposed to rational – reasons would allow his definition to hold true in those accounts. As such, Schmid's view resonates with Wittgenstein's:

> The more narrowly we examine actual language, the sharper becomes the conflict between it and our requirement.... We have got on to slippery ice where there is no friction and so in a certain sense the conditions are ideal, but also, just because of that, we are unable to walk. We want to walk so we need friction. Back to the rough ground!
>
> (Wittgenstein 2001b: §107)

However, this is the extent to which Schmid and Wittgenstein share similarities. For Schmid's answer to the problem is not to 'stop digging' as Wittgenstein would suggest (2001b: §217) but to look to empirical methods via the psychological approach of Self Determination Theory (SDT). For Schmid, SDT enables the conceptualisation of play through collating the motivational reasons people have for participating in particular activities. According to Schmid's theory, the term 'play' can be correctly ascribed to an activity if the reasons a person gives for participating in that activity are founded on both autonomous action and a goal towards satisfaction and well-being. Schmid admits that this account seems quite vague, but says that attempts to be precise in a definition are bound to be unsuccessful. Yet, this merely serves to highlight the issue of attempting to solve a problem of language by turning to empiricism. It remains unsatisfactory in providing us with an adequate account of play itself. As Wittgenstein notes:

> The existence of the experimental method makes us think we have the means of solving the problems which trouble us; though problem and method pass one another by.
>
> (Wittgenstein 2001b: II xiv. 197)

There is one further problem with Suits' definition of play and this is one of Suits' final conclusions; that is, in conceptualising utopia as one that consists entirely of sophisticated play or game-playing.

Suits begins his definition in 'Words on Play' by making an immediate distinction between two types of play: *primitive play* (such as a baby splashing with water in a bath-tub) and *sophisticated play* (such as a game of chess), and it is the latter that leads him to the bold assertion that a utopian existence must necessarily consist in a life of sophisticated play, or game-playing. However, in making this distinction, perhaps Suits is not able to dismiss Wittgenstein as readily as he might have hoped. As Royce (2011) notes, 'primitive play' is defined by Suits as an activity which is 'not engaged in any instrumental enterprise' (Suits 1988: 2) whereas 'sophisticated play' is primitive play but with the addition of skills. This, Royce argues, therefore nullifies his definition, since it is pointing to an instrumental purpose, namely the acquisition and development of skill. 'Primitive play', as Royce understands it, is the purer instance of play, whereas 'sophisticated play' is play plus an additional criterion. Suits attempts to clarify this by identifying 'play' as that which 'is not concerned primarily with the exercise and enjoyment of skills, but with the introduction of new experiences that arise, usually, serendipitously' (Suits 1988: 2). The problem here, as Royce points out, is that Suits weakens his definition by using the terms 'primarily' and 'usually', as it is not clear how one can know whether an activity is an example of the primary or usual unless a definition is already in existence (and use).

This is noted by Allan Bäck in his essay entitled 'The Paper World of Bernard Suits' which focuses on Suits' conceptualisation of play as a relative term that can only be understood in relation to activities that are not play. In attempting to construct a definition, Suits intended to refute the postmodern claim that the world is only as we wish to describe it. Suits says this himself in his 'Words on Play' when he recounts Humpty-Dumpty applying whatever meanings to words that he wished. Suits' analytic approach was an attempt to represent the world as it is which would therefore leave space for a definition of play. Yet Bäck argues that Suits ends up doing exactly the opposite; he constructs a paper world rather than describes the real one.[5]

Although Bäck identifies an inherent flaw in Suits' conception of utopia, he is unreasonable and ungenerous in his criticism. Bäck (2008: 160) describes Suits' definition of play as 'doing things you value for their own sake' – intrinsically valuable activities – in contrast to work, which is 'doing things we value for the sake of something else' – instrumentally valuable activities. Yet, as we have seen, this is not Suits' definition at all. Nevertheless, Bäck uses this misrepresentation to return us to the Huizingan definition that Suits rejected.

It is worth reiterating Huizinga's definition that Bäck points to here:

> [play is] a free activity standing quite consciously outside 'ordinary' life as being 'not serious', but at the same time absorbing the player intensely and utterly. It is an activity connected with no material interest, and no profit can be gained by it. It proceeds within its own proper boundaries of time and space according to fixed rules and in an orderly manner. It promotes the formation of social groupings which tend to surround themselves with secrecy and to stress their difference from the common world by disguise or other means.
>
> (Huizinga 1970: 32)

When considered, this does not seem too far away from Suits' conception. Therefore one must ask: What was it that Suits so disliked about Huizinga's characterisation? Suits agreed with the notion that it must entail some kind of non-seriousness which later became his reallocation of instrumental resources. He recognised it as an autotelic activity similar to Huizinga's non-material interest, and understood that it involved some kind of relation to rules; indeed, he made it a necessary criterion for his definition of game-playing. It seems then that Suits' definition is not too dissimilar from Huizinga's after all. So what is Suits playing at – if you'll excuse the pun?

This is where I return to Bäck's primary criticism of Suits in his conceptualisation of utopia. Bäck argues that Suits' conception of utopia is nonsensical. He goes further in saying that 'the Utopia of the Grasshopper self-destructs into postmodern babble' (2008: 156). This to an extent is true. Suits' utopia does ultimately self-destruct. But I suggest that Suits himself realised this and intended it to be so (Bäck also acknowledges that this may be the case). Suits argues that the term 'play' is a relative one, yet in utopia there is nothing to be relative to, since all instrumental activities are eliminated. Nevertheless, Suits argues that the only activity left in utopia is the play of 'game-playing' when it is engaged in for purely autotelic reasons (that is, when it is not done professionally or to save someone's life). Arguably, Suits recognised the paradox he had created. At the end of his book, the Grasshopper has a final vision of the downfall of Utopia. He notes that eventually, people would come to conclude 'that if their lives were merely games, then those lives [are] scarcely worth living' (2005: 159). As Suits recognised, people want to believe that their lives have a purpose and therefore wish to believe that what they are doing is something more worthwhile than simply playing. But what this ultimate, intrinsically valuable goal is remains as paradoxical as ever, as Suits acknowledged at the end of both *The Grasshopper* and his 'Words on Play'.

Suits was wrong in his criticism of Wittgenstein, but then Wittgenstein himself held various positions in relation to understanding the limits of our language. In his *Tractatus* (the only work he had published within his lifetime) Wittgenstein attempted to clearly delineate the limits of language.[6] However, he later dismissed this attempt at doing so and suggested that language could not be defined in this way – rather, it had to be understood in accordance with the way it is used and with regard to our form of life (social and human context).[7] Wittgenstein's later account seems reasonable in the sense that the meaning of particular words must to some extent be a social activity. Indeed, he makes a very persuasive argument in *Philosophical Investigations* as to why it is impossible to have a private language (2001b: §293). Despite this, however, we are still left with the feeling that there is an essence to the meaning of words, such as 'play', which remains just beyond our grasp, as if we need to try harder to be able to reach it. It is here that *The Grasshopper* really emulates what Wittgenstein was doing in his *Tractatus* when he finishes his work with the following statement:

> My propositions serve as elucidations in the following way: anyone who understands me eventually recognizes them as nonsensical, when he has used them – as steps – to climb up beyond them. (He must, so to speak, throw away the ladder after he has climbed up it.)
>
> (Wittgenstein 2001a: §6.54)

The 'ineffability' reading of the *Tractatus* is that Wittgenstein was attempting to show or gesture at something that could not be said through language but still points to something profound or valuable. Such a reading of the *Tractatus* allows us to overcome the apparent paradoxes within his work and the same may be said for Suits' *Grasshopper*. Arguably, despite what Suits appears to profess in his Prologue, *The Grasshopper* is far more than a straightforward attempt to undermine Wittgenstein by providing an analytic definition of the term 'game'. More than anything else it is a demonstration *in itself* of what Suits defines as a game, and thereby an example of 'sophisticated play' in action.

While Bäck is scathing about Suits' work and brands him an evil genius (2008: 156), it seems that Suits' intent is far from malicious. Rather, *The Grasshopper* and his ripostes to critics seem to be a demonstration of his playful nature. Not with malevolence as Bäck implies but in a much more genial way, with good spirit and humour.

Those who have read Suits' book and have understood it as an attempt to engage Wittgenstein (or at least his supporters) in a game see that perhaps Suits is paying Wittgenstein an honour after all, in 'showing rather than saying', as Wittgenstein himself did with his *Tractatus*. That is arguably the real value and beauty in Suits' work, despite all its limitations and apparent contradictions.

Notes

1 It is necessary to note that the original German word here is 'spiel' which is much broader than the translation into 'game' and would also encompass the English 'play'.
2 Admittedly, it could be argued that there is an opposite of blue in colour theory, although these are generally called complementary colours. It might therefore be better to choose a different example to illustrate, such as 'What is the opposite of a bumblebee?'
3 However, we need to avoid a confusion that stems from the term 'playing a game'; rather, we should think of it as 'participating' or being 'involved' in a game.
4 Schmid's view is in opposition to Morgan's conceptualisation of value as something that can be objectively determined.
5 In fact, much of Bäck's essay is a derisive (and arguably unfair) criticism of Suits' attempt at a definition and of his *Grasshopper*, and furthermore of most of the work done in the *Philosophy of Sport* in looking at these concepts.
6 As may be seen in remarks made in his Preface: 'The whole sense of the book might be summed up in the following words: what can be said at all can be said clearly, and what we cannot talk about we must pass over in silence.' (2001a: 3)
7 As may be seen in the Preface to his later work, *Philosophical Investigations*: 'I have been forced to recognise grave mistakes, in what I wrote in that first book.' (2001b: x).

Bibliography

Bäck, A. (2008) 'The Paper World of Bernard Suits'. *Journal of the Philosophy of Sport*, 35: 156–174.

Huizinga, J. (1970) *Homo Ludens: A Study of the Play Element in Culture*. London: Paladin.

Morgan, W.J. (2008) 'Some Further Words on Suits on Play'. *Journal of the Philosophy of Sport*, 35: 120–141.

Royce, R. (2011) 'Suits, Autotelicity and Defining "Play"'. *Sport, Ethics and Philosophy*, 5: 93–109.

Schmid, S.E. (2011) 'Beyond Autotelic Play'. *Journal of the Philosophy of Sport*, 38: 149–166.

Suits, B. (1977) 'Appendix I: Words on Play'. *Journal of the Philosophy of Sport*, 4: 117–131.

Suits, B. (1978) *The Grasshopper: Games, Life and Utopia*. London: University of Toronto Press.

Suits, B. (1988) 'Tricky Triad: Games, Play and Sport'. *Journal of the Philosophy of Sport*, 15: 1–9.

Suits, B. (2005) *The Grasshopper: Games, Life and Utopia*. Plymouth: Broadview Press.

Wittgenstein, L. (2001a) *Tractatus Logic-Philosophicus*. London: Routledge.

Wittgenstein, L. (2001b) *Philosophical Investigations*. Oxford: Blackwell.

4 Playing well
Wittgenstein's language-games and the ethics of discourse

David Egan

Ludwig Wittgenstein famously compares language to a game, and suggests that language consists of a diverse array of 'language-games' which do not have any essentially common property. The claim that neither language nor games have an essence has been met with resistance. In this chapter I address a particular concern raised by Wittgenstein's pupil Rush Rhees regarding the unity of language. I argue that Wittgenstein's game analogy contains within it the means for addressing the distinction between discussion and sophistry that Rhees thinks Wittgenstein misses. This claim emerges from recognizing how Wittgenstein's understanding of games relates to the regular but unregulated activity of non-game play.

Games and play

Let me begin by drawing some distinctions. Games are a special case of play. Invariably, we 'play' games, but not all play consists of games. The most obvious difference between games and non-game play is that games are constituted and governed by a more or less rigid and explicit set of rules. John R. Searle (1969: 33f.) draws a distinction between constitutive and regulative rules: constitutive rules set up the institution and then the regulative rules lay out what one may, must, or must not do within that institution.[1] For instance, the constitutive rules of football tell us the dimensions of a pitch, the number of players on a team, the aim of the sport, and so on. Outside the institution of football, a football pitch is just a patch of grass and a player is just a person: the constitutive rules establish what Johan Huizinga (1995: 11) calls the 'magic circle' within which the patch of grass becomes a football pitch and the person becomes the player. Regulative rules, on the other hand, place restrictions upon how players can pursue the aim of the game: only the goalkeeper can legitimately handle the ball, for instance, and only within his or her own penalty area.

This notion of placing restrictions upon players is one part of a tripartite definition presented in Bernard Suits' charming book-length analysis of games, entitled *The Grasshopper: Games, Life, and Utopia*. According to Suits, games involve (1) a prelusory goal: an aim that can be defined independent of the regulative rules, whether it be to cross the finish line before everyone else, to checkmate the king, or to get the ball into the net more often than the other team; (2) lusory means: restrictions on how players can achieve this goal, whether it be that one must stay within one's lane, move pieces only according to certain rules, or not touch the ball with one's hands; and (3) a lusory attitude: the game is played for the sake of the game itself, and not due to some outside compulsion. Or, in his pithy summation, 'playing a game is the voluntary attempt to overcome unnecessary obstacles' (Suits 2005: 55).

Suits (and others) take this definition to stand as a knockdown refutation to Wittgenstein's claim that we cannot provide necessary and sufficient conditions for calling something a game. Responding to this challenge directly is not the aim of this chapter: for the moment I want to use Suits' definition simply to draw out the distinction between games and non-game play.

Non-game play is not unstructured – even the sort of child's play described as 'unstructured play' can have a surprisingly finicky structure – but this structure is never made explicit, and it is more fluid. Consider the 'platform and tilt' approach to improvised story-telling discussed by Keith Johnstone (1999: 89–100), one of the great developers and acknowledged masters of improvisational theatre. A story evolves by establishing a platform – a relatively stable world, cast of characters, trajectory, and so on – and then tilting this platform: introducing a new element or twist that disrupts the platform. This tilt then stabilizes into a new platform, which can then be tilted, and so on. A platform without tilts quickly becomes boring, and a series of tilts without any established platforms is disorienting, and also weakens each individual tilt because the tilt has nothing to disrupt. The art of establishing a clear and compelling platform and finding a surprising but appropriate tilt is tremendously complex, and no fixed rules dictate how one must proceed.[2] This sort of play lacks the constitutive or regulative rules of games, sharing with games only what Stanley Cavell (1979: 305) calls principles and maxims of good play.[3] The principles and maxims of improvisation do not direct players towards an already specified prelusory goal, but rather towards the more elusive aesthetic goals of good storytelling.

Not all play has as substantial a narrative element as improvisational theatre, but all play has a rhythm of a sort whose structure bears some resemblance to Johnstone's platforms and tilts. Children's play may shift rapidly in its focus (it may tilt), but at any given moment the children are fully invested in a particular structured activity (it has a platform). The themes and variations of improvising musicians also bear close resemblance to this structure of platform and tilt. To the extent that a platform has structure, it would presumably be possible for an observer to formulate rules that define the platform, but these rules do not explicitly guide the players, and so the observer could never be certain to have characterized the rules accurately. More importantly, no rules guide the direction of tilts. Some tilts may be habitual or predictable, but the creativity of play derives from the freedom players have not only to play within a given platform but to tilt it. The only restrictions guiding tilts is whether a tilt is taken up by the players and does not bring the play to a halt. The capacity for a tilt to perpetuate play depends as much on the players as it does on the particular tilt. One distinction between games and non-game play is that the rules of a game provide a stable platform – and one that is often explicitly formulated – while the platforms of play are constantly changing through unregulated tilts.

Games, play and rules in Wittgenstein

Wittgenstein famously compares language to a game, but much of what he says about language would seem to place his conception of language closer to non-game play. He frequently emphasizes that language users do not need to consult or obey rules in order to speak and that our criteria for using words are fluid. Nevertheless, he claims that the analogy with games still holds. Wittgenstein tells us: 'one can also imagine someone's having learnt the game without ever learning or formulating rules' (Wittgenstein 2009: §31) and returns to this point in §54 of the *Philosophical Investigations*. Several paragraphs later, he claims that games can evolve without anyone ever formulating rules:

> We can easily imagine people amusing themselves in a field by playing with a ball like this: starting various existing games, but playing several without finishing them, and in between throwing the ball aimlessly into the air, chasing one another with the ball, throwing it at one another for a joke, and so on. And now someone says: The whole time they are playing a ball-game and therefore are following definite rules at every throw.
>
> And is there not also the case where we play, and make up the rules as we go along? And even where we alter them – as we go along.
>
> (Wittgenstein 2009: §83)

One of the guiding themes of *On Certainty* is the mutability of our fundamental rules of thought and language. There, he likens the 'propositions describing [our] world-picture' to the rules of a game, and claims that we need never explicitly learn these rules (Wittgenstein 1975: §95). The following two sections lay out the famous river-bed analogy, whereby Wittgenstein claims that these propositions are subject to gradual change. As early as *Philosophical Grammar*, Wittgenstein acknowledges the fluidity of language: 'If we look at the actual use of a word, what we see is something constantly fluctuating' (Wittgenstein 1980: 77).

This conception of language as fluctuating points to a curious tension in Wittgenstein's use of games as an analogy: Wittgenstein uses both chess and open-ended play as examples when discussing games. The differences between the two are striking. The rules of chess are almost entirely constitutive, and regulative rules play a very small part. Illegal moves in chess are ruled out by the constitutive rules, so regulative rules are not required in the way that they are in sports where players have greater freedom of movement. Regulative rules play the much more limited role of requiring that a player say '*j'adoube*' before adjusting a piece, and so on. Chess clearly appeals to Wittgenstein as a source of analogy because language, like chess, is mostly devoid of regulative rules:[4] my conversation partner does not get a free sentence if I misplace a modifier.[5] By contrast, open-ended play has neither constitutive nor regulative rules, and often has only the most faintly defined aims.

This tension between the two sources of analogy, I suggest, is a consequence of Wittgenstein's understanding of rules, which reveals the boundary between games and non-game play to be more fluid than it might appear. In the sections on rule-following in the *Philosophical Investigations*, Wittgenstein suggests that how we follow a rule is a function not just of the rule itself, but also of how we apply the rule in practice. We could imagine a convention according to which we follow a pointing finger not by going in the direction of the outstretched finger, but in the opposite direction, as if following the line from the finger up to the outstretched arm (cf. Wittgenstein 2009: §85). However, just because alternatives are conceivable, we shouldn't conclude that every act of following a rule involves an interpretation. Such a conclusion leads to a regress: the interpretation is itself a rule – a rule telling us how to follow the original rule – and so itself stands as much in need of interpretation as the original rule.

The regress shows that it is not rules all the way down, so to speak: any rule-governed practice in turn manifests certain regularities that are not themselves governed by rules. Games feature rules in the sense that we sometimes appeal to rules in order to teach a game or to work through disputes, but we almost never need to appeal to a further set of rules that would tell us how and when to appeal to rules. People are able to participate in rule-governed practices together because they already share enough common ground that they are predisposed to following rules in similar ways.

This common ground is both discovered and created. In dealing with others, we come to learn how those others behave, how they react, how and towards what they register interest, surprise, fear, and so on. We learn how to deal with others partly through imitation and partly through finding our own ways of behaving, reacting, and so on. We learn to calibrate ourselves to others by interacting with them. This interaction and calibration does not itself follow any set of rules, since rules only emerge as a consequence of this interaction and calibration. It is unregulated activity that nevertheless gives rise to regularity. In a word, it is play. In playing, we discover and create regularities that come to constitute our social lives as criteria and norms. As Huizinga (1995: 10) remarks, play 'creates order, *is* order'. Our ordered world of criteria and norms is not something we are given, but something we play our way into.

In this respect, the regularity of games is not ultimately founded in their rules, but rather the rules themselves are ultimately founded in the unregulated regularity of play. The difference between a game and the sort of play Wittgenstein imagines in §83 of the *Philosophical Investigations*, then, amounts to no more than this: the play is less regular than the play of a game, and players neither teach nor justify their behaviour by appealing to rules that have already been formulated. Chess does not exhibit the irregularities of open-ended play because any attempt to play differently will be met with an objection from the other player, and that objection appeals to the rules. By contrast, open-ended play has as many irregularities as the players will permit without stopping play in disgust. For Wittgenstein, games are not a totally separate category from play, but rather a more regular form of play whose regularity is maintained by certain agreements, which, at a pinch, can be enforced by an appeal to the rules. The place of rules in a game is not as a fixed foundation that somehow stands outside the play of the game itself, but rather rules are a feature of how games are played: resort to rules is one characteristic of games. To echo Wittgenstein, the regularity of games does not reflect the inexorability of their rules, but rather our inexorability in applying them (cf. Wittgenstein 1978: I §118).

Consider the analogous case with language, and the question of how we determine whether a word is used correctly.[6] For the most part we speak freely with one another, without considering or appealing to the criteria that determine the correct use of our words. We teach others new words or new language-games not by providing them with an exhaustive list of rules, but usually through a series of examples or definitions, or whatever else we think is sufficient to ensure that they will go on as we do. Occasionally disputes or uncertainties may arise about whether we are speaking correctly, and one way of addressing these disputes is to appeal to a dictionary or some other equivalent to a rulebook. To what extent our use of words is regular, and to what extent it is open-ended, depends considerably on the language-game we are playing. Mathematicians tend to be very regular in their use of terminology, whereas discussions of ethics or aesthetics often consist of disputes over the very definitions of the words in use. These differences are not (as is sometimes supposed) due to the greater rigour of mathematics, but rather to the way in which the language-game is played and the nature of the criteria at play. Language-games are diverse, and some exhibit greater regularity than others. All we really want when giving and obeying commands on a building site is that we and our interlocutors behave exactly in accordance with the same regular patterns of behaviour that this language-game normally produces. Certain contexts are unfamiliar enough, or call for sufficient individuality of response that we cannot appeal to any practice with the regularity of a game to guide our response. In such cases, our use of language is more like the open-ended play that invites others to follow along with us and introduce their own variants, and where appeals to rules are at best stubbornly dogmatic.

Rhees' challenge

Although he is sympathetic to much of Wittgenstein's philosophy, Rush Rhees expresses concern with the notion that language might be composed of a collection of independent and distinct games. While we might be able to speak of different language-games relating to different aspects of our lives, Rhees maintains that these language-games only have the sense they have because they hang together as part of a unified language. Games lack this essential unity: the sense of chess is not in any important way affected by the way in which it relates to table tennis. For Rhees, the unity of language goes hand in hand with the unity of life: our language-games are connected to the extent that our purposes in playing them are connected, which in turn depends on all the aspects of our lives being connected.

This concern about the unity of language feeds a second concern for Rhees: games do not have a point in the way that language does. Unlike games, language is *about* something. What Rhees (2006) occasionally refers to as 'the reality of language' is closely tied to its capacity to induce learning, understanding, and growth. What we can learn from or through language is not limited by the rules of a game, but only by our own limitations. We might say language is open-ended: it does not itself have a particular subject matter, but is rather the medium in which we can talk about anything.

Rather than consider language in analogy with games, Rhees proposes we use the model of conversation when thinking about language. He does not claim that all language is conversational, or that it consists essentially of conversation, but rather urges that we consider conversation as an important 'centre of variation' (Rhees 1970: 69). Like games, conversations constitute discrete units, bounded in space and time, but unlike games, conversations have repercussions that extend beyond these bounds. The conversations we have pertain to one another (they have unity) and they have a point (they have reality). In engaging in conversation, we can hope to grow in understanding.

For Rhees, the contrast between games and conversation is not simply a quibble over which analogy works the best. In contrasting conversation with games, he takes himself to be engaging in Plato's ancient battle against sophistry. If the words we speak are just moves in a game, skilful deployments of a technique, then 'the growth of understanding could only mean the growth of a skill (efficiency, I suppose) or the multiplication of skills' (Rhees 2006: 3) and the only measure of the worth of the words we speak would be their efficacy in achieving the desired ends. If speaking is simply a means to a desired and predetermined end, language becomes a sophistical battlefield, the site where orators spar and determine whose rhetoric wins out. If every conversation already has a prelusory goal, then we can never truly learn from a conversation, since the only conclusion to a conversation will be the result of victory or defeat.

Sophistry and spoilsports

I think Rhees misplaces the point in characterizing sophistry as treating discussion as simply moves in a game. Playing a game successfully requires coordination and cooperation between players. Rhetorical exchanges between sophists might have many of the characteristics of a game, but presumably what concerns Rhees, as well as Plato, is the challenge sophistry presents to any discussion whatsoever. The challenge that Thrasymachus presents in Book I of the *Republic* is not that he treats as a game what the others take seriously, but rather that he denies the possibility of taking a discussion of justice seriously in the way that Socrates wants to do so. As far as Thrasymachus is concerned, justice is unreal: high-minded talk about justice is just empty chatter, and we could excise the word 'justice' from our vocabulary entirely by simply substituting talk about might and power. Rhees presumably has this sort of challenge in mind when he talks about the reality of language.

The contrast between sophistry and philosophy is not one of play and seriousness – that sophists are playing with language whereas philosophers take their words seriously – because play and seriousness are not opposites. In one sense play contrasts with seriousness, but in another sense seriousness is absolutely essential to play. Huizinga (1995: 5) recognizes this point, and Hans-Georg Gadamer – who acknowledges his debt to Huizinga – links this point to a deeper contrast between sophistry and philosophy: 'seriousness in playing is necessary to make the play wholly play. Someone who doesn't take the game seriously is a spoilsport' (Gadamer 1989: 102). Sophistry is not a matter of playing where others are serious, but rather a matter of playing the spoilsport where others play seriously.

Suits (2005: 60) draws out the following distinction: 'triflers recognize rules but not goals, cheats recognize goals but not rules, players recognize both rules and goals, and spoilsports recognize neither rules nor goals.' Conversations do not have a prelusory goal but they usually have aims, or at least a point: one reason for engaging in conversation, according to Rhees, is so that we can grow in understanding. A sophist both refuses to recognize this goal and denies its very possibility, thereby rejecting the very framework within which these conversations take place: what counts as a pertinent contribution to the conversation, what constitutes a valid argument or objection, and so on. In these respects, a sophist does not resemble a trifler – someone who fails to take the conversation seriously – so much as a spoilsport.

The games analogy does not license sophistry but rather provides within it the tools for thinking about the distinction between sophistry and philosophy, and it does so more cleanly than Rhees' somewhat vague talk about the reality of language. The analogy between language and games does not deny the reality of language, characterizing all discussion as 'just a game', but rather suggests that language derives its reality from being 'in play' in discussion. One of the distinctions Wittgenstein draws with his games analogy is precisely the distinction of various forms of idling and the preliminary work of defining and naming from actually making a move in a language-game, actually saying something. Conversation falls prey to sophistry not when the people engaged in conversation allow the conversation to move according to the dynamic of play, but precisely to the contrary, when one or more people reject the very grounds for holding the conversation, behaving like spoilsports.

Huizinga remarks that spoilsports draw more ire than cheats because cheats at least allow the game to continue, whereas spoilsports bring everything to a halt: the spoilsport 'must be cast out, for he threatens the existence of the play-community' (Huizinga 1995: 11). However, Huizinga sees in discursive spoilsports more noble possibilities than sophistry:

> In the world of high seriousness, too, the cheat and the hypocrite have always had an easier time of it than the spoil-sports, here called apostates, heretics, innovators, prophets, conscientious objectors, etc. It sometimes happens, however, that the spoil-sports in their turn make a new

community with rules of its own. The outlaw, the revolutionary, the cabba-list or member of a secret society, indeed heretics of all kinds are of a highly associative if not sociable disposition, and a certain element of play is prom-inent in all their doings.

(Huizinga 1995: 12)

The sophist and the revolutionary both reject certain operative modes of dis-course as unreal, and their criticism often involves rejecting or defining away key terms in these modes of discourse: compare 'Justice is the advantage of the stronger' and 'Property is theft'. Revolutions – whether they be political or intel-lectual – generally have a positive intent as well: they reject as illegitimate some language-games but seek to establish others in their place.

A discursive spoilsport, then, is not necessarily contemptible. No clear cri-teria distinguish the sophist from the revolutionary, nor the revolutionary we admire from the revolutionary we condemn. What we should make of a discur-sive spoilsport is itself a topic for discussion, with its own norms of appropriate-ness, and its own possibilities for playing the spoilsport, cheat or trifler. Part of what is under discussion in *Republic* I is how the discussion itself ought to proceed, and while such discussions have a structure – Socrates and Thrasy-machus share enough common ground to argue over how much common ground they share – they clearly do not have any hard-and-fast rules.

One of the difficulties with sophistry is that no clear criteria mark it off from serious discourse, certainly not the criterion that they relate to conversation as a game. Which language-game we are playing, and which language-game we should be playing, is not established in advance, but is rather itself a matter open to debate and discussion. This point, however, requires that we see language-games as fluid and based in play. If we neglect this fundamental element of play in Witt-genstein's language-game analogy, we risk developing a conception of discourse that is indeed subject to Rhees' criticism. By taking play into account, however, I believe Wittgenstein's language-games give us fruitful insight into the nature of the growth in understanding that is possible in language.

Play and the ethics of discourse

I argued that the distinction between games and non-game play is fluid with regard to Wittgenstein's analogy with language. Some language-games are more regular than others, and we address controversial moves in different language-games in different ways. Someone who fails to obey an order either misunder-stands the order or refuses to obey it, and we engage with both of these forms of behaviour, and distinguish one from the other, in familiar ways. In moral discus-sion, there is a far greater range of possible responses than in the language-game of giving and obeying orders, and far greater fluidity as to whether interlocutors are cooperating with one another. This greater fluidity in the case of moral dis-cussion gives rise to language-games with far less regularity, where the very nature and structure of the language-games are a part of what is in question.

Cavell (1979: 308) claims that games are the sorts of things that can be *played* because what we *must* do is clearly separated from what we *ought* to do. The constitutive and regulative rules are clearly separated from the principles and maxims that make for skilful play, so that there is no room for *akrasia* in games: as soon as we perceive the most expedient means to a particular end, there is no room for questioning whether this is the end we should be pursuing. By contrast, in matters concerning morality, 'What you say you *must* do is not "defined by the practice", for there is no such practice until you make it one, make it *yours*. We might say, such a declaration defines *you*, establishes your position' (Cavell 1979: 309). What I take to be my moral obligations is a part of my moral life. This is a central respect in which morality – and indeed life more generally – lacks the lusory attitude of games: we accept the rules of a game for the sake of playing the game itself, whereas the reasons we accept certain moral claims as binding upon us are themselves subject to moral evaluation. We do not take on moral responsibilities just for the sake of having moral responsibilities.

Morality does not recognize the sharp distinction between rules on the one hand and principles and maxims on the other because no pre-established rules structure moral discussion. As with open-ended play, the rules with which we accord ourselves are themselves open to being played upon and improvised. We act in accordance with the rules of chess *in order to* play a game of chess. Similarly, we act in accordance with the criteria laid out in a particular language-game *in order to* play that language-game; however, that 'in order to' is not (or not necessarily) justified by appeal to the lusory attitude. Which language-game we should be playing, and why and how, is itself open to debate and question, and this debating and questioning itself takes place in language-games, language-games to which the debating and questioning apply reflexively. To treat our language-games, and the appropriateness of particular language-games to particular circumstances, as already established, misses this crucial point.

That language-games can resemble open-ended play in this respect, such that the structure and appropriateness of a language-game is itself subject to variation, opens up the very possibility of moral debate and discussion. If fixed rules strictly delineated our use of moral concepts, applying those concepts would be as automatic as applying concepts in mathematics. If clear criteria fixed whether and when it was acceptable to break a promise, we would never debate the issue. Rhees is right to note that, if language were like a game in that it had unbending rules and principles, discussion would be impossible. Language is more like a game where a part of the game involves deciding what game to play and agreeing upon the rules. Wittgenstein's analogy works at a deeper level: discussion is possible because, like a game, language is something we play.

Notes

1 Stanley Cavell (1979: 305) draws a similar distinction between rules as defining and rules as regulating.

2 Various theatre and story-telling games impose particular rules on the improvisers. However, precisely by virtue of imposing these rules, the improvisation becomes a game.

3 Suits (2005: 51–52) recognizes these as 'rules of skill'.

4 Does language have regulative rules? One candidate would be the sorts of obligations undertaken in performative speech acts. In making a promise, I undertake the obligation to keep my promise: keeping promises is a regulative rule of the speech act of promising. J.L. Austin (1975: 18) distinguishes between misfires – where, for instance, I declare a couple married without having the authority to do so – and abuses – where, for instance, I make a promise I have no intention of keeping. Misfires violate the constitutive rules of performative utterances, such that the performative utterance is not realized. Abuses, on the other hand, violate the regulative rules of performative utterances: if we violate them, the performative utterance is realized, but in a reproachable manner.

5 Another feature of chess that makes it particularly apt in analogy with language is that it is a perfect information game. Unlike in poker or Battleships, where each player has information that the other lacks, both players in chess see the entire state of play at any given time. With chess as with language, 'nothing is hidden' (Wittgenstein 2009: §435).

6 We could consider the rule-like nature of language on at least two levels: the vocabulary rules that determine the correct uses of words, and the grammatical rules that determine the correct formation of sentences. I will focus here only on the first level.

Bibliography

Austin, J.L. (1975) *How To Do Things With Words* (2nd edn). Cambridge, MA: Harvard University Press.

Cavell, S. (1979) *The Claim of Reason: Wittgenstein, Skepticism, Morality, and Tragedy.* Oxford: Oxford University Press.

Gadamer, H-G. (1989) *Truth and Method* (2nd edn, trans. J. Weinsheimer and D.G. Marshal). London: Sheed & Ward.

Huizinga, J. (1995). *Homo Ludens: A Study of the Play-Element in Culture.* Boston, MA: Beacon Press.

Johnstone, K. (1999) *Impro for Storytellers.* New York: Routledge/Theatre Arts Books.

Plato (1992) *Republic* (2nd edn, trans. G.M.A. Grube and C.D.C. Reeve). Indianapolis, IN: Hackett.

Rhees, R. (1970) 'Wittgenstein's Builders', in *Discussions of Wittgenstein.* London: Routledge & Kegan Paul.

Rhees, R. (2006) *Wittgenstein and the Possibility of Discourse* (2nd edn). Oxford: Blackwell.

Searle, J.R. (1969) *Speech Acts: An Essay in the Philosophy of Language.* Cambridge: Cambridge University Press.

Suits, B. (2005) *The Grasshopper: Games, Life, and Utopia.* Peterborough, ON: Broadview Press.

Wittgenstein, L. (1975) *On Certainty,* trans. G.E.M. Anscombe, G.H. von Wright and D. Paul. Oxford: Blackwell.

Wittgenstein, L. (1978) *Remarks on the Foundations of Mathematics* (3rd edn, trans. G.E.M. Anscombe). Oxford: Blackwell.

Wittgenstein, L. (1980) *Philosophical Grammar,* trans. A. Kenny. Oxford: Blackwell.

Wittgenstein, L. (2009) *Philosophical Investigations* (4th edn, trans. G.E.M. Anscombe, P.M.S. Hacker and J. Schulte). Oxford: Wiley-Blackwell.

5 Gadamer and the game of dialectic in Plato's *Gorgias*

Barry Dixon

In this chapter I will examine Plato's method of dialectic (understood as the method of using dialogue) as it is presented in his *Gorgias*. What I hope to explore are some of the rules of dialectic which I believe are offered to us by Plato through the verbal perambulations of his protagonist, Socrates. Plato is indelibly associated with the method of dialectic he espoused, yet despite the celebrated role of this methodology certain ambiguities arise as to its workings and, indeed, boundaries. For example, are all dialogues of philosophical worth? What is it that distinguishes a dialogue from an argument? What must a discussant bring to a dialogue in order for the discussion to progress, and what is the educative (and philosophical) value of such discussions? I believe that Plato's *Gorgias* addresses these questions and sets the boundaries of dialectic like no other work. Yet I also believe that these boundaries are set in the same way as those of a game. I do not mean that dialectic is similar to any particular game that currently exists (or that existed), but rather that it operates in a common way to games.

Of course, the notion of game-playing, when taken in general and used in this way as a form of comparison, might appear as being rather vague, somewhat broad, and even rather randomly chosen. As a way of countering these issues and providing a more solid frame to this chapter, I will sew my argument with the threads of Hans-Georg Gadamer's conceptual framework of play.[1] I do this as a way of identifying play's most fundamental features, and showing how these features are in fact shared by Platonic dialectic, thereby giving us a better understanding of Plato's method.

The seriousness of game-playing

An important start to any examination of play is how serious a thing it is. Play is such an undeniable part of human culture for Gadamer that he goes so far as to assert that the very idea of culture itself would in fact be unimaginable without our capacity to play.[2] One may say that, as children, we learn how to interact with the world through playing. We learn what is and what is not acceptable, as well as certain cultural motifs and societal expectations through role-playing. There is a safety in play that allows children to experiment with the world and their surroundings. Yet, essentially, we never abandon the conventions of play in our later lives. As Gadamer notes,

> We discover forms of play in the most serious kinds of human activity: In ritual, in the administration of justice, in social behaviour in general, where we even speak of role-playing and so forth.
>
> (Gadamer 1986: 124)[3]

The importance of play is similarly attested to by Plato, who sees it as playing a central role in education.[4] That this same seriousness is required by those engaging in dialectic is no surprise given the fundamental role of dialectic in Plato's philosophical system. Dialectic cannot function without this element of seriousness, a point we see Socrates make when he fears that Callicles is answering just to appease him.

SOCRATES: But are you committed to this view Callicles?
CALLICLES: Yes.
SOCRATES: So we can proceed with our discussion on the assumption that you are serious?
CALLICLES: We certainly can.

(*Gorgias* 495b–c)

All this seems simple enough. It is crucial that Socrates know that his discussants are treating their responses seriously, since without this seriousness the game of dialectic cannot be played. Although Callicles is often seen as being a caustic and downright rude interlocutor, he is treated well by Socrates, precisely because of how seriously he is seen to be treating the discussion. At 486e–487a, for example, Socrates tells us that he is delighted that Callicles is present because he is sure that if Callicles agrees with him he will then know that that which they agree upon will be true. In other words, Socrates takes the force of Callicles' responses as an indication of Callicles' seriousness, a crucial characteristic of any discussant.

The role of the spectators

Let us move from the shared characteristic of seriousness that Plato sees in both play and dialectic to us considering dialectic as a game that one plays. What can this help show us about Plato's conception of dialectic? To start with, let us look at the role of the spectators.

As in any game, the role played by the spectators in dialectic is a crucial one. Yet this role can also be misleading. As with traditional game-playing, although the spectators will often almost quite literally support the efforts of the players, these efforts must never be directed at merely pleasing the crowd. To do this would be to turn the game into a 'show'. For Gadamer, an important element of play is that it never resorts to being a 'show', since in a show the focus is not on the game itself but is either on the attempt to simply 'please' the crowd or is solely on the spectators themselves.[5] All other consequences become secondary to this end. In this way we might imagine a circus act as a good example. Of course, although the players might want to please the spectators of their game, this goal should never be of paramount importance. We see this too in the *Gorgias* and in the difference between the 'displays' or 'shows' of the rhetoricians, and the game of the dialecticians. When Socrates and Chaerephon arrive at the house at the beginning of the dialogue, Callicles wants to ask Gorgias to put on a 'show' for them (447b). Socrates, however, wants no such thing. Instead, he wants to know if Gorgias will engage him in dialogue (447b–c). The difference, then, is in the intentions of the participants. In a 'show', the subject matter is not important so long as the crowd is entertained. This cannot be the intentions of the players in dialectic. In this game the only thing of importance is the subject matter.

The involvement of the spectators is also far more apparent and dynamic in the game of dialectic, since they can even step into the exchange itself at any time. In this way they act almost like substitutions. Before Chaerephon has a chance to ask Gorgias his question at the beginning of the dialogue, Polus inter-jects that as Gorgias seems tired, *he* will answer the questions instead. Polus is therefore answering in place of Gorgias. But as Polus is too concerned with making a speech that skirts around the question, he is eventually ignored by Soc-rates in favour of Gorgias. These 'substitutions' of interlocutors take place throughout the dialogue whenever the direct discussant is seen to be 'failing' in the goal of expounding their position. The whole idea of a substitution in a game is to correct or improve upon a particular failing or weakness and this is no differ-ent in the substitutions in the *Gorgias*. Once substituted, though, and removed from the direct exchange, we note that the players nevertheless remain a keen part of the game, as they can re-enter the fray if they spot a weakness themselves.

Gadamer offers us a similarly critical role for the audience in his philosophy of play, as especially relevant in his treatment of art. In fact, it is because of the direct presence of the spectators at *a* play that what Gadamer calls the 'trans-formation into structure' of art can take place. During this transformation the audience become the players.[6] The fundamental role of the audience, then, comes in their role as participants, the very same role we just saw them play in Platonic dialectic. However, for Gadamer, the most important role of the audi-ence was their simply being there. Gadamer shows the relevance of this in his examination of the term *theoros*. At the Ancient Greek festivals which held the tragic and comedic plays, the *theoroi* were the delegates from the surrounding demes or tribes. Essentially, the only function of the *theoroi* was to be there. They simply bore witness to the festival by their being present, much like wit-nesses to a wedding ceremony. Having no other involvement than to be there gave the *theoroi* their special function.

> *Theoria* is a true participation, not something active but something passive, namely being totally involved in and carried away by what one sees.
>
> (Gadamer 2004: 122)

Thus, although the spectators will not necessarily contribute to the performance of the play, their presence is mandatory for the completion of the play. They are participating, therefore, by being present. Interestingly, their being present is not related to their interpretation of the work, which is a separate issue. It is without question for Gadamer that, 'to be present means to participate', and that 'watching something is a genuine mode of participating' (Gadamer 2004: 122).

But does this idea of an audience being passive not go against my earlier notion of an active audience in the *Gorgias*? I believe it simply points us towards a variegated level of audience. At the direct level we find the live audience, the audience that watches the game. Yet there is a further level of audience, the audience who perhaps watches at home or, in Platonic terms, *hears* about the action of the dialogue and reports it later. That Plato was aware of this differentiated levelling of audience may be seen in how he frames certain dialogues with this very difference. For both the *Phaedo* and the *Symposium*, for example, are dialogues that are being retold by second- or even third-party witnesses. This level of audience cannot take part in the substitutions, a detachment which I believe is similar to that experienced by spectators watching the game at home. The characters of the *Gorgias*, though, are certainly of the first level and, by seeing how they are used much like substitutions, we note an almost direct example of what Gadamer meant by their participation. At 455c we see Socrates point out to Gorgias that there are many people listening to their discussion who want to become his students. His responses, then, as to the content and benefit of training in rhetoric, should be directed at *them*, something which again supports my claim as to a variegated level of audience participation.

Winning and losing

Another central feature of the game of dialectic is how one treats the notion of winning and losing. For Gorgias, rhetoric is like boxing, pankratia and war, in that there are clear winners and losers. In fact, at 456c–d we are told that rhetoric should be used like 'any other competitive skill'.[7] Plato makes sure to tell us that this notion of 'winning and losing' is not to be kept in mind in the same way by dialecticians. The only thing they should be worried about is the subject matter and not in defeating the other. By managing to bring their subject matter to light, all of the participants can be said to win. But this is not at the cost of another participant, since understanding can only come about through the cooperative understanding of all involved. Socrates tells us as much from 453b–c where he notes how much he needs Gorgias in order to find out what rhetoric is. At one stage Callicles mistakenly accuses Socrates of being someone who 'just loves to win arguments' at 515b. Crucially, Socrates responds by saying that he does not just love to win arguments and that 'winning' is never the point.[8] This shows us a crucial difference, then, between traditional games and the game of dialectic, in how one participant cannot be said to win at the expense of another. Perhaps, though, the difference is simply in the goals that lie in dialectic and how one measures one's success. Socrates is not trying to defeat his fellow interlocutors but is trying to defeat any falseness of opinion. What we can say, then, is that in dialectic participants either all win or they all lose, depending on whether or not they reach their goal of revealing the truth of the subject matter.

This same notion of 'winning' in dialectic is of key importance to Gadamer and his theory of the 'fusion of horizons'. Gadamer describes our 'horizons' as follows:

> The horizon is the range of vision that includes everything that can be seen from a particular vantage point. Applying this to the thinking mind, we speak of narrowness of horizon, of the possible expansion of horizon, of the opening up of new horizons, and so forth.
>
> (Gadamer 2004: 301)

In other words, a horizon is a thing's past and ever-flowing present, which projects indeterminably into the future. Although it is our historical embeddedness which creates our horizons, as noted by Lebech (2006), this embeddedness provides the means by which we may critically examine our prejudices, thereby expanding our horizons and broadening our knowledge. Yet, precisely because our history is continuously moving, so too are our horizons, meaning they are not rigid. When we engage with a fellow discussant, or thing, we must take their horizon into account, making sure to remain open at all times. Thus, when we engage in conversation, our worldview is encountering that of another.[9] What happens in agreement, therefore, is a fusion of horizons, a truly common horizon which does not belong to either one of the discussants by themselves, but rather, comes to exist *between* them. It is in reaching this 'common understanding' between discussants which I believe typifies 'winning' in dialectic.

The fairness of the game

Could one not object, though, that it is Socrates who makes up the rules as he goes along? That he simply imposes his own strengths and subsequent will on the others? Once more, Plato goes to great lengths to dispel this. When conversing with Gorgias, Socrates is at pains to say that all that he is doing is 'fair', using this term at 453c5 and 7 and then again at 454a–b with 'doesn't that seem a fair question to you?' It is important for Socrates that nobody thinks that he is unfairly leading Gorgias, a point that Plato pushes home when Gorgias tells us at 451a that Socrates has 'understood his meaning fairly'. What becomes apparent, then, is that Socrates does not castigate the responses of others to massage his own ego. Instead, he is simply imposing the rules of the game. This does not prevent both Polus and Callicles from accusing Socrates of cheating, though (e.g. at 483a).

Another key feature of the 'fairness' of dialectic which is connected to the earlier discussion of 'winning and losing' is that it is not synonymous with an argument. In arguments the subject matter can often be forgotten in the desire to 'defeat' the other. If the game of dialectic is to be fair, it must not serve the egos or alternative agendas of its discussants. From 457c–458b, Socrates describes how discussions can often turn into arguments. When people do not agree it makes it hard for them to learn from each other. What happens, then, is that these people set out to try and 'win' the argument without looking into the issue under discussion.[10] At 457d the discussants make it known that they must avoid 'abuse', which is one of the key features of arguments (see also *Laches*, 195a). These abusive discussants become 'lovers of victory'. The term has a negative connotation of one who is contentious for the sake of contentiousness. Socrates tells us at 457d that these lovers of victory do not seek the subject matter, but merely pursue their personal agendas. We have found, then, an intriguing rule to the game of dialectic. Winning is never at the cost of beating an opponent, but is simply found in a successful co-achievement among players. Those whose aim is solely to beat the other will therefore never 'win' at dialectic as they will never admit the *need* for their opponents. Being more used to playing dialectic, Socrates spends a lot of time explaining the rules to his discussants, offering them advice on how they should approach and frame their contributions (e.g. from 451a–c and 452a–c).

Types of players

We can often tell most about a game by the types of characters who play it. Socrates tells us what types of players are needed for dialogue from 457d–458a. They must be happy to be proven wrong if they make a mistake but similarly happy to prove someone else wrong if they make a mistake. Crucially, they must not be less happy to be proven wrong, as they will then have learned something. One of the clearest reasons why Polus is a weak dialectician is his unwillingness to answer lest he be proven wrong. At 474a–b, for example, Socrates needs to ask Polus to be more forthcoming with his answers. When Socrates eventually shows Polus' position on doing wrong and suffering wrong to be contradictory (at 475d), Polus does not want to answer and admit the contradiction. He has to be dragged to answer by Socrates, a feature of Polus we already see when at 468c and d he hesitates in answering Socrates.[11] The way discussants should act may be seen at 504c when Callicles turns questioner and asks Socrates what he thinks the effects of organization and order on the mind are, asking what the equivalent term to 'health' is in this case. Although Socrates agrees to answer, he adds: 'If you think I'm right, please tell me; but if you think I'm wrong, don't let me get away with it – show me why I'm wrong.' This attribute is so necessary for playing that it is only after Gorgias agrees to proceed in this way at 458b that the dialogue can move forward.

Yet the *Gorgias* also gives us an even more explicit description of the types of characters needed for the game of dialectic. At 492d, Socrates outlines for us three qualities that are necessary for such players. They must have: (1) knowledge, (2) goodwill, and (3) frankness in expression. According to Socrates,

Callicles has all three of these qualities. In fact, one of the reasons Socrates likes Callicles is that he has the courage to say what others are thinking but are afraid to say (492d). Even when Callicles gets himself worked up at 489d and is asked by Socrates to calm himself a little, this is not as serious a criticism as at 495a when Socrates believes Callicles is offering a response he does not truly believe in. As we saw, contentiousness for the sake of contentiousness is suited more to an argument than a discussion. We can see that Callicles is not like this at 510b when he calls one of Socrates' points 'excellent'. Callicles himself makes a point of this, pointing out that he is willing to compliment Socrates but only when he deems it deserving.

The ontological being of dialogue

While I have shown only some elements of Gadamer's work so far, I turn now to possibly the most important feature of his treatment of play. It is with showing the Platonic significance of this most prominent element of Gadamer's that I will finish. The concern in question is with the ontological being of the game. For Gadamer, the game exists over and above its players. We never change a game by taking part. Rather, it is we who are changed. We must submit ourselves to the rules of the game, allowing these rules to shape and move our contributions. We get taken in by the game, becoming a part of its world. For Gadamer, the structure of play 'absorbs the player into itself' (Gadamer 2004: 105). Yet this is a world we can only attempt to belong to, meaning it is not a world we can own or govern. For Gadamer, truly to participate in the game one must belong to it. The player 'conforms to the game or subjects himself to it, that is, he relinquishes the autonomy of his own will' (Gadamer 1976: 53). Of course, as noted by Lebech (2006), this requirement of belonging to the game is not a wholly one-sided relationship which robs the players of any contributive involvement. Rather the relationship must be seen *dialectically*, a term of great significance here.[12] So, the opposition involved in the game of dialectic is of course in keeping within its rules and in breaking down the 'hiddenness' of the subject under discussion. Of especial importance, then, is once more seeing how the participants are not the controlling elements, but are more facilitators in the coming-into-being of that which is under discussion.

> To conduct a conversation means to allow oneself to be conducted by the subject-matter to which the partners in the dialogue are oriented.
>
> (Gadamer 2004: 383)

Throughout the *Gorgias*, and throughout Plato's other works, Socrates puts the progression of the dialogue ahead of the egos of the discussants. The subject matter is what is of key importance, and as dialogue is the only way of reaching it, it too must be played in just the right way. Socrates often treats the progression of the dialogue as something of an independent being which, much like a game, takes its own course through the efforts of the participants. We can see this when Socrates asks Gorgias what he thinks rhetoric is the persuasion of, rather than offer Gorgias an explanation of it himself. Socrates tells us that he does this because he wants 'the course of the discussion to show us as clearly as possible what it is we're talking about' (453c). The course of the discussion is treated here as something that is almost separate from the participants. If it is played the right way it will show its subject matter to the players, seemingly taking on a life of its own.

The openness of dialectic is lacking in a craft like sophistry. Perhaps the paradigmatic example of this method is seen in the *Euthydemus*, where Euthydemus and Dionysodorus display their 'craft' to Socrates and the unsuspecting Cleinias. At the very beginning of the dialogue we are shown how Cleinias cannot win in such a discussion.

> In the meantime, Dionysodorus had leaned a little over to my ear, with a big grin on his face. 'In fact, Socrates,', he said, 'I can tell you now that whichever answer the lad (Cleinias) gives, he will be proved wrong'.
>
> (*Euthydemus*, 275e)

This purely sophistic method of discussion acts like a 'fixed' or crooked game of play, whereby all the various machinations surrounding the event, as well as the action which occupies the event, are of no progressive consequence. Although it seems to the audience members and the unsuspecting members of the discussion that the exchange is free, this is not, in fact, the case. For, as we see in the case of Euthydemus and Dionysodorus, the prerehearsed outcome of the discussion is of secondary importance when compared to the way in which they achieve their goal. Unlike the shadowy, concealed involvement of one who usually fixes games of play, these two celebrate their con, displaying pride at its effectiveness. Although his interlocutors often feel as if they have been trapped by Socrates, Plato works hard to show us that the interlocutors brought themselves to this position. Had they answered differently they would not necessarily have ended up in the position they now find themselves. If we ever find ourselves frustrated by our position while game-playing, our first thought is often an impetuous accusation of cheating. More often than not, though, our contribution has been free but simply lacking. The superior ability of Socrates within the game of dialectic is even expressly drawn by Adeimantus in the *Republic*:

> [A]nd like those who are left unable to continue by those skilled in draughts, being shut out and not able to move, so they too [Socrates' fellow discussants] are in this way shut out and don't have anything to say by this different type of draughts, played not with discs but with words.
>
> (*Republic*, 487b–c)[13]

I must state again, however, that this ability of Socrates is not in any way argumentative and sophistic but is rather designed to keep his participants within the rules of the game. In this respect Socrates is seen as being like a referee who, though unable to play the game perfectly, knows when the rules have been broken. In fact, we even find direct evidence of this role in the *Laches* where Socrates is asked by Lysimachus to join in with the discussion and 'act as referee' (*Laches*, 184d).[14] The reason Socrates is needed is because neither Laches nor Nicias could agree on the nature of courage and whether or not it can be taught. Although Lysimachus oversimplifies the matter, asking Socrates to add his vote to either one of the positions raised previously, thus giving that view the majority vote, the point remains that Socrates is needed to help bring all discussants to agreement. A better example of this Socratic role as referee, perhaps, is in the more everyday, non-professional game-playing, whereby the players *themselves* act as the referee. Though they may not all like it, they know when the rules have been broken. Gadamer calls this the 'non-purposive rationality' of play, a 'self-discipline and order that we impose on our movements when playing, as if particular purposes were involved' (Gadamer 1986: 23). A certain degree of pliability is thereby requested where those involved cannot enforce their own rules but must rather allow their ideas, beliefs and arguments to be shaped by the dialogical model.

Conclusion

Gadamer's conceptual framework of game-playing allows an exploration of some of the 'rules' and characteristics of Platonic dialectic. These included the role of the spectators, the notion of winning and losing, the importance of fairness and the types of players needed to play the game well. Finally, it explored how the ontological mode of being of dialogue absorbed its participants into itself, existing over and above them. This was shown to operate in the same way as game-playing, whereby the players truly take part in the game. They do not change the game but are themselves changed by it.

Notes

1   What I believe makes Gadamer's philosophical hermeneutics suitable for this endeavour is his own celebration of dialogue. There is a fascinating interplay between Gadamer's treatment of dialogue and play that I feel warrants the use of his work in this way.
2   'The first thing we must make clear to ourselves is that play is so elementary a function of human life that culture is quite inconceivable without it' (Gadamer 1986: 22). Gadamer states that he drew influence on this aspect of play from Huizinga (1955) and of course from Heidegger. Burwick (1990), however, believes that Gadamer took even stronger influence from Herder.
3   Gadamer suggests that it is an illusion 'to think that we can separate play from seriousness, and only admit it to segregated areas peripheral to real life, like our leisure time which comes to resemble a relic of lost freedom' (Gadamer 1986: 130). The seriousness of play is a consistent feature of Gadamer's treatment which may also be seen in *Truth and Method* where we find that 'play itself contains its own, even sacred seriousness', and 'seriousness in playing is necessary to make the play wholly play' (Gadamer 2004: 103).

4 In the *Republic* we find: 'Then whenever children play well from the beginning, and are imbued with a good sense of law through music and poetry, it follows them in every-thing and nurtures their growth, correcting anything which may have gone wrong in the other city' (*Republic*, 425a). In the *Laws* we find a similar sentiment: 'I say that there is a lack of knowledge in every city about children's games, that they are so important in lawgiving as to determine whether the laws be permanent or not' (*Laws*, 797a). This argument is also seen in the *Laws* at 643d and followed up from 797b–c.

5 For Gadamer, 'contests are in danger of losing their real play character precisely by becoming shows' (Gadamer 2004: 109).

6 'A complete change takes place when play, as such, becomes a play. It puts the spec-tator in the place of the player. He – and not the player – is the person for and in whom the play is played' (Gadamer 2004: 109). As noted by Lebech (2006), 'the spectator is not simply a disinterested observer, but a participant who belongs to play and is active in playing' (p. 226).

7 This point is reiterated at 457b when Gorgias again calls rhetoric 'a competitive skill'.

8 This is a refreshing viewpoint given the results-driven big business of modern games. For a similar discussion of competition as 'the mutual quest for excellence through challenge', see Simon (2004).

9 Gadamer explains this in a short essay entitled 'The Incapacity for Conversation'. 'When two people come together and enter into an exchange with one another, then there is always an encounter between, as it were, two worlds, two world-views, and two world pictures' (Gadamer 2006).

10 A similar distinction is made at *Republic* 454a and 499a. As noted by Kastely (1991), the desire for victory is a feature of Polus which detracts from his ability to play the game of dialectic fairly. 'Since his sole criterion is victory, for him the interaction between two people in a discourse can only be competitive and can only close with the triumph of one and the defeat of the other' (p. 99).

11 Klosko (1983) also sees the dialectical relationship breaking down if no genuine will-ingness to answer exists. 'It is especially apparent that the dialectical relationship does not exist when we see various interlocutors either refusing to state their true convictions on matters under discussion, or simply refusing to answer Socrates' ques-tions' (p. 586).

12 'The primacy of play over the players is therefore relative. Rather, that which is truly primary is the dialectical relation between, and mutual conditioning of, play and the players themselves' (Lebech 2006: 225–226).

13 Dialectic is also directly compared to a game in the *Theaetetus*. While trying to initiate the dialogue in question Socrates asks, 'Who of us would like to speak first? He who makes a mistake, and he who makes a mistake thereafter, will sit down and be "donkey", as the children say when playing ball' (*Theaetetus*, 146a).

14 In the *Laches* in particular, however, Socrates does take a more visibly regulatory role. For Nicias and Laches do not pull any punches in their discussion, accusing the other at numerous times of 'talking rubbish'. Socrates has to make sure that the participants do not get abusive (195a) but rather work together in coming to agreement.

Bibliography

Burwick, F. (1990) 'The Plagiarism of Play: The Unacknowledged Source of Gadamer's Ontological Argument in Truth and Method'. *Pacific Coast Philology*, 25(1/2): 60–68.

Gadamer, H. (1976) *Philosophical Hermeneutics*, trans. and ed. David E. Linge. Berkeley and Los Angeles: University of California Press.

Gadamer, H. (1986) *The Relevance of the Beautiful and Other Essays*, trans. Nicholas Walker, ed. and intro. Robert Bernasconi. Cambridge: Cambridge University Press.

Gadamer, H. (2004) *Truth and Method* (2nd revised edn), trans. Joel Weinsheimer and Donald G. Marshall). London: Continuum.

Gadamer, H. (2006) 'The Incapacity for Conversation', trans. David Vessey and Chris Blauwkamp. *Continental Philosophy Review*, 39: 351–359.

Huizinga, J. (1955) *Homo Ludens: A Study of the Play Element in Culture*. London: Beacon Press.

Kastely, J.L. (1991) 'In Defense of Plato's Gorgias'. *PMLA*, 106(1): 96–109.

Klosko, G. (1983) 'The Insufficiency of Reason in Plato's Gorgias'. *Western Political Quarterly*, 36: 579–595.

Klosko, G. (1984) 'The Refutation of Callicles in Plato's Gorgias'. *Greece and Rome*, second series, 31(2): 126–139.

Lebech, F. (2006) 'The Concept of the Subject in the Philosophical Hermeneutics of Hans-Georg Gadamer'. *International Journal of Philosophical Studies*, 14(2): 221–236.

Mitscherling, J. (2002) 'Gadamer's Legacy in Aesthetics and Plato Studies: Play and Participation in the Work of Art'. *Symposium*, 6(2): 149–165.

Plato, *Republic*, Loeb Classical Library, trans. Paul Shorey. Cambridge, MA: Harvard University Press, 1930.

Plato, *Laws*, Loeb Classical Library, trans. R.G. Bury. London: William Heinemann, 1926.

Plato, *Laches · Protagoras · Meno · Euthydemus*, Loeb Classical Library, trans. W.R.M. Lamb. Cambridge, MA: Harvard University Press, 1925.

Plato, *Lysis · Symposium · Gorgias*, Loeb Classical Library, trans. W.R.M. Lamb. Cambridge, MA: Harvard University Press, 1925.

Plato, *Theaetetus · Sophist*, Loeb Classical Library, trans. Harold North Fowler. Cambridge, MA: Harvard University Press, 1921.

Reichling, M.J. (1997) 'Music, Imagination, and Play'. *Journal of Aesthetic Education*, 31(1): 41–55.

Simon, R.L. (2004) *Fair Play: The Ethics of Sport* (2nd edn). Oxford: Westview Press.

6   Gadamer and the game of understanding

Dialogue-play and opening to the Other

Monica Vilhauer

A breakdown in genuine dialogue and understanding increasingly plagues communication today, in both political and personal contexts. The popular sense that we simply cannot understand each other because of differences in gender, race, class, religion, sexual orientation, political affiliation, etc. discourages us, more and more, from even trying to communicate with those we consider to be our 'Other'. This leads frequently to the abandonment of dialogue, and to either a kind of isolationism or resort to force as a response to conflict. Considering the ever more global nature of our society, and the need to find ways to fully understand and act upon shared concerns, the abandonment of dialogue has become all the more troubling. We are thus faced with the pressing questions: What causes dialogue to break down? And what do we do once it has broken down?

Hans-Georg Gadamer's philosophical hermeneutics offers a philosophy rich in resources for grappling with questions surrounding communication, understanding, and the varying approaches we might take to others whose lives and ideas are considerably different from our own. While Gadamer's magnum opus *Truth and Method* (originally published in German in 1960) explicitly concerns itself with discovering how understanding works and what makes understanding possible, it simultaneously offers a distinctive philosophy of genuine human engagement in which true dialogue and understanding can be achieved. It is in the concept of play (*Spiel*) that we find the key, in Gadamer's philosophy, to understanding how it is that we must approach 'the Other' for dialogue to be a fruitful and transformative event, in which interlocutors truly communicate with each other and develop a higher shared grasp of the subject matter at hand. It is by focusing on what is required to create and sustain the back-and-forth linguistic play-movement between human beings, which represents the very process of understanding itself for Gadamer, that one can best see the ethical conditions[1] for genuine dialogue and understanding, and grasp what happens when the game of understanding goes right, versus what happens when it gets blocked or breaks down. Gadamer's phenomenological (descriptive) account of genuine play – that dance of presenting and recognizing meaning – is ultimately meant to serve as move us past the recurring blocks to dialogue we set for ourselves, and move us towards the sorts of interpersonal engagements that best facilitate mutual understanding for our common good. I say 'for our common good' because I find in Gadamer's philosophical hermeneutics an implicit lesson that preserving an authentic engagement in dialogue-play with the Other is crucial for our education, development, and our very existence as human beings. Implicit in Gadamer's philosophical hermeneutics, I find an 'ethics of play' in three senses. First, Gadamer's phenomenological analysis of how understanding works in terms of play reveals to us that there are crucial ethical conditions that must be met for genuine dialogic play to succeed. Second, there is an implicit value claim in Gadamer's work that genuine play with the Other is ultimately good for us, as the interactive path of our development as human beings. Third, Gadamer's theory of understanding as a process of play is meant, *as practical philosophy* (in the style of the older Aristotelian tradition), to guide our concrete dialogical relations with others so that we may understand better, and – insofar as understanding is conceived by Gadamer as our very mode of being and developing in the world – so that we may come to live better.[2] This chapter begins with a discussion of what play means for Gadamer and how it relates to the process of understanding in all its forms. It then develops the ethical conditions of dialogue-play by focusing on how it is that we must approach the Other for genuine understanding to occur. Finally, the chapter illuminates how Gadamer's philosophy is itself a practical philosophy in the Aristotelian sense.

The concept of play

Essential to Gadamer's concept of play, as Gadamer explains in his *Truth and Method,* is that play is not a subjective act or attitude – not something that happens in the mind, impulses or conduct of the subject – but is, rather, an activity that goes on between the players, reaches beyond the behaviour or consciousness of any individual player, and has a life, meaning, essence or spirit of its own that emerges from the players' back-and-forth movement (Gadamer 2000: 101–110). This life or meaning of a particular occurrence of play is what Gadamer calls the true subject or subject matter (*Sache*) of play, which reaches presentation (*Darstellung*) only in and through the players' movement. The subject matter of play, according to Gadamer, is the game itself (*das Spiel selbst*), which has the character of an event (*Geschehen*). This event must be understood as a dynamic process, whose back-and-forth movement involves spontaneity and variability. As Gadamer emphasizes, no one knows ahead of time what will ultmately come out of a particular event of play. Play, thus, is a movement that is neither mechanical nor fully determined. The very movement of play requires respondents whose movements are not identical, but differ from each other enough to keep the game going.

Although Gadamer recognizes that the movement of play is present in all of nature, he perceives that what is peculiar about human play is that 'the structure of movement to which it submits has a definite quality which the player "chooses." First, he expressly separates his playing behaviour from his other behaviour by *wanting* to play. But even within his readiness to play he makes a choice' (Gadamer 2000: 107). Human play, thus, involves the intention, willingness or choice to constrain one's own freedom to the rules of a game. Human play has the special quality of human freedom, which is not simply the freedom of randomness or caprice, but is a freedom that involves the intentional self-restraint that goes along with any effort to accomplish something. It involves what Gadamer refers to as a profound commitment.

Now, it is true that in his description of play, Gadamer emphasizes the *'primacy of play over the consciousness of the player'* (Gadamer 2000: 104), and describes play as absorbing the players into itself. He explains that play is less of a thing a person does and more of a thing done to him. Gadamer declares that 'all playing is a being-played ... the game masters the players' (Gadamer 2000: 106). We should not conclude from these remarks, though, that the players become quite passive in play; rather, they become a part of an activity that is bigger than their own personal, active roles. Each player must actively approach the game with the seriousness of a fully engaged participant – since, as Gadamer observes, 'seriousness in playing is necessary to make the play wholly play. Someone who doesn't take the game seriously is a spoilsport' (Gadamer 2000: 102). It is essential to the existence of the game that the player *comport himself* in his playing in such a way that he attends whole-heartedly to the tasks required of him. This comportment is, in fact, what allows him to become wrapped up in the game. Thus, although Gadamer locates play in the back-and-forth movement that occurs between the players, and not in the intentional consciousness of any one of them, we must notice that such a genuine move-ment cannot occur unless the players actively comport themselves in such a way that they become fully involved or immersed in the game. They must have, we might say, seriously playful attitudes and intentions in order to give themselves over to the game and fully engage in it.[3] Gadamer states: 'A person playing is, even in his play, still someone who comports himself, even if the proper essence of the game consists in his disburdening himself of the tension he feels in his purposive comportment' (Gadamer 2000: 107). To put this another way, one cannot truly participate in play in a half-committed manner. The game requires the players' full involvement.

The play-process of understanding: understanding art, text, tradition and living speech

Just as play has the fundamental structure of a dynamic movement that occurs in and through the engaged participation of players, understanding too for Gadamer must be conceived as such an interactive event that takes place in the basic back-and-forth process of someone trying to understand someone else about something. In language – whether the language of art, text, tradition or living speech – interlocutors become players in the shared game of a joint artic-ulation of truth.

In the encounter with a work of art, Gadamer finds work and spectator to be players and participants in a continuous to-and-fro dance of presentation and recognition, out of which the meaning of the work of art emerges and is understood. The work of art, according to Gadamer, makes a claim to truth (*Wahrheitsanspruch*) about our common world, which it presents to us for our recognition. The work of art points to something in our shared world and articulates it in a specific way. But it is only in our ability to see or recognize the subject articulated as 'the way things are' that the event of understanding takes place and the achievement of communication that Gadamer calls total mediation (*totale Vermittlung*) occurs.

The same is the case if the work we are encountering is a text, since the literary text also finds its life in the event in which its meaning is grasped by an audience. According to Gadamer, the reader plays just as much of an active role in the meaning of the text as the spectator does in the life of an artwork. Readers enter into play with texts, and through a back-and-forth movement of speaking and listening they form a communicative event in which meaning is shared. To begin with, the text addresses us (the readers) with its message, with its claim to truth. We come to the text with our own set of assumptions, which make up a kind of background understanding, or a context of meaning, in which we integrate new experiences. We take a stab at interpretation based on what we already know, and the text replies ('that's not yet what I mean'). Our present understanding now enters into play. Through our experience of the other meaning the text offers, which resists or denies our projected presuppositions, our presuppositions become foregrounded, provoked, or called into question in a way that makes us aware of them, able to examine them (their origin and validity), and finally able to transform them so that we may improve our understanding (Gadamer 2000: 267) – so that we may 'know better'.[4] We continue a back-and-forth process of revising our prejudices until the meaningful whole we project is confirmed by all the details of the text. We are close, now, to grasping the claim to truth made on us; but we must, finally, answer the claim by interpreting its contemporary relevance *to us*. We must critically appropriate it or apply it. We must understand it in terms of the world in which we live (Gadamer 2000: 308). It is in this back-and-forth process of engagement – of absorption in new meaning and return with an enriched sense of our world and ourselves – that the play-process or event of understanding takes place.

This event of understanding cannot take place without the commitment of the engaged player. A true spectator of an artwork is not one who simply happens to be in the room in a quite casual way while the performance is going on; rather, his participation requires what Gadamer calls 'a subjective accomplishment in human conduct' (*eine subjektive Leistung menschlichen Verhaltens*) (Gadamer 2000: 125), where he must devote his full attention to the articulated subject matter before him. Likewise, a good reader of a text must involve himself in the subject matter in a way that allows the other meaning coming from the pages to speak to him and address him. This means he must be willing to hear something different from what he already thinks, test his own prejudices, risk himself and his prior understanding, become aware of his old biases, and allow himself to be affected by new meaning. Gadamer refers to this willingness of the fully engaged interpreter as a comportment of openness. This openness is necessary if we are to understand the meaning of an artwork, a text, a tradition or some Other in dialogue.

The artwork and text are conceived by Gadamer as two forms of tradition that we attempt to understand through the same play-process. In the play-process of understanding, grasping what tradition communicates in terms of our own time and place is itself part of the event of its meaning. (Gadamer famously terms this process of understanding a 'fusion of past and present horizons'.) In tradition, Gadamer asserts, a voice speaks to us. Tradition 'expresses itself like a Thou. A Thou is not an object; it relates itself to us' (Gadamer 2000: 358). Understanding tradition, thus, is not a matter of an active subject knowing some dead thing. Understanding is, rather, an interactive, communicative process between I and Thou (*Ich und Du*). Tradition, as Gadamer insists, is for us 'a genuine partner in dialogue' (Gadamer 2000: 358). The experience we have with the traditionary work of art or text is an experience whose play-structure is ultimately that of dialogue (*Gespräch*).

In Gadamer's shift to describing the event of understanding in terms of a conversation or dialogue, we hear his original description of authentic participation in play reverberate. Just as the genuine player had to engage the other players and fully involve himself in the game, the genuine interlocutor must listen carefully to the Other and allow the subject matter and its truth to be his guide in the conversation. Gadamer explains:

> To conduct a conversation means to allow oneself to be conducted by the subject matter to which the partners in the dialogue are oriented (Gadamer, 2000: 367).... To reach an understanding in a dialogue is not merely a matter of putting oneself forward and successfully asserting one's own point of view, but being transformed into a communion in which we do not remain what we were.
>
> (Gadamer 2000: 379)

The communion is a shared language between I and Thou in which a common understanding of some truth about our world develops.

Gadamer's ethics of play

The ethical conditions of dialogue-play

Just as any play-movement is a dynamic process or event that takes place between players, goes beyond any individual player, and allows something new to reach presentation, dialogue-play requires that we move beyond a preoccupation with ourselves, and lend ourselves to a game that is larger than our own individual roles in it – the game of articulating truth. Just as any play-movement has a life of its own that takes hold of the players, dialogue-play requires that interlocutors give up a certain level of control and allow the subject matter to guide them. Just as any play-movement involves a reciprocal responsiveness, dialogue-play requires that interlocutors not hold back as observing spectators, but instead contribute to the undertaking of the conversation. Just as any human game demands that the players make a choice to play and deliberately constrain their conduct and attention to the tasks of the game, dialogue-play requires that we be willing to do the work of interpretation – the work of active listening, of asking questions, and of trying, risking and revising our prejudices until we finally comprehend what each other is trying to say. Just as any human player must take the game seriously – as not to be, as Gadamer puts it, a spoil-sport – the game of understanding requires of us a profound commitment – a commitment to listen with care, to be sensitive to the alterity of what each other has to say, to take seriously each other's claims to truth, and to stand ready to be challenged and truly transformed in our own thinking. Embodying these commitments, these behaviours, these postures when approaching each other in conversation is what Gadamer refers to (as mentioned above) as a comportment of openness towards the Other. This comportment of openness characterizes in a general way the ethical conditions which must be met by both/all parties involved for genuine dialogue and a common understanding of some truth about our world to take place.[5] Gadamer proclaims:

> In human relations the important thing is, as we have seen, to experience the Thou truly as a Thou – i.e., not to overlook his claim but to let him really say something to us. Here is where openness belongs.... Without such openness to one another there is no genuine human bond.
>
> (Gadamer 2000: 361)

The open approach to the Other involves a fundamental recognition of the Other as a crucial partner and participant in the process of articulating truth, and produces a deep engagement in which the Other's claim to truth receives a full hearing (or is fully 'played out' as Gadamer puts it). Only when the Other's claim receives a full hearing can it truly affect us, educate us, and contribute to building a common ground of meaning that puts us in an even better position to communicate and act with others.

This 'open' approach to the Other is contrasted by Gadamer with three other approaches or I–Thou relations, all of which are characterized by levels of 'closedness', distance and postures of dominance over the Other that hinder the back-and-forth movement of dialogue-play and the understanding that can be achieved in it.[6] I refer to these three I–Thou relations (or forms of 'foul play') as (1) the scientific approach to the Other, (2) the psychological approach to the Other, and (3) the sophistic approach to the Other.

In the scientific approach to the Other, the Other is treated as an object to be observed and examined from a distance, for the purpose of anticipating its future behaviour and developing some sort of mastery or control over it. By approaching the Other as a thing, rather than as a person who has something significant to say, one immediately closes one's ears to the Other's claim to truth and blocks the sort of conversation that would allow for a mutual understanding to develop. The Other, under this approach, is allowed to make sounds but not to speak meaningfully; he is used as a means to the end of one's own knowledge or one's own control, and is denied the kind of recognition that is involved in taking seriously what he has to say. The posture of dominance taken in this I–Thou relation, which is really reduced to an I–It relation, severs the basic moral relation (of subject to subject), according to Gadamer, which is needed if we are to enter into a mutually transforming dialogue. Gadamer states: 'From the moral point of view this orientation toward the Thou is purely self-regarding and contradicts the moral definition of man' (Gadamer 2000: 358).

The psychological approach to the Other is a derivative of the scientific approach. Although it appears to treat the Other as a human being rather than as an object, it really just treats the Other as a peculiar kind of object – a 'psychological thing'. In this I–Thou relation one hears what the Other says as a meaningful statement – even as a unique enunciation of meaning other than one's own – but one takes the Other's statement to be the expression of his personal attitude, an expression of his life (*Lebensäußerung*), or of his life experience (*Erlebnis*), and attempts to understand it only as his idiosyncratic point of view. The 'I', under this model, does not recognize the 'Thou' as a being that has something meaningful to say about the way the world is, about the truth of things, but only as a being that is capable of expressing the way he feels, or the way he sees things as a result of his personal life history. The 'I' even claims to know the 'Thou', through a psychological-biographical study, better than the Thou knows himself. But, Gadamer explains: 'By understanding the other, by claiming to know him, one robs his claims of their legitimacy .... The claim to understand the other person in advance functions to keep the other person's claim at a distance' (Gadamer 2000: 360). The problem, in short, is that the I, here, does not take what the Thou says seriously – that is, as a potential *truth* that could apply to any of us and transform the way we think and act. Rather, the I sees what the Thou says as a mere attitude, a subjective reflection, or a product of some life event which colours all of his thoughts. The psychological approach to the Other, like the scientific approach to the Other, is characterized by a kind of distance in which the I remains removed from a real engagement with the Thou due to the I's unwillingness to recognize the Thou's truth claims. This distance keeps the I from being affected, transformed or educated in his encounter with the Thou.[7] The psychological approach to the Other, like the scientific approach, is a relationship in which mastery, control and dominance is attempted over the Other. The I takes himself to be the knower while the Thou is the known. What the Thou knows himself, and what might be learned from him, is ignored. A relationship of mutual understanding, teaching and learning is neither recognized nor achieved.

Finally, the sophistic approach to the Other, as we know from its depiction in Plato's dialogues, is one of argumentative attack and conquer. The goal, simply, is to overpower the Other in a debate and to 'win' for the purpose of acquiring honour, money, votes or some other award. In this case, the Other is listened to only long enough to discover the vulnerable spot in his argument, so that he may be refuted. The sophist, instead of engaging and taking seriously what his adversary says, stands back at a competitive distance where he remains unaffected by the possible truth of his partner's words. This sophistic, competitive game is contrasted by Gadamer with the play of dialectic, or that 'art of conducting a real dialogue', of which Socrates is quintessential master. In the case of the dialectical dialogue, the aim is not to outdo each other but to reach agreement at every step in the argument, so that there is always a common subject matter being worked through. Socratic dialectic

> consists in not trying to discover the weakness of what is said, but in bringing out its real strength. It is not the art of arguing (which can make a strong case out of a weak one) but the art of thinking (which can strengthen objections by referring to the subject matter).
>
> (Gadamer 2000: 367)

Simply put, the goal is a joint grasp of truth. As the example of the Socratic dialectical dialogue shows, this cooperative and collaborative pursuit requires what I like to call a 'double openness': an openness to the Other and what he has to say (what Gadamer often refers to as a 'good will to understand') and an openness towards truth as the ultimate goal. Interlocutors' shared double openness creates the kind of friendship, in Plato's texts, that lies at the root of the upward-moving Socratic philosophical conversation. This friendship is the model for the ethical conditions of genuine dialogue-play we find in Gadamer – conditions that must be met if a higher, joint understanding of some truth is to take place. In the end, it is the comportment of openness that leads us, as Gadamer puts it (appropriating Hegel, but echoing insights found in Plato), to move beyond the nearsightedness of our own individual perspectives and towards more universal points of view with regard to the subject matter.

The value of dialogue-play

There is an implicit lesson in Gadamer's hermeneutics that preserving an authentic engagement in genuine dialogue-play with the Other is crucial for our education, development and our very existence as human beings.[8] The movement in which we open ourselves to new and strange meaning, offered by the Other, is the very activity in which human beings undergo rich, transformative experience (*Erfahrung*) and cultivation (*Bildung*). It is the path by which we learn, grow and flourish as human beings. A failure to engage in play, or a refusal to work through new meaning with others (with all the risks and growing pains involved) results in a kind of stunted growth, alienation, and even a limitation of our own possibilities (as a higher understanding and comfort level with the subject matter is related to a higher freedom by Gadamer, again appropriating Hegel). Genuine dialogue-play, I think we are justified in asserting, is ultimately *good for us*!

Furthermore, since understanding is considered to be our fundamental *mode of being* in the world, according to Gadamer, being a participant in genuine dialogue-play with the Other is crucial for what it means to be a human being, or to live a fully human life. This life is not the life of a subject at a distance from the objects and other subjects of the world. It is not the life of an observing spectator, nor the life of a mind alone enveloped in its own thoughts (as the Cartesian tradition has trained us to believe). It is the life of a fundamentally open, involved, receptive and responsive being-in-the-world, primordially in contact with the meaningful subject matter of the world, moving in a back-and-forth communicative dance with others. Now, although we may always be understanding beings-in-the-world – or, as I would like to put it, understanding 'beings-at-play-in-the-world' with others – we can always enrich this understanding and this way of being. This enrichment is, I take it, one of the primary goals of hermeneutics as a theory and practice of understanding and correct interpretation. When we consider that understanding for Gadamer represents both what or who we already are and, simultaneously, an achievement that we want to reach with each other, we can see that in an important sense the goal of hermeneutic understanding is to be who we are more genuinely, more authentically – to be who we are *better*. I do not know of a goal more ethical in character.

Phenomenology of dialogue-play as practical philosophy

Finally, in connection with this last point, Gadamer's laborious efforts to develop a phenomenological analysis of genuine dialogue-play is offered to us, in the form of a practical philosophy, as a guide to help us improve our dialogic relations with Others so that a higher shared understanding can truly develop. [9] This is not a guide in the form of a 'how-to' book that offers rules or formulas for us to follow. It is a guide in the (distinctively Aristotelian) style of a description of the kinds of practices (that we know from experience) promote and preserve the process of dialogue and understanding, and a description of the kinds of contrasting practices (that we know from experience) lead dialogue and understanding to break down. As with Aristotle's ethics – which can only offer guidelines in the form of an outline or sketch, due to the ever-changing reality of situations in which humans must act – Gadamer's hermeneutics also offers an outline for how we can best approach the Other in dialogue. Just as Aristotle teaches us from observation and experience that virtue is preserved by 'the mean' and destroyed by excess and defect, Gadamer teaches us from observation and experience that genuine dialogue-play and understanding are preserved by a comportment of openness to the Other, and are destroyed by various attempts to objectify or overpower the Other. This truth communicated to us about the ethical conditions of dialogue and understanding, like Aristotle's truth about the mean, is meant to be recognized and applied by us in our own lives, and so is offered as a guide to praxis, a practical philosophy, or an ethical philosophy in its distinctively ancient form. This reading is confirmed by Gadamer in his 'Hermeneutics as Practical Philosophy', written in 1976, where he states: 'The great tradition of practical philosophy lives on in a hermeneutics that becomes aware of its philosophic implications … in both cases we have the same mutual implication between theoretical interest and practical action' (Gadamer 1981: 111). In this essay Gadamer establishes explicitly the connection between hermeneutics and practical philosophy, which both ask 'the question of the good' (Gadamer 1981: 93).

Conclusion

Gadamer shows us throughout his *Truth and Method* what is really at stake in his project of developing an accurate account of understanding. He shows us that a proper notion of understanding is needed if our efforts to grasp the subject matter of our world with others, in a more complete and profound way, are to be given proper direction. In accounting for the ethical conditions that make the play-process of understanding possible, Gadamer guides us past the sorts of road-blocks we set for ourselves that cause communication breakdown – in particular, those that occur when we approach the Other in various postures of dominance and close ourselves off from being affected by what the Other has to say.

What is particularly troubling, though, is our more and more frequent experience of a kind of 'radical closedness' to the Other; a flat refusal to even try to speak or listen to those who one considers to be their Other. In political, religious or ethical debates in particular, we encounter a popular attitude that one should not even *want* to understand their Other out of a belief that either such understanding is impossible (so that there is 'no point' in even trying), or that reaching an understanding with one's Other would mean having one's own beliefs somehow 'perverted' by those one already knows one disagrees with. Although Gadamer is able to offer guidance to those who still *want* to develop understanding with each other, and who generally view mutual understanding as a valuable pursuit for our common good, he is unable to help us past the obstacle of radical closedness, since he always begins his discussion where a shared 'willingness to try' is already in place. Thus, our biggest and most threatening contemporary obstacle to genuine dialogue and understanding – the refusal to take part in dialogue, and the immediate withdrawal or use of force that follows it – remains unexamined and undealt with. Our new task must be to find a way to reopen dialogue where it has become radically closed, and go beyond Gadamer to develop an ethics of human engagement that can cultivate dialogue where it has been totally blocked. We stand in need of a broadened ethics of play.

Notes

1   I call these conditions for dialogic play 'ethical' conditions because (1) they represent the manner in which human interlocutors *must treat each other* for dialogic play to continue and flourish; (2) these I–Thou relations create an encounter with the Other that is characterized by mutual *respect* (i.e. treating the Other like a human being who has something meaningful to say, rather than as an object to be dominated); (3) these I–Thou relations require a shared *commitment* and *self-disciplined conduct* to be

achieved; and (4) these I–Thou relations ultimately provide for a process in which mutual human growth can occur, making them I–Thou relations that are ultimately *directed towards our common human good.*

2 I offer my thanks to Lexington Books for allowing me to borrow sections from my book *Gadamer's Ethics of Play: Hermeneutics and the Other* (2010) in order to craft a condensed version of some of my main arguments in a form that is meant for a broad interdisciplinary audience.

3 Drew Hyland, in his book *The Question of Play*, argues that Gadamer denies the intentional character of play, and that for him 'play simply "happens" to the player independently of his or her intentions' (Hyland 1984: 88) and further that 'the attitude of the player has nothing to do with whether or not there is play' (Hyland 1984: 89). I think this depiction misses a crucial aspect of play. Although the players' intentions and attitudes are not the locale of play, no play can take place without seriously playful attitudes and intentions. The players' shared comportment towards each other and towards the game is a crucial condition for the possibility of any genuine play at all. Although it cannot be fully developed here, I would venture to say that Hyland's own articulation of play as involving the 'stance of responsive openness' actually shares much more in common with Gadamer's notion of play than he recognizes.

4 Although Gadamer is often accused of promoting a theory of understanding that does not adequately preserve difference, we can see that difference is really the life-blood of the play-movement of understanding in which we revise our prejudices and enrich our knowledge. See the last section of Chapter 5 in *Gadamer's Ethics of Play: Hermeneutics and the Other* (Vilhauer 2010) for the full argument.

5 Although Gadamer often speaks from the perspective of what the 'I' does (or must do) in relation to the 'Other' for genuine dialogue to occur, we should remember that both interlocutors must operate with a reciprocal openness and shared commitment to understanding for the play-process of genuine dialogue to occur. Certainly, I only have control over my own behaviour in a dialogue and I cannot control whether the Other is open towards me, is committed to understanding each other, is a good listener, etc. But what the Other does (or does not do) is just as important for the functioning of the dialogue as what I do. I cannot create genuine dialogue-play on my own. The movement of genuine dialogue will only occur if there is a shared openness between interlocutors, and if their commitment to understanding each other is reciprocal.

6 Although Gadamer is often accused of being generally ignorant of the power relations that underlie dialogue, we can see in Gadamer's description of less than genuine dialogues that he is, in fact, concerned very much with the problem of uneven power relations and their effect on dialogue. All three forms of what I call 'foul play' are driven by an attempt to dominate the Other. This means that it is in fact an imbalance of power, caused by the way in which one person approaches another, that is a main root of communication breakdown. Gadamer's goal in his phenomenological study of genuine dialogue is to take the phenomenon of genuine dialogue as it actually occurs in our experience, to describe it, and to analyse what it is that makes such genuine dialogue possible. One of the important conditions of genuine dialogue that comes to light through Gadamer's analysis is that interlocutors (regardless of the social/political standing they might hold in their culture) treat each other in the conversation as equals (as human beings worthy of respect, and as people whose 'claims to truth' deserve serious consideration).

7 The problems Gadamer sees with the psychological approach to the Other are developed also in his critique of Schleiermacher's influential conception of, and approach to, interpersonal understanding, which suggests that understanding the meaning of a text requires understanding the intention or psychological state of the author – or, in other words, *who* he or she was.

8 See Chapter 7 of *Gadamer's Ethics of Play: Hermeneutics and the Other* (Vilhauer 2010) for the full argument.

9 See Chapter 8 of *Gadamer's Ethics of Play: Hermeneutics and the Other* (Vilhauer 2010) for the full argument.

Bibliography

Aristotle (1962) *Nicomachean Ethics*, trans. Martin Ostwald. New York: Macmillan.

Gadamer, H-G. (1981) *Reason in the Age of Science*, trans. F.G. Lawrence. Cambridge, MA: MIT Press.

Gadamer, H-G. (1986) *The Relevance of the Beautiful and Other Essays*, trans. N. Walker, ed. R. Bernasconi. Cambridge: Cambridge University Press.

Gadamer, H-G. (2000) *Truth and Method* (2nd edn), trans. J. Weinsheimer and D.G. Marshall. New York: Continuum.

Hyland, D. (1984) *The Question of Play*. Lanham, MD: University Press of America.

Ormiston, G.L and Schrift, A.D. (eds) (1990) *The Hermeneutic Tradition: From Ast to Ricouer*. Albany, NY: SUNY Press.

Schmidt, L. (ed.) (1995) *The Specter of Relativism: Truth, Dialogue, and Phronesis in Philosophical Hermeneutics*. Evanston: Northwestern University Press.

Vilhauer, M. (2010) *Gadamer's Ethics of Play: Hermeneutics and the Other*. Lanham, MD: Lexington Books.

7 Language at play

Games and the linguistic turn after Wittgenstein and Gadamer

Núria Sara Miras Boronat

Wittgenstein and Gadamer: the impossible encounter

If there ever was a philosopher whose personality could be exactly the opposite of Ludwig Wittgenstein's radical temperament, it must be Hans-Georg Gadamer. Wittgenstein's life was intense and often dramatic, whereas the days of Gadamer were joyful and calm. When Wittgenstein attained recognition in the philosophical world he was barely thirty years old and had not applied for any academic positions, while when Gadamer received major attention he was more than sixty and occupied a comfortable position as a professor in Heidelberg. These differences in temperament become more obvious when comparing the *pathos* of their 'official' biographies: Ray Monk's (1991) thrilling examination of Wittgenstein's life contrasts with Jean Grondin's (1994) symphonic account of Gadamer. But there are more than just differences in their respective personalities; these two thinkers differ in philosophical style. Gadamer was a scholar: erudite and meticulous. Wittgenstein, on the other hand, was an anarchistic spirit who wrote in feverous floods of thought, without giving them any systematic form.[1]

Despite the fact that they were two of the most important philosophers of the twentieth century and that they were, specifically, two major thinkers of the so-called *linguistic turn*, Wittgenstein and Gadamer never had any personal contact. It is doubtful that they had even been aware of each other's existence. It was not until Wittgenstein died in 1951 and became world famous that Gadamer became aware of Wittgenstein's revolutionary philosophy. Both philosophers also had a major influence in parallel but separate schools of philosophy. Philosophy departments all over the world declared Wittgenstein the founding father of analytical philosophy. Gadamer saw his philosophical hermeneutics as a possible development of a tradition of more than 2000 years of continental thought (although it was not called 'continental' until 'analytic philosophy' invented these labels).[2]

For all of these reasons, it might seem nonsensical to try and compare these philosophers. In fact, few writers have attempted to do so,[3] although such comparisons across traditions are becoming not only common, but interesting and desirable.[4] A pluralistic tone is dominant nowadays and this is good news for philosophical dialogue as well as for integrative perspectives. Therefore I attempt to show that if we aim for a complete picture of the philosophical world during the early 1930s, and in particular the history of the philosophy of language, there is a need for an integrated approach to Wittgenstein and Gadamer. Their writings present fundamental convergences, as Gadamer appreciated many decades later. They shared the intuition that philosophy had to move beyond the solitary *Geist* to ordinary language if proper access to philosophical problems was to be found. As Wittgenstein once stated: 'When philosophizing you have to descend into the old chaos & feel at home there' (CV: 74). Both believed that one of the main problems of philosophy is how to describe the nature of language. Language and history are the stuff we are made of, but what if language keeps playing tricks on us and hiding its very essence? Thus their first concern was to clarify how language shapes our mind, instead of assuming that our words are mere 'translations' of our ideas, as modern epistemology did. The focus has changed: instead of searching for a mental connection with an ethereal and ideal world of meanings, we have to look at language working in ordinary communicative contexts. For this task we can use the concepts of games and play,[5] since the inner structure of these phenomena allows for a more accurate explanation of the functioning of language.

Wittgenstein's 'language-games' as theoretical instruments for the study of language

Wittgenstein's first mention of games appears in 1933 as he tries to elucidate how small pieces of communicative acts function. During 1933 and 1934 Wittgenstein explored many such examples, often through discussion with his students. The notes of these classes were later known as *The Blue Book* and *The Brown Book*. The discussion on language-games is given a broader theoretical context in the *Philosophical Investigations*, where Wittgenstein examines some examples from Augustine's *Confessions* on learning language. Wittgenstein takes Augustine's work as an example that fits with his own earlier conception of meaning described in the *Tractatus Logico-Philosophicus* (published in 1922). The problem with his earlier theory of meaning is that it can only explain how a specific class of propositions, *declarative propositions* or *assertions*, make sense and distinguishes between true and false propositions. Such assertions are typically the propositions that refer to concrete objects (e.g. 'the hut is red') or relationships between objects (e.g. 'the hut is on the table'). But Wittgenstein's theory fails to explain how other types of proposition (that express desires, orders or hypotheses, e.g. 'I wish I had a red hut') can be meaningful for others. Wittgenstein had to admit that not all propositions are reducible to propositions about objects. Immersed in this crisis of the *Tractatus* paradigm, he invented the concept of a 'language-game'. 'Language-games' do not correlate to any particular linguistic reality but are rather a simplified reconstruction of a common linguistic situation. As Wittgenstein defines them, language-games are:

ways of using signs simpler than those in which we use the signs of our highly complicated everyday language. Language-games are the forms of language with which a child begins to make use of words. The study of language-games is the study of primitive forms of language or primitive languages.

(BIB: 17)

Thus, language-games are primarily devised as a model or object of comparison[6] for the purposes of showing how *plural* our actual use of language is. Wittgenstein describes in the famous aphorism 23 of the *Philosophical Investigations* the different language-games he tries to study. They include activities such as giving orders, reporting an event, making up a story, making a joke, thanking, greeting or praying, among others.[7] But in using the phrase 'language-game', Wittgenstein never intended to reduce linguistic acts to games, nor did he assume that language-games are any kind of metaphysical entities. The phrase 'language-games' may be understood as a *metaphor*, or more properly as an *instrument* for the study of language. In the phrase 'language-game', the first term has priority over the second. Wittgenstein does not provide any definition of games. He only states that we use the term 'game' in very different situations, and that therefore what a 'game' is, is open to interpretation.[8] What is essential for any given game is that the game is constituted by its rules: the rules define the game.[9] Furthermore, games are activities that take place in specific contexts. Subsequently, language-games refer to the totality composed by language and the activities with which language is interwoven.[10] A language-game refers to a communicative situation which involves individuals, objects, relationships and contexts: its goal is to represent synoptically how all these elements interact. Performance criteria are essential to understanding linguistic utterances. When we communicate we give life to words; we play with them. It is such a performance that transforms something in the world. If communication is successful, things should never be as they were before.

Wittgenstein's language-games became powerful conceptual tools in the philosophy of language during the 1960s. But a question still remains: How did Wittgenstein get the inspiration to talk about language as a game? Wittgenstein never gave any indication of where his idea of language as a game originated. There were, indeed, other theorists working on games and play during this time who expressed similar ideas to Wittgenstein; for example, Johan Huizinga, George Herbert Mead and Hans-Georg Gadamer. Since there is no indication that Wittgenstein engaged with any of these thinkers in his writings, the inspiration must have come to him through other paths. The most common example used by these thinkers is, as Gunter Gebauer (2009: 22) recalls, a game like chess, where the role of every piece defines its function in the whole.[11] Monk's (1991) biography of Wittgenstein discusses the purpose of language-games, but says nothing concrete about where the concept originates from. Language-games are described as a technique for dissolving philosophical confusion. In Allan Janik's (2006) opinion, the most direct influence appears to be Heinrich Hertz's mechanical models, but Wittgenstein does not mention him in the *Investiga-tions*. Elsewhere, Norman Malcolm (1962) claims that Wittgenstein had his idea as he was observing a football match. Such a hypothesis would be undoubtedly more attractive than that offered by Janik; however, it is difficult to support it with textual evidence.[12]

Gadamer: Games, play, artworks and language

Gadamer's first mention of play and games occurred in the late 1920s as he was finishing his first large philosophical work: the *Phenomenological Interpretations Relating to the 'Philebus'* (1929).[13] In this work, Gadamer mentions play and games by pointing to Heidegger's brief observation in his lectures on Leibniz, that the existence of the *Dasein* (our being in the world) is a game.[14] The purpose of Gadamer's lectures on Ancient Greek philosophy was to regain the original sense of Plato's dialectics in order to present a dialectical form of wisdom which could be set against the *monological* model of modern science. This first approach to games and play was not strictly thought to be applicable to language, so I will not consider it further in this chapter. Gadamer's second attempt to analyse games and play would occur thirty years after these lectures.

Gadamer's analysis of the word *Spiel* (which means both games and play)[15] is detailed in two sections of his most important philosophical work *Truth and Method* (1960). Here Gadamer reflects on the nature of aesthetic experience and previous enquiries into the nature of language. Originally Gadamer conceived *Truth and Method* as wanting to show the ontological relationship between art-works, *Spiel* and language. This relationship can be explained in an intuitive manner: when we contemplate an artwork, we often feel that the artist is trying to say something to us. We are immediately involved in a conversational game between the meaning of the piece of art and its potential audience. Immanuel Kant, one of Gadamer's references, described how, in the *Critique of Judgment*, the experience of beauty is the result of the interplay of our cognitive faculties. Nevertheless, the application of the ontology of games and artworks to language was not properly detailed by Gadamer because he assumed it was self-evident.

In order to understand what the nature of play is, Gadamer begins with an examination of our everyday uses of the terms 'play' and 'games'. In language we find plenty of phrases that express the joy and ease of play. We play the piano, the waves play with the sand, the bees play among the flowers, and so on. Within this context, the idea of a 'game' mostly refers to *aimless, effortlessly per-formed movements, which are constantly repeated*.[16]

If we examine Gadamer's definition of play, we can see how the analogy between language and play actually works. Language refers to a movement, to something occurring between two or more people. When we are competent speakers of a language, we are aware of grammatical rules (i.e. the rules that define what a meaningful utterance is and what it is not) but we speak without being aware of them all the time. It is as if we were playing: we manage to form meaningful utterances spontaneously, without having the feeling that we need to make considerable effort.[17] We also find repetition in language. Words have to have fixed meanings, so that we can be sure that in future uses our expressions mean the same things.[18] Language is an instrument for communication but it does not belong to an individual or to any social institution. Language is the common property of a community of speakers and has an independent life beyond that community: in this sense the movement has no definite aims; its aim is in itself. Although Gadamer does not pay as much attention to (as Wittgenstein does) the criteria for defining a 'game', he does acknowledge that rules are an important part of any game. The moves within a game, which are a priori potentially infinite, are restricted by the rules, which define the space or universe of the game. The player who does not respect the rules is either (1) not playing the same game as others, or (2) spoiling the game by their refusal to follow the rules of the game. This is also the case with language. If we are not respectful of grammatical rules, we may (1) not be speaking the same language, or (2) ruin the possibility of true communication.

Gadamer's reading of Wittgenstein

It took Gadamer around ten years to write *Truth and Method*. After all, he was trying to summarize decades of teaching experience and intellectual work. He experienced the completion of this – his *opus magnum* – as an awakening to the world after a long period of reclusion. While he was writing *Truth and Method* very interesting philosophical debates were taking place. As he recounted many years later,[19] the first works that caught his attention during this period were the poetry of Paul Celan, the essay 'Ousia and Gramme' by Jacques Derrida[20] and Wittgenstein's *Philosophical Investigations*. As he read Wittgenstein he was astonished. The coincidences were striking. Wittgenstein had written about 'language-games' (*Sprachspiele*) and Gadamer had finished his work with a lyrical note about wordplay and language-games (*sprachliche Spiele*), through which we, as learners, develop our understanding of the world.[21] But, at the same time, some important differences between his own work and that of Wittgenstein became clear to Gadamer. His reading in the 1960s now gives the impression of having been superficial. Two themes are central to Gadamer's disagreement with Wittgenstein: a critique of metaphysics and a critique of language.[22] By focusing on these areas, there are strong parallels between Gadamer's own critique and the wider interpretation of Wittgenstein's work as positivistic during the 1960s to the 1980s.

Gadamer shares with Wittgenstein the conviction that language was not created originally for the purpose of doing philosophy. As Gadamer sees it, the desire to capture reality with abstract concepts has always been something tragic and desperate: we live in a kind of constant linguistic poverty.[23] But Gadamer did not understand Wittgenstein's refusal of all metaphysical questions. For Gadamer, metaphysics is part of human intellectual history, and, while we may have to live in linguistic poverty, we do have the possibility to find new languages and to enrich our actual language use too. Perhaps if he had read the

Philosophical Investigations more closely, Gadamer might have recognized that Wittgenstein's spirit was not only critical, but also radical in the original sense of the word. Wittgenstein was trying to go back to the *roots* of philosophical puzzles, which is close to the hermeneutic method of analysis in our conventional interpretation of these concepts.

Almost twenty-five years elapsed before Gadamer returned seriously to Wittgenstein. *Truth and Method* had become the centre of many philosophical debates: a fact that surprised Gadamer, who was not expecting so much attention. By the 1980s, Gadamer's hermeneutics was so popular that Gianni Vattimo (1989) declared it the 'new *koiné*' (a term used by the Ancient Greeks to refer to the 'common language') of philosophy. Since Gadamer was defending the idea that language gives us access to the world, he may have been pleased with Vattimo's declaration. All these debates forced Gadamer to examine the key concepts of philosophical hermeneutics in order to come to terms with his critics. Over time, Gadamer became particularly concerned about the precarious application of aesthetic experience analysis, which was based on the ontological discussion of games and play, and the universal linguisticality (*Sprachlichkeit*) of our world experience. After all, world experience and language is something that we learn through imitating others.[24] Nevertheless, these examples are few and far between: there are only a few examples of Gadamer moving in this direction.

In the 1990s Gadamer published his essay entitled 'Towards a Phenomenology of Ritual and Language' (1992, in GW8) where he seeks an anthropological foundation to his philosophical hermeneutics via the analysis of rituals, celebrations and symbols. In order to emphasize the priority of conversation over other basic forms of life, such as rituals or habits, Gadamer uses Giambattista Vico's concept of 'rhetoric'. Originally, Vico used the term 'rhetoric' to refer to our primary and linguistically articulated access to the world. It is important to note that in this case Gadamer considers not only verbal or spoken language but every simple form of exchange. The life of any given community is considered from two points of view: *Mitsamt* (which could correspond to our 'natural', instinctive behaviour) and *Miteinander* (which could be called 'hermeneutic' behaviour, i.e. oriented to mutual understanding). These forms of communal life encompass everything from animalistic rituals to the highest tiers of literature. We could say: from the material basis to the spirit. These forms could also include all sorts of games and play, from the most rudimentary, childish games to the most complex and elevated. Wittgenstein is mentioned in this essay and we can feel his implicit influence on Gadamer as he pays attention to the ways in which we acquire language in our childhood. Although Gadamer could have opened a promising line of enquiry from this essay, these notes remained marginal in the context of his main philosophical focus: hermeneutics.

Perhaps the lack of success in Gadamer's attempt to integrate Wittgensteinian concepts was due to historical circumstances. In these years, Gadamer was involved in two crucial polemics: one with the critics of ideology (Apel and

Habermas, among others, in the 1970s), another with the deconstructionists (mainly Derrida in the 1980s). Perhaps the *kairós* (the right moment) had not arrived yet, since the debate in Europe and America insisted on maintaining the chasm between analytic and continental philosophy. Furthermore, Gadamer could have profited more from Wittgenstein's aphorisms on certainty, but they remained unpublished until 1969. He probably would have realized how close his own concept of tradition as the hermeneutic background for common life and language was to concepts of the late Wittgenstein, such as in the form of life and world picture.

In one of his last interviews with Riccardo Dottori, the centenarian Gadamer looks back on his philosophical career and again mentions his deep intellectual kinship with Wittgenstein. Gadamer states that there are two concepts which give credibility to the claim that he and Wittgenstein could be seen as counterparts in the history of philosophy: the concept of game and the concept of individuality.[25] Reconstructing their analogies between language and the games we play allows us to reveal ways in which their concepts of game may be unified.

Language, games and play: limits and virtues of the analogy

Wittgenstein and Gadamer were working in different conceptual frameworks, but their analyses of play and games in the context of the study of language are significantly similar. These similarities have to do with the function of the analogy between the language and the games we usually play.

In the first instance, an analysis of games and play in relation to language is meant to be strictly *phenomenological*, i.e. *descriptive*. Play activities have structural parallels with the sort of activity that language is and therefore play is a good way in which to explain the nature of language, but language should be more than merely a game we play. In other words, initially, Wittgenstein and Gadamer try to avoid the 'ontological temptation' to identify the object with the model. Language-games are not autonomous entities; they do not exist as such in the real world. On this point Wittgenstein was more consistent. In his analysis Gadamer uses language to explain what games are, and later returns to language through the perspective of an everlasting game that is played and that recreates itself beyond the intentions of the speakers.

The second similarity between Gadamer and Wittgenstein relates to the inner structure of games that helps both philosophers to stress the following aspects of language: its *normativity*, *social character* and *creativity*. Normativity refers to the existence of rules that define what is allowed in a game, and what is not. The rules define the game, so that, when we stop playing, we are sure we can play the same game in the future. To take an example: Today I can play chess online with someone living in Barcelona. I am sure that the rules of the game we are playing will not change tomorrow and that we will be playing chess when we meet online next week. As sure as we are that we play the same game on different occasions, the normativity of the meaning (the fact that a word always denotes the same class of objects) is what makes us sure that the same word has the same meaning in its different contexts of use. As there is no game without potential partners, even if we play alone, language is a *social* phenomenon that needs other potential speakers to exist. Solitary games are only possible because 'normal' games exist. Solitary use of language is a secondary use, derived from normal uses. Although rules restrict movement within the game so that not everything is possible, they also still allow for surprises, and this creativity is the joy of the game. This is also the case in language: we can introduce new, unexpected uses of words.

Furthermore, these three aspects of language (normativity, sociality and creativity) are internally linked. A norm cannot exist without a community that accepts it and supports it. In addition, any society cannot exist without sanctioning behaviour as appropriate or otherwise. A creative pattern of behaviour (linguistic or not) can have its source in the genius of a single personality experimenting with the possibility of new patterns, but it will not be more than a solitary experiment if there is no society that acknowledges it and if it is incompatible with the rest of the socially sanctioned patterns.

The *social* aspect of the game is perhaps one of its most important features, as it has consequences for the concept of language. If language, as games, is primarily social, that means that its existence and nature depends on a collective. In modern epistemology, language is a 'mere' translation of the ideas of the transcendental subject referring to objects of the world. But there are many uses of words that do not fit into this schema. What Wittgenstein and Gadamer are saying is that our language conforms to the way in which transcendental subjects cope with the world, and in doing so they manage to overcome the strict subject–object schema regarding community, history and dynamics for the study of language. Language is no longer the 'mirror of nature' or the 'incarnation of mind'. Language, as Gadamer beautifully states, *is* only in the conversation.[26]

Gadamer's link to this analogical case is, as Walter Schulz (1970: 311) points out, his claim that the terms 'history', 'language', 'conversation' and 'game' all end up being synonymous. All these terms can be equated to the concept of game. Indeed, one of Gadamer's favourite poems is the *Friedensfeier* by Friedrich Hölderlin. *Seit ein Gespräch wir sind* ('since we are a conversation') is one of the *leitmotivs* of Gadamer's work and life. Gadamer chose for the opening of *Truth and Method* Rilke's poem on an 'eternal partner in the game'. Gadamer's interpretation of Rilke's metaphor consists in a personification of the whole tradition to which we belong, and with whom we keep playing in an endless conversation.

Unfortunately, Gadamer and Wittgenstein never had the occasion to meet in person or to discuss each other's ideas. However, there is a pertinent remark by Wittgenstein around 1948 that reminds us of the spirit of Gadamer's philosophical hermeneutics: 'In a conversation: One person throws a ball; the other does not know: is he to throw it back, throw it to a third person, or leave it lying, or pick it up & put it in his pocket, etc.' (CV: 84). The analogy between games and language has proven to be a good starting point for this conversation between philosophical traditions. The next move is our turn.

Notes

1 Wittgenstein confesses in the opening of the *Philosophical Investigations*: 'The best I could write would never be more than philosophical remarks; my thoughts were soon crippled if I tried to force them on in any single direction against their natural inclination' (PI: viii).

2 As Jean Grondin (2003) tells the story.

3 I base my reflections mainly in Apel (1976), Arnswald (2002), Del Castillo (2001), Habermas (1985, 1999, 2001), Kambartel (1991), Tietz (2000) and Zimmermann (1975).

4 See e.g. Grondin (1994), Hacking (1975), Stekeler-Weithofer (2004).

5 I am going to use the English words 'play' and 'game' as equivalents to the German word *Spiel*, which is the term used by both. A comparative linguistic study of the terms in the semantic field of play activities is to be found in Huizinga (1962). Perhaps the most important difference between the terms 'game' and 'play' is that in 'game' the rule component seems to be stronger, whereas in 'play' the component of creativity and freedom seems to have more weight. Play also relates to the performative element in the arts (music, drama, etc.). I use the phrase 'play activities' to refer to all the phenomena that fall under the German substantive *Spiel*. George (2011) refers only to the concept of play by Gadamer but in the context of the aesthetic experience. Since Gadamer uses 'game' sometimes related to language, I use the term in this context too.

6 Cfr. PI, 130: 50.

7 Cfr. PI, 23: 11.

8 Cfr. PI, 69: 33.

9 Cfr. PG, I, II, 26: 63.

10 Cfr. PI, 7: 5.

11 See e.g. PG, I, II, 31: 67.

12 Malcolm had never heard this story from Wittgenstein. It seems that Wittgenstein mentioned it to Freeman Dyson, a young physics student who was staying at the Trinity College:

> Dyson recalled one anecdote of Wittgenstein's which is of considerable interest: One day when Wittgenstein was passing a field where a football game was in progress the thought first struck him that in language we play *games* with *words*. A central idea of his philosophy, the notion of a 'language-game', apparently had its genesis in this incident
>
> (Malcolm 1962: 65)

13 This work was later revised and published as *Platos dialektische Ethik* (1931).

14 Cfr. Heidegger (1990). See also Fink (1969), Kusch (1989) and Zúñiga (1995).

15 See n. 3 above.

16 Although Gadamer has other important sources, his phenomenological analysis of play and game is directly taken from Johan Huizinga's definition in *Homo Ludens*. See Huizinga (1962).

17 This is the case when we use our mother tongue or when we speak a language with which we feel confident. It might not be the case when we speak foreign languages at the beginner's level.

18 The constant repetition of the game is explained through the concept of celebration (*Fest*). The performance character, whose origin comes from the inside of the movement, is linked to the categories of the autorepresentation (*Selbstdarstellung*) and execution (*Vollzug*). These categories are more related to the specifity of aesthetic experience and they are difficult to translate in the terms of linguistic normativity.

19 In his essay 'Hermeneutik auf der Spur' of 1994 (GW10: 149).

20 Published in Derrida's collection *Margins of Philosophy*.

21 Cfr. TM: 484. Unfortunately, the English translation cannot reflect the German nuances. Wittgenstein's *Sprachspiele* are technical concepts invented by him. When Gadamer writes *sprachliche Spiele* he means the games language plays, as if language itself were a character acting.
22 The most important essay by Gadamer mentioning Wittgenstein in the 1960s is *The Phenomenological Movement* (1963, see GW3).
23 Cfr. GW2: 83
24 Cfr. GW2: 5. The most important development of the aesthetic concept of play is the work *The Relevance of the Beautiful* (1986, see RB).
25 Cfr. CP: 74–75.
26 Cfr. GW8: 369.

Abbreviations used for Wittgenstein's works

[BIB] (1964) *The Blue and Brown Books*. Oxford: Blackwell.
[CV] (1998) *Culture and Value*. Oxford: Blackwell.
[OC] (1972) *On Certainty*. New York: Harper.
[PG] (2005) *Philosophical Grammar*. Berkeley: University of California Press.
[PI] (1999) *Philosophical Investigations*. Oxford: Blackwell.

Abbreviations used for Gadamer's works

[CP] (2003) *A Century of Philosophy. A Conversation with Riccardo Dottori*. London: Continuum.
[PH] (1976) *Philosophical Hermeneutics*. Berkeley: University of California Press.
[GW2] (1999) *Wahrheit und Methode. Ergänzungen*. Tübingen: Mohr Siebeck.
[GW3] (1999) *Neuere Philosophie I. Hegel-Husserl-Heidegger*. Tübingen: Mohr Siebeck.
[GW8] (1999) *Ästhetik und Poetik I. Kunst als Aussage*. Tübingen: Mohr Siebeck.
[GW10] (1999) *Hermeneutik im Rückblick. Nachträge und Verzeichnisse*. Tübingen: Mohr Siebeck.
[RB] (1986) *The Relevance of the Beautiful*. Cambridge: Cambridge University Press.
[TM] (2004) *Truth and Method*. London: Continuum.

Bibliography

Apel, K.-O. (1976) *Transformation der Philosophie*. Frankfurt am Main: Suhrkamp.
Arnswald, U. (2002) 'On the Certainty of Uncertainty: Language Games and Forms of Life in Gadamer and Wittgenstein', in J. Malpas, U. Arnswald and J. Kertscher (eds) *Gadamer's Century*. Cambridge, MA: MIT Press, pp. 25–44.
Del Castillo, R. (2001) 'Juegos, diálogos, historia: Gadamer y Wittgenstein en discusión', in L. Vega, E. Rada and S. Mas (eds) *Del pensar y su memoria*. Madrid: Publicaciones UNED, pp. 475–496.
Fink, E. (1969) *Spiel als Weltsymbol*. Stuttgart: W. Kohlhammer Verlag.
Gebauer, G. (2009) *Wittgensteins Anthropologisches Denken*. Munich: Beck.
George, Th. (2011) 'From Work to Play. Gadamer on the Affinity of Art, Truth and Beauty'. *Internationales Jahrubuch für Hermeneutik*, 10: 107–122.
Grondin, J. (1994) *Introduction to Philosophical Hermeneutics*. New Haven, CT: Yale University Press.

Grondin, J. (2003) *Hans-Georg Gadamer. A Biography*. New Haven, CT: Yale University Press.

Habermas, J. (1985) *Zur Logik der Sozialwissenschaften*. Frankfurt am Main: Suhrkamp.

Habermas, J. (1999) *Wahrheit und Rechtfertigung*. Frankfurt am Main: Suhrkamp.

Habermas, J. (2001) *Kommunikatives Handeln und detranszendentalisierte Vernunft*. Stuttgart: Reclam.

Hacking, I. (1975) *Why Does Language Matter to Philosophy?* Cambridge: Cambridge University Press.

Huizinga, J. (1962) *Homo Ludens. A Study of the Play Element in Culture*. Boston, MA: The Beacon Press.

Janik, A. (2006) *Assembling Reminders. Studies in the Genesis of Wittgenstein's Concept of Philosophy*. Stockholm: Santérus Academic.

Kambartel, F. (1991) 'Versuch über das Verstehen', in B. McGuiness (ed.) *Der Löwe spricht . . . und wir können ihn nicht verstehen*. Frankfurt am Main: Suhrkamp, pp. 121–137.

Kusch, M. (1989) *Language as Calculus vs. Language as Universal Medium. A Study in Husserl, Heidegger, and Gadamer*. Dordrecht: Kluwer.

Malcolm, N. (1962) *Ludwig Wittgenstein. A Memoir*. London: Oxford University Press.

Monk, R. (1991) *Ludwig Wittgenstein: The Duty of Genius*. London: Vintage.

Stekeler-Weithofer, P. (2004) 'A Second Wave of Enlightenment: Kant, Wittgenstein and the Contintental Tradition', in M. Kölbel and B. Weiss (eds) *Wittgenstein's Lasting Significance*. London: Routledge, pp. 282–300.

Tietz, U. (2000) *Hans-Georg Gadamer zur Einführung*. Hamburg: Junius.

Vattimo, G. (1989) *Etica dell'interpretazione*. Turin: Rosenberg & Sellier.

Zimmermann, J. (1975) *Wittgensteins sprachphilosophische Hermeneutik*. Frankfurt am Main: Vittorio Klostermann.

Zúñiga, J.F. (1995) *El diálogo como juego. La hermenéutica filosófica de Hans-Georg Gadamer*. Granada: Universidad de Granada.

8 Whoever cannot give, also receives nothing

Nietzsche's playful spectator

Catherine Homan

In his account of aesthetics, the German philosopher Friedrich Nietzsche argues that to be an artist is not merely to create a work of art, but also to lead one's life in a particular, namely artistic, way. This way of life is characterized by creativity, independence and an active will to give shape to one's life in the same way that one gives shape to a sculpture or a poem. Thus the artist is characterized as active rather than passive. Ultimately, Nietzsche sees artistic activity as fundamentally playful. The difficulty of Nietzsche's work, though, is that he says very little about how non-artists relate to art and whether they are capable of leading their lives in the same way as artists. In other words, Nietzsche does not explain whether art has any influence on life for those who are not artists. Furthermore, Nietzsche seems to equate non-artists with critics, who are diametrically opposed to artists. Yet by looking specifically at the role of play both in artistic creation and artistic life, I argue that we gain a clearer sense both of the role of the spectator as non-artist and non-critic and the significance of art for such a spectator.

Hans-Georg Gadamer, who has also written extensively on play and art, helps shed light on how the spectator or non-artist also participates in this play. Both Nietzsche and Gadamer believe that our experience of art can never be one of disinterested objectivity. Instead, we stand in an intentional relation to works of art and can be transformed by them. Thus, although the spectator has not created the artwork, her experience of the work is still transformative and enables her to create and give shape to her life in the same way as the artist does. Because of this, the spectator is not passive, but an active participant in her self-creation. Although Nietzsche is more likely to see this playful activity of the artist in agonistic terms, primarily as the artist struggling against society, and Gadamer is more likely to see this play as collaborative and communal, they agree that both play and art afford unique opportunities for opening up a space that enables perspectives and possibilities we could not otherwise have. This play space always has boundaries and is guided by particular rules, yet these rules do not dictate our responses. We experience freedom through this playful nego-tiation between necessity and contingency. By looking at play, we can better understand how it is that art opens up such a space. Furthermore, this account of the relation among art, play and life enables us to see that play is not merely frivolous but very serious, since it affords the possibility to determine who we are and who we might be. I would like to suggest that we understand the spectator not as the passive recipient, but as an active, playful participant who stands, like the artist, in an essential relationship to art and life.

Nietzsche's artist

To begin, we should first consider Nietzsche's discussion of the artist. In 'The Will to Power as Art' we find that the artist stands apart from the rest of society, that is, belongs to a different race, and so is to be distinguished from those who are not artists. Whereas the non-artists remain passive or part of the herd, the artists engage in active creation and giving. As Nietzsche writes,

> This is what distinguishes the artist from laymen (those susceptible to art): the latter reach the high point of their susceptibility when they receive; the former as they give – so that antagonism between these two gifts is not only natural but desirable. The perspectives of these two states are opposite: to demand of the artist that he should practice the perspective of the audience (of the critic –) means to demand that he should impoverish himself and his creative power – ... that he should receive.
>
> (Nietzsche 1968b: 811)[1]

Here Nietzsche quite clearly draws a boundary between artists and laypeople. Artists create from 'the inner need to make of things a reflex of one's own fullness and perfection' (ibid.: 812). The expression of this drive is found in giving: the artist gives shape to the work of art and, in the process, gives shape to this fullness and life. This marks the artist's will to power. Conversely, the non-artists, as described, lack these feelings and creative power and thus have neither the possibility of experiencing the artistic will to power nor the possibility to give. If the artist were to be like the audience, then he would be an impoverished form of himself.

However, if we pay attention to the language Nietzsche uses, we see he does not state that every non-artist or audience can and does only receive. Rather he states that the artist cannot 'practice the perspective of the audience (of the critic –)' and that 'it is to the honour of an artist if he is unable to be a critic'.[2] There is an important distinction to be made between the critic as receiver and the spectator. By critic, Nietzsche has in mind the disinterested critic who believes aesthetic judgements can be made objectively if one assumes a critical distance from the work of art. This critic is, on every account from Nietzsche, in fact untenable. To assert some critical distance or objectivity ignores that such objectivity is a myth; every interpretation, and even reception, involves making use of particular interests, prejudices and additions. Furthermore, Nietzsche writes, 'whoever cannot give, also receives nothing' (ibid.: 801). The sober, weary, dried-up or disinterested non-artist who receives art objectively cannot exist, since this critic gives nothing and so ultimately receives nothing. As we will see, the spectator does not match this description of the critic.

The artist is capable of this giving through superabundance, as well as by the waking of basic instincts, 'of power, nature, etc.!' (ibid.: 797). Nietzsche also draws our attention to the instinct of play. He writes of play as 'the "childlikeness" of God, *pais paizon*' (ibid.). Regarding artists, he describes 'Their habitual manner, their unreasonableness, their ignorance about themselves, their indifference to "eternal values," their seriousness in "play"' (ibid.: 816). The affirmation of these basic instincts encourages the rejection of disinterested objectivity in favour of a dynamic and intentional relationship of the artist to her creation and the world. Because one who is disinterested could never play or be active, such a person also could not have this creative, artistic attitude. The artist's playfulness also demonstrates that this attitude is not one of domination or strictly individual, but of a relation with and towards what is other than the artist, since play is always play with or of something.

The seriousness of play

Particularly interesting in these descriptions of the artist is the idea of 'seriousness of play': play is something intentional insofar as it is serious, but play is also 'useless'. Play is not directed towards an eventual goal, but intends a different sort of activity itself. I suggest that play best describes the nature not only of artistic creation, but also of artistic reception. In both cases we find that play indicates a certain comportment of the participant to the activity that is dynamic, intentional and open.

In 'The Relevance of the Beautiful' Gadamer writes, 'play appears as a self-movement that does not pursue any particular end or purpose so much as movement *as* movement, exhibiting so to speak a phenomenon of excess, of living self-representation' (Gadamer 1986c: 23). The player intends the activity itself. Just as a child intends the game of leap-frog, so the artist intends the creation of art, and so intends the spectator the participatory experience of art. Thus to speak of play as non-purposive is not to say that it lacks any purpose, rather the activity is its own purpose. As we have seen in Nietzsche, art does not expressly fulfil a function, but instead arises from the superabundance that is beyond strict utility. The activity of creating is the purpose of artistic creation. Similarly, the player can choose to pursue something non-purposive because she is not bound to a specific goal. Indeed, she pursues rather a goal that she sets for herself.

Although play is non-purposive, it is not simply arbitrary. Play is always carried out within a certain play space (*Spielraum*) and within the realm of different rules and boundaries. All play involves free movement, but always within a particular context; this is the 'seriousness of play'. When engaged in play, persons take seriously the play space and the activity at hand. Not only do they choose to play, but they choose to play *in this way*. A child, for example, becomes incensed when someone claims her game is not 'real', or a group bristles when another player ignores the rules. The rules and boundaries of play thus do not inhibit or stifle the movement; rather these boundaries are what enable play in the first place. A person may choose to flout the rules, but then we might say she is no longer playing the game. The rules themselves might be changed or challenged by the players, but these changes always occur within this play space, which is itself bound and given shape, though not rendered static, by rules and limits. It is important to note, however, that this play space only arises through play, meaning that the play space cannot exist without the active participation of players. As Gadamer rightly notes, 'the purpose of the game is not really solving the task, but ordering and shaping the movement of the game itself' (Gadamer 2004: 107). Play marks a negotiation between the boundaries of the game and the free movement of the player, and is always a matter of play *with* and *of*. The player thus dynamically and creatively plays with and within this space, or, more strongly, 'the player belongs to the play' (Gadamer 1986c: 26).

The parallel between play and Nietzsche's artist crystallizes on this point: the artist engages the world in a way that intends creative production itself while navigating within a particular space. Furthermore, the giving superabundance is not exhausted by the creation of a work, but spills over into the way the artist comports herself, i.e. the will to power. Yet it was suggested before that the spectator also participates through play. In order for a reception of art to be possible, there must be something received, so here I would like first to draw our attention to the nature of art in order to understand better its interplay with the spectator.

The play of art

Since the work is the play space for the creative act, the work and artist stand in a mutual relationship. For Gadamer, this mutuality holds between the spectator and work as well. When we encounter a work of art, we encounter it *as* a work of art. We recognize that 'something stands before us' (Gadamer 1986c: 25), namely that world that 'issues a challenge which expects to be me' (ibid.: 26). This very act of recognition and identification already involves participation and interpretation. Nietzsche writes, for example, 'We do not always keep our eyes from rounding off something and, as it were, finishing the poem' (Nietzsche 1974: 107). Our experience of a work also has this to-and-fro character of play. We anticipate something about the work, but we must in a sense let it present itself, and we respond in our interpretation. We take notice of certain boundaries of the work while playing. We cannot impose any particular meaning on the work, since to do so would be to treat the work as merely instrumental. Nor may we think of the work as merely given. If the spectator were an objective, disinterested spectator, then the work would be self-sufficient, self-contained and there would be nothing for the spectator to bring to it. We take notice of the certain boundaries of the work while playing within the space it opens up for us and, through play, we hold open. In this way, our play with the work opens up a particular world, in the sense that this space is not meaningless, but, like the everyday world, is bound by time and space and is a locus of meaning and understanding. We comport ourselves in a way that intends this relation with the work; we do not think of it only as a stimulant for thought, nor do we stamp any particular meaning on the work. This play does not end after the initial exchange, but continues as long as we remain with it, work and spectator both giving and receiving.

Art as transformative

The world that the work of art sets up is not the everyday world and, in some cases, it may be a world that we have never before experienced. Even non-representational art such as a work by Rothko or Mondrian marks a break with the everyday by drawing our attention away from what is immediately present. Experiences that would never be available to us before now become so. Even if what is portrayed is familiar, the work enables us to see it in a new way or draws our attention to something we might have otherwise overlooked. The relations familiar to us have become transformed. The possibilities opened before us allow us to navigate, to play, between that which is necessary and that which is contingent.

This distance from the everyday is neither an absolute break, nor is the distance disinterested or objective. Instead, we remain in a productive tension with what is distant from us, and what is distant from us actually draws us to it. We do not leave it behind, but continue to hold it in our sight from another perspective. Our relationship to that from which we gain distance becomes transformed. Changes in perspective and productive distance are vital for Nietzsche and appear in several of his discussions of art. In the section entitled 'Our Ultimate Gratitude to Art' in *The Gay Science*, Nietzsche addresses this very topic:

> [Art] furnishes us with eyes and hands and above all the good conscience to be able to turn ourselves into such [an aesthetic] phenomenon. At times we need a rest from ourselves by looking upon, by looking *down* upon ourselves and, from an artistic distance, laughing *over* ourselves or weeping *over* ourselves.... [W]e need all exuberant, floating, dancing, mocking, childish, and blissful art lest we lose the *freedom above things* that our ideal demands of us.... We should be *able* also to ... *float* above it and *play*.
>
> (ibid.)

Art allows us perspective on the world and practices, such that we can stand above them, but also that we gain a perspective on ourselves. The play spaces or worlds brought forth in art present possibilities of experiences we might not otherwise have; for example, of historical periods or melodies, or tragic situations, but they also present possibilities for our own life.

The experience of art always demands our interpretation, and as we respond to this demand we present ourselves. This presentation is part of the play between us and the work. As the play continues, we catch sight of ourselves. The work is not simply a reflection of our projected image, but in opening up a world the work shows us something we recognize and provides us with another interpretation. We need art in order to be ourselves, to gain perspective on our very selves, to see a world of possibility that we may not otherwise see. Thus we may also say that the spectator's understanding and interpretation are manifested in the work too. The work of art, when engaged in play rather than in disinterestedness, becomes and remains a play space and world for the spectator as a constellation of possibilities. To float above ourselves is to engage ourselves dynamically neither as a mere copy of ourselves nor with an objective grand view, but in a 'transformed reality in which the transformation points back to what has been transformed in and through it' (Gadamer 1986a: 64). In play we see explicitly what we already implicitly know.

Not only does the work of art demand an interpretation, a creative response, but so too does the everyday world that has become transformed for us. Thus, to think of art as an escape from the self is misguided; aesthetic experience is not from a safe distance or an objective perspective. Neither can art be an escape from everyday life to liberate the self. Gadamer writes,

> [T]he play of art is a mirror that through the centuries constantly arises anew, and in which we catch sight of ourselves in a way that is often unexpected or unfamiliar: what we are, what we might be, and what we are about. In the last analysis, is it not an illusion to think that we can separate play from seriousness and only admit it to segregated areas peripheral to real life?
>
> (ibid.)

Because of its transformative nature, what arises from the play of art cannot be bracketed from the rest of life. Art and play both prompt us to action and towards creativity in the other areas of life. Similarly, our experiences of everyday life cannot also be bracketed from our play, since play gives us new insights into that everyday life. We have something to say about the work of art, and the art has something to say about us as well. As Nietzsche writes,

> *Artists* ... at least fix an image of that which ought to be; they are productive, to the extent that they actually alter and transform; unlike men of knowledge, who leave everything as it is.
>
> (Nietzsche 1968b: 585)

With art, then, we play not only with the necessity and contingency that happens in every interpretation of a work, but also with the necessity and contingency that arise from the transformed reality of ourselves. The 'men of knowledge', conversely, attempt to leave everything as it is so that they can gain objective knowledge, but this attempt leaves them paralysed, since to act would automatically alter what they were trying to fix in place. However, Nietzsche and Gadamer demonstrate that we can still gain knowledge through our participation, as is evidenced in play, and that we can act on that understanding. We gain perspective on how we comport ourselves, how we attune ourselves to certain possibilities, and how we shape and engage our lives.

To know how to comport ourselves requires mastery and command over oneself to act in a particular way. Mastery means not domination, but letting something be, which is still a form of willing. The focus, however, is not on giving oneself a set of directions, but on the decisiveness and self-formation that follows. The way in which one learns how to play with a work of art can be translated to the way one learns to play with life: not by conquering or dominating it, but by maintaining an open, but decisive, spirit of delight and possibility. Gadamer speaks to this idea, writing, 'Play is less the opposite of seriousness than the vital ground of spirit as nature, a form of restraint and freedom at one and the same time' (Gadamer 1986b: 130). Nietzsche thus still understands mastery as playful, since it is the negotiation between restraint and freedom and as the impulse to create within this space.

In *The Gay Science* Nietzsche illustrates the need to translate the creativity of art to life by declaring that 'to give style to one's character' is 'a great and rare art' that is achieved through an artistic plan and self-mastery (Nietzsche 1974: 290). Thus giving style is the ultimate task of human beings; the will to power is to give oneself one's own law and to make one's life both the form and content of one's creation, so that life, too, is a 'reflex of one's own fullness and perfection' (Nietzsche 1986b: 811). Giving style to one's life is a form of self-formation and self-mastery. Life itself becomes a work of art. This is not reserved only for the artist, since, as we have seen, the spectator too is an active participant as she can participate in transformative play with art, and thus can give style to her life and character. To speak of the artist means more to speak of the artistic state, which may certainly be achieved by the spectator. The inartistic state should not be equated with non-artists, but with the particular attitude towards life that effectively denies life by denying play and thus the ability to make life a work of art.

Although Gadamer and Nietzsche hold similar positions on the transformative power of art, there still seems to be a tension regarding how such transformation fits with or against everyday life. Gadamer does not deny the distance from the everyday world, but he hesitates to think of it as something discontinuous or as divorced from the community from which it arose. The everyday does transform into something new, but it still maintains a continuity of meaning for the self, community and everyday life. The work of art changes our fleeting experiences into 'coherent creation' (Gadamer 1986b: 53). For Gadamer, then, the self-formation is less individualistic than it is for Nietzsche.

Although Nietzsche agrees with Gadamer that to float above one's life and play with reality seems to suggest no absolute break with the everyday, the transformation he identifies is more radical. The distance occurring between the aesthetic experience and the world is what actually enables contact with the world and with life. Turning oneself into an aesthetic phenomenon and giving style to oneself thus require a continuity of the self. Nietzsche writes,

> All this we should learn from artists while being wiser than they are in other matters. For with them this subtle power usually comes to an end

where art ends and life begins; but we want to be the poets of our life – first of all in the smallest, most everyday matters.

(Nietzsche 1974: 299)

Artists, and here perhaps more in the sense of the professional artist, have the subtle power to make beautiful what is not, to conceal some things in order to highlight others, or to see through a particular frame or light. Artistic production demands this certain eye. But, as Nietzsche states, life itself also needs this eye, and to be an artist in the fullest sense requires the translation from creativity in art to creativity in life. What we learn from the artist is what we learn from the work of art: how to engage possibilities dynamically and playfully such that we can become poets of our lives. Thus even the spectator is called to be the poet or artist of her life. Furthermore, Nietzsche emphasizes that the artistic state is not a series of discrete transformations but a continuous willing transformation which prevents the artist from becoming dried-up or expended. Through a process that constantly reaffirms life, the artist creates not out of hunger but out of abundance.

Nietzsche shares Gadamer's idea that art enables a direct transformative relationship with the everyday through play, although he speaks more of dramatic recreation. Although Nietzsche's artist stands apart from the larger community, I propose that she does maintain a community, but one that arises from and continues to foster self-creation through play. The way in which Nietzsche and Gadamer identify this transformation also parallels the way each describes play. Gadamer sees transformation as more communal and anchored in tradition, so he describes play as more irenic; that is, as more collaborative and peaceful. Since Nietzsche is more concerned about the artist's resistance to objective knowledge and the herd-mentality of society, he more frequently speaks of an agonistic play, describing players in terms of strength and power and in opposition in their play towards society. What is essential for both, however, is that it is this play that yields such transformation and self-creation.

This transformation cannot occur automatically or identically for all involved. There is no guarantee that any spectator will succeed at this task, nor that anyone who calls himself an artist is in fact an artist in the Nietzschean sense. To give style to one's life requires both courage and vulnerability. The artist, despite all the gaiety and playfulness of self-creation, must still recognize the immense task involved in this creation and cannot shy away from this responsibility. Gadamer uses a poem from Rilke to illustrate the play of self-creation through the willingness to throw back the ball of existence; that is, to enter into the play of self-creation:

[T]hen, that gamble, is the first moment/you too can be said to play. You/ unburden yourself of the throw no longer; you burden/yourself with the throw no longer. Out of your hands steps/the meteor and it races into its skies.

(Rilke 2010: 9)

Thus through such playful daring the artist responds to the call of the universe to create. In so doing, the possibility of suffering cannot, according to Nietzsche, be denied: 'A highest state of affirmation of existence is conceived from which the highest degree of pain cannot be excluded' (Nietzsche 1986b: 853). The affirmation that comes forth from creative production does not result from an abandonment of the everyday or escape from the self. Instead it is the very engagement with the self and resoluteness in the face of potentially over-whelming possibilities. The artists say Yes to these very possibilities[3] and art does seem to be the real task of life (ibid.).

When Nietzsche writes,

> All art exercises the power of suggestion over the muscles and sense, which in the artistic temperament are originally active: it always speaks only to artists – it speaks to this kind of a subtle flexibility of the body.
>
> (ibid.: 809)

I propose that here he is not stating that art exercises this power and speaks only to artists *qua* artists, but only to artists as those who say Yes to life and give style to themselves. In fact, there seems to be no strict line between artist and spec-tator, since even the spectator wills to be artist of her own life and express her creative and giving power. Heidegger, too, draws upon the blurring of this dis-tinction, stating that although Nietzsche conceives of aesthetics in terms of the artist, his emphasis is much more on the artistic versus the inartistic, i.e. the state of creativity, movement and growth versus the state of receptivity and stagnation (Heidegger 1991: 96).

One of Nietzsche's final assertions in the section 'The Will to Power as Art' is that 'whenever man rejoices, he is always the same in his rejoicing: he rejoices as an artist, he enjoys himself as power, he enjoys the lie as his form of power ... art as the real task to life' (Nietzsche 1968b: 853). To think of Nietzsche's artist as diametrically opposed to the spectator is to preclude the power that art has for artist and spectator alike, as well as the fundamental interplay of art and life. For Nietzsche, art cannot be separated from life. If we think of the spectator as player, as Gadamer suggests, we find that this spectator, too, does not separate art from life. As such, the spectator fits into Nietzsche's artist aesthetics as an active parti-cipant in an artistic state. Ultimately, the idea of artist seems less a professional designation and more a way of life marked by creativity, giving, resoluteness, willing and play, open to traditional artists and spectators alike. Gadamer writes,

> For we read in Nietzsche, 'Mature manhood: that means to have found again the seriousness one had as a child – in play.' Nietzsche also knew the reverse of this as well, and celebrated the creative power of life – and of art – in the divine ease of play,
>
> (Gadamer 1986a: 130)

What life requires is art and play alike, manifested in the will to power as art.

This willing and giving style always requires a negotiation between necessity and contingency and the play between them as we give shape to our lives. Gadamer concludes his essay on play and art by reaffirming, 'For these our forms of play are forms of our freedom' (ibid.). To give style to one's character is the exercise of this freedom; this play brought forth in works of art opens up the very possibilities to make our own lives works of art. The gravity of everyday life risks overwhelming us, but the change in perspective brought forth in art prevents us from suffocating from life and instead enables us to play with it, to will it, and indeed, to love it.

Notes

1 All Nietzsche references are to aphorism, rather than to page number.
2 Nietzsche's objection to the critic as devoid of interest is due, in part, to what Heidegger takes to be a misreading of Kant: 'Had Nietzsche inquired of Kant himself, instead of trusting in Schopenhauer's guidance, then he would have had to recognize that Kant grasped the essence of what Nietzsche in his own way wanted to comprehend regarding the decisive aspects of the beautiful' (Heidegger 1991: 111).
3 The third metamorphosis Nietzsche discusses in *Thus Spoke Zarathustra* is the child:

> The child is innocence and forgetting, a new beginning, a game, a self-propelled wheel, a first movement, a sacred 'Yes.' For the game of creation, my brothers, a sacred 'Yes' is needed: the spirit now wills his own will, and he who had been lost to the world now conquers his own world.
>
> (Nietzsche 1968a: 139)

Creation bears the quality of a game, of childlike playfulness, and needs Yes-saying. Nietzsche echoes this in *The Gay Science*:

> I want to learn more and more to see as beautiful what is necessary in things; then I shall be one of those who makes things beautiful. *Amor fati*: let that be my love henceforth!.... And all in all and on the whole: some day I wish to be only a Yes-sayer!
>
> (Nietzsche 1974: 276)

Bibliography

Gadamer, H.-G. (1986a) 'The Festive Character of Theater', in R. Bernasconi (ed.) *The Relevance of the Beautiful*. New York: Cambridge University Press, pp. 57–65.
Gadamer, H.-G. (1986b) 'The Play of Art', in R. Bernasconi (ed.) *The Relevance of the Beautiful*. New York: Cambridge University Press, pp. 123–130.
Gadamer, H.-G. (1986c) 'The Relevance of the Beautiful', in R. Bernasconi (ed.) *The Relevance of the Beautiful*. New York: Cambridge University Press, pp. 1–56.
Gadamer, H.-G. (2004) *Truth and Method*, trans. J. Weinsheimer. New York: Continuum.
Heidegger, M. (1991) *Nietzsche Vol. I: The Will to Power as Art*, trans. David Farrell Krell. New York: HarperOne.
Heidegger, M. (2002) 'The Origin of the Work of Art', in J. Young and K. Haynes (eds) *Off the Beaten Track*. New York: Cambridge University Press, pp. 1–56.
Nietzsche, F. (1974) *The Gay Science*, trans. W. Kaufmann. New York: Vintage Books.

Nietzsche, F. (1968a) 'Thus Spoke Zarathustra', in W. Kaufmann (ed.) *The Portable Nietzsche*. New York: Viking Penguin, pp. 103–439.

Nietzsche, F. (1968b) *The Will To Power*, trans. W. Kaufmann. New York: Vintage Books.

Rilke, R.M. (2010) 'As Long As You Catch What You've Thrown Yourself', in D. Searls (ed.) *Inner Sky: Poems, Dreams, Note*. Jaffrey: David R. Godine, pp. 9–10.

9 Play and being in Jean-Paul Sartre's *Being and Nothingness*[1]

Rebecca Pitt

The twentieth-century French philosopher Jean-Paul Sartre (1905–1980) is best known for his writing on freedom, controversial political development (particularly his relationship with Marxism, and his later writings on emancipatory violence) and extensive oeuvre, which covers a vast terrain: from the life of Flaubert, documentation of his trips to the USA and Cuba, to plays and his extensive philosophical output. But what contribution can Sartre make to current debates on the concept of play? While a feeling of freedom is often described as occurring through play, what philosophical implications does such a claim have? And what does this tell us about non-playful existence?

Sartre's first major philosophical work, *Being and Nothingness* (BN), presents his theory of human existence, or ontology. The world of BN is one in which we live primarily in 'bad faith'. It is a world usually described as one where we deceive ourselves: we deny that we are freedom itself (we are 'condemned to be free'), and fail to take responsibility for our choices and actions, deliberate or otherwise. It is also a world of conflict with fellow human beings, or what Sartre calls *for-itselves* (often characterised as an 'embodied consciousness' Sartre's *for-itself* is necessarily situated in the world).

Contained within BN is a largely unacknowledged analysis of play, the most pointed and developed discussion of which takes place in fewer than two pages (BN: Sartre 1996: 580–581). Here Sartre presents and develops his own analysis of the *play/seriousness* dichotomy. Yet while the inconclusive analyses offered by BN might give the impression that play is a minor, and unimportant, part of the text, to adopt such a reading would be to underestimate play's specific, and specialised, role in Sartre's philosophy. While common interpretations of BN frequently imply that the world of *bad faith* and conflict is inevitable, there remains much dispute among scholars as to whether play indicates that there is the possibility of transforming certain aspects, or even eradicating what Sartre describes as the desire to 'try-to-be-God'. It is this type of 'fundamental project' which gives us the seemingly endless task of trying to give permanence to our being, while we simultaneously suppress ourselves as freedom.

Sartre's discussion of play reveals BN as a critique of, rather than statement about, our existence. Furthermore, play tentatively indicates the parameters for Sartre's developing emancipatory theory. Consequently, this use of play enables us to broaden and situate this concept beyond just a list of characteristics which fail to acknowledge the wider context in which play takes place. It is precisely this wider critique of existence, and because of play's specialised role in Sartre's ontology, which means that while Sartrean play utilises similar terminology to many other thinkers who write on this topic (e.g. it is different from normal activity, gratuitous, etc.), Sartre's use of such terms is quite specialised, and has the potential to inform or reorientate other discussions on play.

The following description of play in Sartre's work is exploratory: I offer an interpretation of play's essential characteristics, the reason for play's inclusion in the text and note some contentious areas of this concept. For reasons of space I do not fully evaluate the central, and often diverse, concerns of the few commentators who do write on Sartrean play (primarily Thomas Anderson (1993), Linda Bell (1989) and Yiwei Zheng (2001, 2002, 2005)), or exhaustively cover the terrain and implicit connections between different characteristics of play.

'An ontology before conversion ...'

Central to understanding Sartrean play is *how* one interprets the description of our existence in BN: as above, this remains a source of contention in secondary scholarship. It is also a question central to the few commentators that examine play at any length, and at the heart of Zheng's criticisms of Anderson. The focus of this debate is the meaning and implications of Sartre's description of BN in the later, posthumously published *Notebooks for an Ethics* (NE). In the opening pages of the text Sartre notes: 'The very fact that *Being and Nothingness* is an ontology before conversion takes for granted that a conversion is necessary' (Sartre 1992: 5–6).

Here it is clear that Sartre himself rejects conventional interpretations of BN by stressing that *conversion* is both possible and desirable. As Anderson (1993) reveals, NE's claim is supported by the relation between earlier variants of *reflection* to *conversion* in Sartre's early writing which makes 'recognition of this ... crucial for a proper interpretation of much of that [BN's] ontology, for it means that it generally describes human reality, its relation to others and to the world, from the perspective of impure reflection' (Anderson 1993: 54).

Zheng, by contrast, directly challenges Anderson's claims regarding the eradication of the *fundamental project* of trying-to-be-God in *authenticity* by contending their compatibility. While it is contestable that BN assumes a 'perspective of impure reflection' (Zheng 2002: 128) – Sartre appears to be describing, rather than assuming as absolute, the world of 'hell' in BN – Anderson is correct I believe to contest that the *project* of trying-to-be-God is not 'inevitable' and is in fact related to a particular ontology.

Sartre's statement in NE therefore appears to make two claims. First, that BN represents a theory of being that is illustrative of a pre-transformative state of existence. Second, that the world described in BN is one that implicitly argues for the need to transform that world. In other words, all the seemingly negative statements Sartre makes about human existence in the text are actually *only* illustrative of one possible, but not necessary, way of existing. That this is the case appears to be reinforced in a number of ways throughout BN.

First, Sartre's theory of consciousness describes us as 'a lived relation' (Sartre 1996: 575), a claim that reflects the nature of consciousness both as necessarily embodied and in the world, and lacking any possibility of 'inertia' (Sartre 1996: 61). Consequently 'activity' is fundamental to the *for-itself* or what Sartre describes as a 'detotalised totality' (e.g. the possibility of living this apparent 'tension' between subjectivity and objectivity). Indeed, the discussion of *play* takes place within the wider context of an examination of the question of 'action'. As we are freedom Sartre cannot give any ground to determinism: consciousness as freedom means that, by extension, we cannot declare that this way of collectively existing is inevitable. It is, however, a pervasive and well-established way of existing both through the structure and way in which we collectively give meaning to the world, and how we choose to perpetuate this state of being.

The 'disturbing analyses' (Detmer 2009: 134) presented to the reader of BN are simultaneously supported, and rejected, by Sartre himself. They are 'supported' in the sense that, as the citation notes, Sartre believes what he describes in BN 'takes for granted that a conversion is necessary'. BN, Sartre appears to contend, presents evidence in and of itself that change is necessary: no additional statements regarding, for example, the 'violent' intersubjectivity and 'inevitable' *bad faith* as undesirable are thus perceived as necessary. Yet while the force of Sartre's claims elsewhere (the well-known references to BN as 'the Hell of passions' (Sartre 1992: 499), 'man is a useless passion' (Sartre 1996: 615), 'the pursuit of Being is hell' (Sartre 1992: 37), and the infamous statement from the play *Huis Clos*: 'hell is other people') are perhaps, through their negative connotations, indicative of a need to transform the status quo, one does not necessarily conclude that 'another ontology is possible'.[2] Given that BN is often interpreted as Sartre's definitive description of *human reality*, his assumption of how the reader would interpret the text may have been overly optimistic.

Provisionally, it could be claimed that Sartre at least indicates the outcome or conceptual form of an *unconverted ontology*.[3] What is less clear, and less explicated in the secondary literature, however, is the remit, foundation or divergence point in the text for the 'converted' and 'unconverted' versions of BN's ontology, or the conditions/process by which this 'conversion' takes place. Why is *human reality* the way it is described in the text and, if an alternative is possible, as indeed the quotations above seem to indicate, then both why and how this is possible should at least be implicit in the text.

Reflection

Pure reflection is the central focus for Zheng's 2001 claims, and is described as both 'ontologically' and 'ethically' important.[4] In addition to the ontological status of the *project-of-trying-to-be-God*, reflection is the second focus of secondary commentators on *play*, as there is a strong correlation between *reflection* and *authenticity* in BN. Refuting Anderson's claim by emphasising both aspects of Sartre's thought (and they are necessarily related) Zheng argues that the *project* of *trying-to-be-God* is compatible with the idea of 'authenticity'.[5] Moreover, by developing the initial claim made in his 2002 paper (that *pure reflection* is associated with 'good faith' and is a developing concept in his early writings), Zheng develops an account of *play* as 'lead[ing] to pure reflection' but in which the *for-itself* retains its *fundamental project* of *trying-to-be-God*. Later Zheng will claim 'that in authenticity we have a passion to revive the childish heart' which (among a reiteration of the characteristics used to define *play* also describes 'process ... [as] more important than result' (Zheng 2005: 132)). In this instance however there is a further implicit problem, particularly when contextualised within sports/games: that of idealising child's *play* as somehow uncontaminated or more 'real' than other forms of play.

To make his claim that *play* is related to *authenticity* (according to Zheng, described in NE as 'pure reflection') but not synonymous with it, Zheng characterises the former as 'unreflective' and the latter as 'reflective' (Zheng 2005: 119). However, this appears to simplify Zheng's earlier claims in which *play* can be broader than just 'ordinary games. We can transform any project-related consciousness into play. All we need to do is insert the playful attitude and let it take over all other attitudes.'[6] How does this claim correlate with *play* as 'unreflective'? Given the special and rare occurrence of *play* as presented in BN it must be the case that any infusion of our existence with the 'attitude' of *play* is 'reflective' at some level.

Moreover, the terminology and description of *play* in BN suggests that this is the case. Sartre characterises play as 'apprehension'; a contrast to the passivity and 'fundamental' or initial *project* of *trying-to-be-God* which frames the *unconverted ontology* of BN. Play is indicative of a *for-itself* as 'reflecting' on both *human reality* and 'discovering himself as free in his very action, he certainly could not be concerned with *possessing* a being in the world' (Sartre 1996: 581). The 'activity' and 'attitude' of *play* arises from 'man ... wish[ing] to use his freedom' (Sartre 1996: 580). This is critical: it is not necessarily the case that *play* as we normally think of it, or even the realisation that consciousness *is* freedom, is Sartrean *play*. By failing to acknowledge these characteristics Zheng both fails to contextualise the *project* of *trying-to-be-God* and is unable to account for the origin and inclusion of other characteristics of *play* such as the *for-itself* 'escap[ing] his natural nature' which is 'the first principle of play' (Sartre 1996: 581) or the connection between *appropriation* and *play* noted in Sartre's account, and which has wider ontological import.

Although Anderson does not develop his claims regarding *unconverted ontology*, it could be argued that in *play* there is a sense of something more akin to a *converted* 'relation to the world' through a transformation of our relationship with our own body: a denial of the 'being-for-others' which Sartre describes in the *body* earlier in BN. It is our attempt to understand ourselves through others (e.g. to perpetuate a certain kind of *mediation*) that is problematic. As Sartre describes it, 'these difficulties all stem from the fact that I try to unite my con-sciousness not with *my* body but with the body *of others*' (Sartre 1996: 303).

Situating play

Sartre is obviously not the first philosopher to either write on *play* or discuss its relationship with *seriousness*. This dichotomy of play/seriousness is explicitly noted in his main discussion of play but is also implicit elsewhere in BN, while providing a case for strong parallels between Sartre and other thinkers such as Johan Huizinga (1950). More explicitly, as Sartre noted during the Second World War:

> Renouncing the ivory tower, I should like the world to appear to me in its full, threatening reality – but I do not, therefore, want my life to stop being a game. That's why I subscribe whole-heartedly to Schiller's phrase: 'Man is fully a man only when he plays.'
>
> (Sartre 1999: 327)[7]

Sartre does not acknowledge his debt to Schiller in BN. Neither does he acknowledge his critical addendum to Schiller's statement, that of the 'world appearing in its full, threatening reality' in this later text. Instead, the idea of 'threat' gives Sartre's account a critical uniqueness – play itself stands opposed to the usual way in which we relate to the world, the 'reassuring' (Sartre 1996: 38) and 'comforting' existence of *bad faith*. It is the description of the *for-itself* as constantly 'anguished' (Sartre 1996: 43; an apt description for the constant, hidden existential discord that is integral to the *for-itself* engaged in the *funda-mental project* of *trying-to-be-God*: an attempt to be both *for-itself* and an object or *in-itself*) which explicitly results in commentators drawing attention to *play's* uniqueness when contrasted with the 'fundamental project'. As Sartre describes this rare occurrence, 'anguish is precisely my consciousness of being my own future, in the mode of non-being' (Sartre 1996: 556, 32).

As Sartre notes later in BN: 'I am condemned to exist forever beyond my essence, beyond the causes and motives of my act. I am condemned to be free … [but] we are not free to cease being free' (Sartre 1996: 439). Sartre does not revoke *essence* as 'possibility' here but instead makes it clear that, first, we are not the 'end' at which we aim in an action (hence *play*, while 'releasing subjectivity', is not concerned with the goal of the *self*) and that because we cannot 'be' 'possib-ility', we are always *surpassing*; in other words transcending our possibilities to new situations. Furthermore, we transcend 'the causes and motives of my act' because I cannot grasp fully their *meaning*; to do so would mean that my actions only have *meaning* for myself. Given that Sartre's *for-itself* is not solipsistic we are 'con-demned' to assume responsibility for how we respond to this state of affairs and whatever happens, unexpected or otherwise, as a consequence of our actions.

Likewise, *anguish* is 'the fear which I have of being suddenly exorcized (*i.e.* of becoming radically other)' (Sartre 1996: 475). This appears to render *anguish* as specific to the context of the pervasiveness of the *project-of-trying-to-be-God*. As one can only become 'radically other' under certain conditions, there appears to be an implicit sense of danger: I could be 'possessed' by Others and therefore have my *subjectivity* nullified. I would therefore no longer be 'haunted by being' as I would become *in-itself*. Yet while, as a number of commentators have noted within the context of 'being-for-others' (Sartre 1996: 280), this is impossible, there remains a sense that *alienation* is a constant threat to the *for-itself*. How does this relate to Sartre's seemingly contradictory claims in *War Diaries* (WD)? Can 'life' really be a 'game' *and* expose the 'full, threatening reality' of our existence?

Sartre's discussion of *play* is situated in the final part of BN which examines the meaning and relationship between 'having', 'doing' and 'being'. In describing what 'action' is, we clarify the relation between the *for-itself* and *in-itself* by revealing the foundation for transformation as being integral to ourselves: 'the perpetual possibility of *acting* ... must evidently be considered as an essential characteristic of the for-itself' (Sartre 1996: 430). Moreover, it appears that it is action itself which, as emphasised in the description of *play*, offers a way of transforming the *unconverted for-itself* and which has an emancipatory role. However, the role of play remains inconclusive: although it is undeniable that the *for-itself* is *always* 'doing' in the sense that we can never be 'inert' or 'passive', it is clear within the context of *play* that action remains subordinate to what Sartre describes as *appropriation* and *possession*, and cannot destroy the dominance of an ontology which perpetuates the *project-of-trying-to-be-God*.

The reason for this is twofold. First, *play* is the counter-example to *seriousness*, the highly criticised and commonly acknowledged, primary way of relating to the world in BN. Related to the infamous *bad faith* which dominates the text, and when 'contrasted with the spirit of seriousness', play, according to Sartre, 'appears to be the least possessive attitude' (Sartre 1996: 580). Here it is worth stressing that although *seriousness* receives more attention than either *appropriation* or *possession* in Sartre's work, it is, as scholars such as Danielle LaSuza noted, an important overlooked concept.[8]

Second, within the 'unconverted' context of BN, 'doing' or 'making'[9] are only intermediary, or reducible, to 'being' or 'having' – they are illustrative of a particular type of 'relation'. This 'relation' appears to be one of a *pre-conversion* ontology type, the definition of which may be extended through understanding the specifics of what 'being' and 'having' mean within the context of this type of 'relation'. It is what Sartre calls 'appropriation' in which all types of *action* reveal a particular 'pursuit of being', that of the *project-of-trying-to-be-God*. In describing 'the world of tasks' which characterises BN, Sartre notes that

> each of these functions has its existence justified by its end ... [but] freedom can not determine its existence by the end which it posits ... it determines itself by its very upsurge as a 'doing' ... *to do* supposes the nihilation of a given ... freedom is a lack of being in relation to a given being; it is not the upsurge of a full being.
>
> (Sartre 1996: 485)

In other words, 'doing' or 'making' have a specific meaning: they are only applicable to 'action' in which consciousness in some way is aware that it is *freedom*[10] and in which the *mediation* of Otherness with all its 'duty' and 'demand' is rejected. As Sartre will describe it in both BN and NE, we usually adopt a *serious* attitude towards, and identify ourselves with, the *in-itself*: 'The goal is appropriation, that is, the assimilation to Me of objects that will thereby become visible qualities. These objects are ready-made' (Sartre 1996: 580 and 1992: 513).

Towards the end of his description of *play* Sartre notes that '"to do" is purely transitional. Ultimately a desire can only be the desire *to be* or *to have* ... it is seldom that play is pure of all appropriative tendency' (Sartre 1996: 581). Revealing *play* as individualistic, Sartre is clear that, while the framework of *desire* and therefore *appropriation* remains, *play* is 'transitional' because it does not eradicate the way in which we have conceived of ourselves as *lack* and our aim to *totalise* ourselves as *detotalised totality*. Thus the importance of the terminology used by Sartre in the description 'escaping of our natural nature' (which is 'the first principle of play') (Sartre 1996: 581) is revealed: we can run from *fundamental alienation* and the *project-of-trying-to-be-God* (as our 'natural nature') through 'releasing subjectivity' but this is not a permanent solution to the 'hell' of BN.

Play emphasises 'doing' rather than 'being' and 'the being of man [as] action' (Sartre 1992: 473). In other words, play is 'the least possessive attitude' (Sartre 1996: 580) one can adopt towards *human reality* as depicted in BN. There are a number of distinctive qualities associated with *play* beyond those highlighted in WD. 'Man ... escapes his natural nature' in Sartrean *play* (Sartre 1996: 581). *Play* is different in the *project* of which it (as both 'attitude' and 'activity') is illustrative: the expression 'freedom for its foundation and its goal' (Sartre 1996: 580–581)[11] implies the absence of both the *fundamental project* and, through *freedom* as a 'goal', the destruction of appropriative 'ends'. Moreover, specific changes not only occur in terms of *appropriation* but also in the type of *reflection* of the *for-itself*.[12]

Implicit in the idea of 'natural nature' of the *project-of-trying-to-be-God*, and prior to the discussion of play in BN, many of the characteristics of the *for-itself* in an *unconverted ontology* have been described as 'natural', 'primitive', 'original' or 'fundamental' (Sartre 1996: 560, 456, 407). These terms appear to indicate particular structures integral to this mode of being, and appear as a priori because they are both pervasive and condition our *upsurge*. However, while the task of understanding *play's* distinctiveness is made easier by the way in which Sartre clearly contrasts concepts in his discussion, we cannot rely on these comparisons alone to give credibility to a purely self-referential assessment of this concept. The need to assess play within the context of an *unconverted ontology* is therefore necessary.

One important concept within this context is *mediation*. In contrast to the emphasis on *objectivity*, 'play ... releases subjectivity' and is 'an activity of which man is the first origin ... sets the rules, and [whose action] has no consequence except according to the rules posited' (Sartre 1996: 580–581). *Play* is the counter-example to those who 'make the Not a part of their very subjectivity, establish their human personality as a perpetual negation' (Sartre 1996: 47), or, in other words, objectify themselves. As originator of the 'rules' one rejects the 'duty' and 'demand' of the Other – one 'strips the real of its reality' – and consequently 'there is in a sense 'little reality' in the world' (Sartre 1996: 580–581).

What do these claims really mean? Should we conclude, like Zheng, that 'adoption of the playful attitude across the board is unfeasible in practical life' (Zheng 2002: 136)? Or instead, like Joseph Catalano (1996: 54) and others, read Sartrean *play* as either/both a viable political strategy and/or post-*conversion* status quo?

'Full, threatening reality'

One indication that an *anguished* realisation of 'the world [as] full threatening reality' must be compatible with 'life' as a 'game' is the non-specificity of what type of action is required for play. For this reason it is clear that Sartre's description of *play* (despite the depictions of sport which surround and illustrate his discussion) does not apply exclusively to 'games' and sport in an everyday sense.

It is similarly clear, as indicated in WD and within the context of 'ends', that *play* also needs to be an opening of oneself up to 'threatening reality' in the ways described above (e.g. in relation to *gratuity*, etc.).[13] By approaching Sartre's discussion of *play* within this context it becomes clear that both the claims that 'there is always in sport an appropriative component' and 'it is seldom that play is pure of all appropriative tendency' (BN 581) are indicative of a particular type of *play* which, as Ralph Netzky (1974) notes within the context of sports, are 'safe' and have very clear ends, i.e. it is controlled in some sense.[14] Roger Caillois (1959), who responds directly to Huizinga's famous account of *play*, while noting that *play* is an eschewing of responsibility, makes a similar point: *play* 'constitutes a kind of haven in which one is master of destiny. There, the player himself chooses his risks, which, since they are determined in advance, cannot exceed what he has exactly agreed to put into play.'[15] Yet the relation between Cailloisian *play* and Sartrean *play* is ambiguous when placed in the wider context of Sartre's ontology. While I cannot be 'master of destiny' as my *destiny* is integrally linked to that of every human being, it appears that, in both types of *play* described here, I can choose the framework, limits and outcome of my action. *Play* therefore appears deficient as it reflects the 'individualism' that Sartre criticises in his account of our fundamental project. Moreover, as Linda Bell indicates, *play* does not eradicate the structures which frame our existence and support oppression.[16]

Besides concurrence with Netzky, it is important to note the idea of the 'haven' which appears implicit in Sartre's depiction of *play*. There is no mention of the 'being-for-others' which provides the framework for the existence of the *for-itself* as alienated here. Whereas for Sartre 'we are all destiny for ourselves' (Sartre 1992: 47 and 1996: 53), here 'one is master of destiny' to use Caillois' phrase.[17] Again *play* appears a purely individualised experience. The possibility of *pure reflection* remains, but whether it is synonymous with *non-appropriativeness* remains worthy of further investigation. Thus, while a number of commentators describe *play* as *conversion*, this cannot be extended to *play* as *radical conversion*, which appears to involve *reciprocity* (Sartre 1992: 369). There is no evidence in *play* for 'radical conversion' which Sartre has described as 'necessary' 'if he [the Other] is to escape objectivity' (Sartre 1996: 257). Neither can one limit the remit of this 'escape' to purely oneself, as in Caillois' and Netzky's description: 'The Other is ... the condition of my being un-revealed ... the concrete, par-ticular condition of it' (Sartre 1996: 269). Again, just as 'morality ... must be a choice of a world, not of a self' (Sartre 1992: 3), similarly it would appear that *fundamental alienation* as 'objectification' (Bell 1989: 149) can be challenged.

The persistent Sartrean caricature of quintessential individualism and idea of *play* as detachment from 'the world' is reflected in Zheng's claim that *play* is a form of detachment that necessarily causes a rupture in personal relations (Zheng, 2002, 136). However, within a wider context such expressions as *play* 'strip[ping] the real of the reality' which originates from the 'least possessive atti-tude', the 'little reality' in the world', 'no consequences except according to the rules posited' (Sartre 1996: 580–581) and the 'nothingness [which] mak[es] the world iridescent, casting a shimmer over things' (Sartre 1996: 23–24)[18] can be reinterpreted. Such statements reveal that not only is detachment necessary (the question is *what* is one detaching oneself from rather than detachment per se) but that subsequently the insight one has into *human reality* is one which does not fall prey to the mysticism which Sartre condemns elsewhere.

While Sartre's description remains at the level of the *for-itself* it does not rule out collective *play* per se; there is no clear evidence for the abstract, isolated *for-itself* or *emancipation* from *inauthenticity* as a purely individualistic phenomenon. It is clear that when we question our being in some way (via *anguish*) we there-fore potentially challenge our *fundamental project* and the 'milieu' of *alienation* in some way. There is thus always the possibility, but never the inevitability, of *play* via *anguish*; after all we can always *flee* the realisation of ourselves as *freedom*. Hence in the statements cited above, a demystification appears to take place: there is 'little reality' and a 'stripping' because we encounter and have some insight into the 'full, threatening reality' of existence: a world without 'guardrails against anguish', an exposure to the *truth* of our existence as *freedom*, a 'lack' of *reality* because *play* is the antithesis of the dominant and pervasive way in which we understand our existence through *bad faith* and *seriousness*. In other words, while 'life is a game' it is also a *risk* (as noted in a citation Bell uses)[19] and a *challenge*: we are undetermined, yet dependent on our situatedness to understand ourselves as freedom itself, and must assume responsibility for our existence, whatever the outcome of our 'actions' (e.g. Sartre 1996: 555).

Conclusion

It is clear that play has a specialised role in BN, and that Sartre's account reveals the need to both situate and reassess play more widely. While the preceding analysis is far from conclusive – there is much to say on how Sartre develops the characteristics associated with play in his later writing, for example – it is of note that Sartre both critiques and radicalises the concept of play simultaneously. Such an assessment has the potential to develop or challenge other definitions of play.

Notes

1 This chapter is a partially revised and shortened version of part of my Ph.D. thesis (Pitt 2012: ch. 3), an early version of which was presented at the *Philosophy at Play* conference at The University of Gloucestershire during April 2011. Some sections are reproduced verbatim from the former. I would like to thank the organisers for such an enjoyable conference, the participants for their feedback, and the editors of this book for all their advice and help in preparing the following text.

2 A play on the slogan 'another world is possible'.

3 See Bell 1989: 92.

4 See Zheng 2001: 19.

5 See Zheng 2005: ch. 6; Daigle 2011: 6.

6 See also Marcuse 1948: 325.

7 See Schiller 1794: Book XV. See also Sartre's diary entry made two days prior: Sartre 1999: 313. The connection between Schiller and Sartre is similarly noted by Netzky (1974: 135).

8 The North American Sartre Society conference 2011.

9 The French word '*faire*', as Barnes notes in her footnote, means both 'doing' and 'making' (Sartre 1996: 431).

10 This appears to be another example where Sartre's terminology is unique, and not synonymous with our everyday, common understanding of language (e.g. in defining *freedom*: 'Common opinion does not hold that to be free means only to choose oneself. A *choice* is said to be free if it is said that it could have been other than what it is' (Sartre 1996: 453)).

11 For this reason 'play is vital to ethics' claims Bell (1989: 112).

12 A particular focus for many commentators who work on play (e.g. Zheng 2001, 2002).

13 In other words, as the well-cited statement regarding 'it amounts to the same thing whether one gets drunk alone or is a leader of nations' (Sartre 1996: 627) makes clear, one realises that one's existence is 'gratuitous' and the *meaning* of our lives is entirely dependent on the *value* we give to it. This is 'threatening', since it undermines our collective *value* system which would propose that the activities of the 'leader' are always of more worth than those of the 'drunk'.

14 Netzky 1974: 126.

15 Caillois 1959: 159; see also Manser 1966: 151.

16 See Catalano 1996: 55.

17 This claim appears to be a different/similar spin to the analyses of mastery that other commentators have remarked upon (e.g. Fisher 2009: 89) on the actor compared with the *bad faith waiter*.

18 This citation originates from a counter-example to *seriousness* and therefore may be allied with *play*.

19 Bell 1989: 120 (re: Genet); see also the wonderfully concise statement from Linsenbard (citing Beauvoir): 'For Sartre, conversion to authenticity is consciousness's *willed resolve* to accept itself as *at risk* before the world and, in doing so, it accepts and values itself as the gratuitous freedom it is' (2007: 14).

Bibliography

Anderson, T.C. (1993) *Sartre's Two Ethics: From Authenticity to Integral Humanity.* Chicago, IL: Open Court.

Bell, L.A. (1989) *Sartre's Ethics of Authenticity.* London: The University of Alabama Press.

Caillois, R. (1959) *Man and the Sacred*, trans. M. Barash. Glencoe, IL: The Free Press of Glencoe.

Catalano, J.S. (1996) *Good Faith and Other Essays.* London: Rowman and Littlefield.

Daigle, C. (2011) *The Ethics of Authenticity. Reading Sartre: On Phenomenology & Existentialism*, ed. J. Webber. London: Routledge.

Detmer, D. (2009) *Sartre Explained: From Bad Faith to Authenticity,* Vol. 6 (Ideas Explained series). Chicago and La Salle, IL: Open Court.

Fisher, T. (2009) 'Bad Faith and the Actor: Onto-mimetology from a Sartrean Point of View'. *Sartre Studies International*, 15(1): 74–91.

Huizinga, J. (1950) *Homo Ludens: A Study of the Play-element in Culture.* Boston, MA: Beacon Press.

Linsenbard, G.E. (2007) *Morality and Authenticity in Sartre's Notebooks for an Ethics. 14th Annual Conference of the UK Sartre Society.* London.

Manser, A. (1966) *Sartre: A Philosophic Study.* London: University of London.

Marcuse, H. (1948) 'Existentialism: Remarks on Jean-Paul Sartre's L'etre et le neant'. *Philosophy and Phenomenological Research,* 8(3): 309–336.

Netzky, R. (1974) 'Sartre's Ontology Re-appraised: Playful Freedom'. *Philosophy Today*, 18(2): 125–136.

Pitt, R. (2012) *Jean-Paul Sartre and the Question of Emancipation.* Ph.D. thesis. University of Essex.

Sartre, J.-P. (1992). *Notebooks for an Ethics*, trans. D. Pellauer. Chicago, IL: University of Chicago Press.

Sartre, J.-P. (1996) *Being and Nothingness*, trans. H.E. Barnes. London: Routledge.

Sartre, J.-P. (1999) *War Diaries: Notebooks from a Phoney War 1939–40*, trans. Q. Hoare. London: Verso.

Schiller, J.C.F. von (1794) *Letters upon the Aesthetic Education of Man.* Whitefish, MT: Kessinger.

Zheng, Y. (2001) 'On Pure Reflection in Sartre's Being and Nothingness'. *Sartre Studies International*, 7(1): 19–42.

Zheng, Y. (2002) 'Sartre on Authenticity'. *Sartre Studies International*, 8(2): 127–140.

Zheng, Y. (2005) *Ontology and Ethics in Sartre's Early Philosophy.* Oxford: Lexington Books.

10 Passion play

Play, free will and the sublime

Thomas Hackett

At the heart of the human experience is a seeming contradiction: we are often healthiest and happiest when our suffering is most acute. More to the point, suffering can restore happiness. The eighteenth-century philosopher Edmund Burke was not the first to notice this phenomenon – Plato and Aristotle touch on the matter, as do Seneca and Spinoza – but he may have described it most pithily in his *Enquiry into the Origin of our Ideas of the Beautiful and Sublime*. 'Whatever is in any sort terrible,' he writes, 'or is conversant about terrible objects, or operates in a manner analogous to terror, is a source of the sublime, that is, it is productive of the strongest emotion which the mind is capable of feeling' (Burke 1757: 86). Here Burke is using the word 'sublime' in a way we seldom do any more, not as a synonym for 'inspiring' or 'magnificent' but to identify an experience of pleasure paradoxically predicated on pain, danger and trepidation. The immensities and power of nature (say, a raging river) can evoke these thrilling feelings. We feel at once fragile and invigorated. Even the hardships and challenges of daily life can arouse these contradictory feelings. 'Without all doubt', he continues,

> the torments which we may be made to suffer are much greater in their effect on the body and mind than any pleasures which the most learned voluptuary could suggest, or than the liveliest imagination and exquisitely sensible body could enjoy.
>
> (Burke 1757: 86)

Not all such torments produce pleasure, of course. Some 'are simply terrible'. However, 'at certain distances and with certain modifications,' other torments to mind and body 'are delightful, as we every day experience' (Burke 1757: 86). Indeed, it is precisely the *absence* of more pointed difficulties that creates physical and psychological disorder, Burke contends. We fall prey to anxiety, depression and despair. His enquiry does not take into account the psychological processes that lead to that emotional debilitation. He leaps over that more confounding question to propose a quick and effective fix. The 'best remedy' to what ails us emotionally and spiritually is 'the surmounting of difficulties', an experience that 'resembles pain' (Burke 1757: 164).

Although I discuss the work of philosophers, my primary interest here is psychological, as I examine exactly what that remedy addresses and why it works. I argue that freedom is both what ails us and what cures us. Our deepest anxieties originate in the fact that we are essentially free beings, but they are also eradicated by acts of free will. Play, which at first glance seems so wasteful and insignificant, turns out to be the realm of life best suited to objectifying and confronting our existential apprehensions, for the freedom and courage necessary to play is also the freedom and courage necessary to being.

Burke's counter-intuitive logic is echoed by the philosopher and theologian Paul Tillich and by the existential psychologist Rollo May. In *The Courage to Be* (Tillich 1952), *The Meaning of Anxiety* (May 1950) and *The Courage to Create* (May 1975), these two friends each propose a philosophy of human fulfilment achieved by doing what is most difficult – living life courageously, in full recognition of one's essential freedom. The rival force to that courage may be called cowardice, but cowardice is really only a symptom of the more insidious emotional malady of anxiety. And anxiety is native to the human condition, they argue. In the simplest terms, it comes from feeling uncertain about our ability to cope with a situation of some personal importance. We may feel anxious about a collapsing stock market or a dicey side-hill putt in golf – natural reactions, made vivid by the wish that things were otherwise, that we were immune to economic vicissitudes, that we had only a tap-in to close out the match. Tillich would put such apprehensions, however big or small, in the less insidious category of fear. After all, a fear can be identified, objectified and bravely met. But existential apprehensions that go by the names of anxiety, angst or dread are more difficult to 'passionately challenge' (Tillich 1952: 42). That is because, as Tillich sees it, they originate in the ever-present spectre of non-being, in the horror of 'nothingness' that shrouds everyone's life and pervades human consciousness and unconsciousness. It is not merely that we have fears that 'we may cease to be' (1848), as John Keats puts it, or that, in our trepidation, we can only hear the 'melancholy, long withdrawing roar' of a civilization's dying faith in some higher purpose, as Matthew Arnold writes (1867). It is, rather, that there is a negation of life – a nothingness – before which we seem to stand helpless. To Tillich, the origins of existential anxiety lie in this knowledge, in this profound sense of helplessness.

May confronts a similar conundrum. Along with Kierkegaard, he argues that anxiety begins and ends in freedom. 'Anxiety is the state of man ... when he confronts freedom', he writes (May 1950: 33). What distresses the would-be writer is not that he is somehow barred from writing a novel; it is that nothing is really stopping him doing so. We are afraid of our freedom, and the only answer to that fear is to challenge it. Needless to say, that is easier said than done. After all, it is only natural that we would try to avoid or escape what causes us distress. Because we can readily discern the negative consequences of giving into our escapist urges, we generally rise to life's quotidian challenges. '*A person is subjectively prepared to confront unavoidable anxiety constructively when he is convinced (consciously or unconsciously) that the values to be gained in moving ahead are greater than those to be gained by escape*', May writes (1950: 229; italics in original). Writing a term paper may make a university student anxious; however, she accepts that anxiety because she understands that *not* writing the paper would only cause greater feelings of distress, not the least of which would be a sense of shame and guilt. We would not need to bother explaining the dynamics of that emotional economics but for the fact that they also obtain on a more profound existential level. What about anxieties that are less specific and identifiable? What about the anxiety occasioned by our very freedom? There, the economics of anxiety are not so easily calculated.

Implicit in freedom is possibility, and in May's view 'there is anxiety in any actualizing of possibility'. Paraphrasing Kierkegaard, he adds that 'the more possibility (creativity) an individual has, the more potential anxiety he has at the same time' (May 1950: 33). Thus, we feel a powerful urge to forsake our individual freedom. The problem is, while shirking the risks and responsibilities concomitant with freedom may bring temporary relief, doing so only arouses the more profound anxiety of a largely unconscious guilt, not regarding our conduct towards others but towards ourselves. For we will have betrayed ourselves. We will have fled from doing the difficult, courageous thing of actualizing our freedom (a task that inevitably threatens stability and security), and we will therefore have refused to actualize ourselves. In forsaking freedom, we forsake our essential selves. Or, to use Tillich's metaphor, we cage ourselves in neurotic behaviour 'comparable to the security of a prison' (Tillich 1952: 75) guarded vigilantly by no one but ourselves.

'Life must be lived as play,' Plato writes: 'playing certain games, making sacrifices, singing and dancing, and then a man will be able to propitiate the gods, and defend himself against his enemies, and win in the contest' (Plato, *Laws*: vii). The words could easily be used as advertising copy for a Club Med-style retreat. But for Plato and others after him (Kant, Schiller, Freud, Winnicott, Klein, Caillois, Derrida, Lacan, Gadamer, to name a few), play means something more complex than simple hedonism, as the most cursory appraisal of the subject makes clear. The Dutch cultural historian Johan Huizinga, one of the few people outside child psychiatry to devote a book specifically to the subject, calls play 'an absolutely primary category of life' (Huizinga 1938: 3). Many commentators on the subject, though, have defined play by either what it is not (i.e. work, seriousness, rationality, authenticity) or by how it facilitates and accommodates some other aspect of living, such as learning or instinctual aggression. It has also been viewed as a mere waste product of life, a discharge of excess energy, sometimes linked to masturbation. Yet the closer we look at it, the clearer it becomes that play is autotelic, sui generis, not a means to an end but a thing in itself. Beyond the exigencies of meeting our somatic, material and procreative needs, and beyond economic, politics and status concerns, there is everything else – everything we do above and beyond what is necessary for survival, material comfort and social positioning, things done for no apparent or logical reason, that often involve strife and struggle, if not pain and suffering but that give life meaning and value, that bring satisfaction and joy, that allow us to explore and experience the various aspects of our identities, and that reveal the paradoxes of freedom and being. In a word, play.

Whether it is Mozart or marbles, Shakespeare or soccer, all play forms are equally impractical to the immediate needs of life. In their purest form, none follow an ulterior imperative or serve a necessary material purpose (Huizinga 1938: 13). While the competitive and antagonistic aspect of, say, a political election may at times be playful, politics is not play since it clearly serves a purpose. Neither is work, though a job may well be enjoyable. Nor sex, which has as its basis a biological imperative. To be sure, the distinction between what is and what is not play can be fuzzy. And though anyone who thinks for a moment about the subject of play quickly discards notions that it is childish, frivolous or inconsequential, he must also recognize that, as Oscar Wilde and W.H. Auden have noted, play is in fact useless, that it makes nothing happen.[1] Practical and monetary considerations obviously impinge on and derive from the play experience. Sports, art and entertainment can confer significant financial and social advantages on any number of participants. However, even a professional athletic contest, for all the anguished excitement it generates and despite the exorbitant salaries and profits, is ultimately inconsequential. The stakes of a game are really just a contrivance, a dramatic fiction, brought into play to create tension, which produces enjoyment (all meaningful play entails contrived tension of one sort or another; the 'fun' or enjoyment of play is in the release of that tension). For most athletes the simple desire to win still precedes and exceeds monetary concerns, yet they are not deluded: they understand as well as anyone that a victory changes nothing, practically speaking. In the end, as Caillois writes in *Man, Play and Games*, the conclusions of the nihilist who refuses to play or watch the game because it is pointless are irrefutable (Caillois 1961: 7). 'Play is an occasion of pure waste,' he writes. '[A] waste of time, energy, ingenuity, skill, and often money' (Caillois 1961: 5–6). Which is not to imply that play (or art, a species of play) is meaningless. 'In play there is something "at play" which transcends the immediate needs of life and imparts meaning to action,' Huizinga writes. 'All play means something' (Huizinga 1938: 1). This is the operative principle of child psychiatry and cultural anthropology: the idea that the play of children or of communities manifests psychological and social concerns, and that the job of the therapist or ethnographer is to 'gain access' to the symbolic articulation of those concerns.[2]

At times, I have rather casually defined play as everything we do for no good reason. That is not quite right, however. There are excellent reasons to play; they just are not self-evidently rational, considering the physical and emotional hardships play imposes on participants. Yet we do engage in it freely. There are degrees of volition involved, as well as degrees of engagement. Children who play the piano probably do so at their parents' urging, even if they enjoy practising. The money and prestige that professional athletes enjoy are no doubt motivating factors; they duly expect to profit from their efforts, so the purity of their play is somewhat tainted by practical considerations. Sports are also often put in the direct service of ideological agendas – political, economic, ethnic and religious. The 1936 Berlin Olympic Games are a vivid example. But these concerns are an extrinsic contamination of play properly understood.

Of course, our motives are invariably mixed and often obscure, especially to ourselves. They also change. We are often asked to perform a task, and it seems that we should distinguish that activity from play as it satisfies a clear purpose. Yet it often happens that we make a greater effort than a situation requires, or needlessly complicate the process, driven by some other, ineffable satisfaction. The person who takes up jogging for health considerations but then enters marathons is an example. Procrastination seems a related phenomenon. And artists are famous for extending themselves not just beyond, but also often in direct defiance of, what would be needed to reap the rewards of wealth and fame.

In pure play (e.g. autotelic play, play without ulterior motive), an individual not only chooses to enter into the experience of her own accord; she also accepts the terms and rules, as well as the hardships and disappointments of playing. In competitive sports, players choose to accept severe and regular blows to body and ego. In play characterized by ordeal, such as mountain climbing or marathon running, players choose to suffer. The concert violinist chooses to endure the acute anxieties of a public performance. Play is sublime, in other words. Sublime in the Burkean sense – in one way or another, to greater and lesser degrees, it hurts. Play is also 'deep' in the Jeremy Bentham sense: practically speaking, the expense of time, effort, money, spirit, etc. is often greater than the return. The two concepts are related. When play is deep it is also sublime. Transcending utilitarian considerations and inviting hardship, play brings about the existential satisfaction of restoring us to ourselves. Never mind skydiving, bungee jumping, marathon running or mountain climbing; even more passive forms of play, such as watching a romantic movie like *Titanic* or taking in the histrionic agonies of an opera like *Tristan and Iseult*, evoke sublime pleasures, since our enjoyment comes not from the success and happiness of the relationship these dramas depict but, rather, from the exquisite pain of its failure.[3] Indeed, in art as in religion we do more than witness suffering; we participate in it willingly, as irrationally, it would seem, as the skydiver leaping out of an aeroplane. The Christian personally participates in Christ's crucifixion; he isn't a mere spectator to that suffering; he is meant to feel it himself and, consequently, to be similarly exalted by it. This, in a nutshell, is the paradoxical logic of many of our most cherished literary and liturgical traditions: pain is pleasure.[4]

Play is fundamentally paradoxical in another sense as well. To play, one must freely choose to suspend his freedom. The skydiver is free, but only until the moment when he leaves the aeroplane. But it is a temporary captivity; and for this reason, to truly play one must also be able to stop playing. The addict conspicuously lacks that agency. The drug use that begins as a free activity soon ceases to be play, as addiction takes over and the ability to quit using diminishes. The masochistic element is not often enough discussed in the literature of play. Karl Groos' *The Play of Man* (1899) perhaps set the tone. Throughout, Groos characterizes pleasure in the narrowest sense, arguing absurdly (ignoring abundant evidence to the contrary) that pleasure disappears and play ceases when it is either taken seriously, requires technique or effort, or depends on rules and restrictions. Likewise, Huizinga mostly emphasizes the 'fun' of play – that is, pleasure in the conventional and immediate sense. The line of thought proceeds from a Platonic privileging of rationality in all things, straining to justify play as an eminently reasonable activity. Educators and child psychiatrists follow suit, positing that play's *raison d'être* is to prepare both individuals and societies for the various challenges of life. Enjoyment facilitates what might otherwise be an arduous learning process, the thinking goes. But these theories confuse effect for cause. Many kinds of play do teach children important life skills, of course. In playing, we come to know our limitations and potentialities and, accordingly, come to know ourselves. But that is not *why* children play. Nor does the educational model explain why adults run marathons or write sestinas.

The fact that not everything we do in the spirit of play is pleasurable or fun suggests that play operates outside the realm of rational self-interest. To Huizinga, this remarkable phenomenon is sufficient proof that man is more than a rational being (Huizinga 1938: 4). We are, Huizinga implies and I argue, often driven by spiritual concerns that resist and transcend rational considerations. Psychoanalytic theory, emphasizing unconscious motives, provides tempting explanations for the masochistic element of play. We have ego needs; we are driven by dark fears and wishes; the id and the superego make conflicting and inexorable demands on us, warping our behaviour; we are not really free; we are at the mercy of our past, of our unconscious; what seems an occasion of unpleasure upon closer examination satisfies obscure but ultimately explicable desires; we temporarily tolerate unpleasure only 'as a step on the long indirect road to pleasure' (Freud 1920: 596) and so on. Throughout his work, particularly his case studies, Freud deftly illustrated many instances of these psychological processes. Yet the more he thought about it, the more it seemed that some behaviour clearly contradicted his cherished pleasure principle, revealing 'mysterious masochistic trends of the ego' (Freud 1920: 598). The play of his eighteen-month-old grandson provides one example. Again and again, the child repeats a game that could not possibly give him pleasure, prompting Freud to note with some surprise that 'the unpleasurable nature of an experience does not always unsuit it for play' (Freud 1920: 601). It would seem, in other words, that there is something in us that 'overrides the pleasure principle', and that not all play corrects an unsatisfying reality, as he had earlier argued in 'Creative Writers and Day Dreaming' (Freud 1907: 439). Rather, it seems that 'some 'daemonic' force [is] at work' in how we play (Freud 1920: 625). He calls that force the death instinct, which is less a matter of aggression than 'an urge inherent in all organic life to restore to early state of thing … to the quiescence of the inorganic world' (Freud 1920: 625) – that is, to the state of non-being.

Which brings us back to anxiety. Once again, according to Tillich, a semi-conscious sense of the nothingness that subtends life is the source of our deepest, most entrenched anxieties. For May, it is the knowledge of our essential freedom that stirs up anxiety.[5] Both men propose similar answers to that anxiety, which relate to play and the experiences of the sublime it affords. In a sense, the answer to anxiety is anxiety. Or rather anxiety transformed, objectified and bravely met. Courage conquers anxiety. So does embracing one's freedom, argues May, even as that freedom is the source of our anxieties. Only in confronting anxiety, they contend, is man able to achieve selfhood, actualize freedom, unburden himself of existential guilt and shame and, finally, overcome the terrors of nothingness. But how exactly are we to do this when the sources of these anxieties are so vague and elusive? Karen Horney says that 'anxiety indicates the presence of a problem which needs to be solved' (May's paraphrase, 1950: 45). But existential despair is difficult to locate and identify. As T.S. Eliot might have put it, we require an 'objective correlative' to these apprehensions. The phrase appears in Eliot's essay 'Hamlet and His Problems'. As the tragedy appears to lack this quality, Eliot deems it an 'artistic failure' (Eliot 1919: 123). But the failures of the play (if failures they are) should perhaps be taken as evidence of Shakespeare's psychological perspicacity, for what they reveal are not so much the failures of a playwright to concretize vague but no less distressing emotional experiences but, rather, the frustrations of man to understand his tortured psychological processes. Most of us can no better discern an objective correlative to our existential anxieties than Hamlet can adequately identify and address his.

What then are we to do? Again, Plato provides the answer: Live life as play. Only then, he says, are we able to 'propitiate the gods'. Only then, that is, are we able to objectify and confront existential anxieties and actualize what is essential in each of us. That is the gist of Tillich and May's exhortations to courage, although instead of focusing on play per se they emphasize spirituality, creativity and acts of self-affirmation. They also don't specifically invoke Burke's notion of the sublime. Indeed, at first glance, they seem to propose a less severe kick in the ass. Tillich speaks of the 'Yes to one's true being' (Tillich 1952: 14). May writes about the courage of 'sensitivity' (May 1975: 15). (One can see how both writers became inspirational figures of the New Age movement. Theirs is undoubtedly a romantic vision of human potential.) Even so, concerned as they are with the self-affirming joy of creative expression, neither minimizes the hardships one needs to endure to achieve happiness. 'Joy is a "severe matter"', says Tillich, quoting Seneca. It is 'difficult and therefore rare, like everything sublime', he adds, now paraphrasing Spinoza. Paradoxically, it also requires self-negation, he notes, drawing on Nietzsche. Joy doesn't escape fear; it 'passionately challenge[s]' fear (Tillich 1952: 14, 24, 29, 42).

This is precisely the course Burke prescribes: experiencing the sublime ordeal to achieve the delight of well-being. The sublime provides the necessary objective correlative to vague but no less insidious anxieties, and therefore calls for a courageous response – the courage of will, of freedom, necessary to vanquish the dread of nothingness.

How to go about this? In the Middle Ages, people assuaged their anxieties by often extreme ascetic exercises of penance. A later age made a cult of the suffering artist, inspiring others who were less artistically inclined to wrestle with their own demons. Those practices and preoccupations are no less strange or narcissistic – and no less psychologically efficacious – than the extreme sports that millions of people engage in today. Many mental health professionals look askance at the risk-seeking behaviour of extreme athletes. Conscious, wilful behavior inimical to a supposed imperative to health is often seen as evidence of deep psychic (if not psychopathic) conflicts, in dire need of therapeutic attention. But the psychologist Carla Willig points out that skydivers, bungee jumpers and rock climbers report achieving something profoundly therapeutic in their practices. Interestingly, though, 'participants did not engage in extreme sports to produce pleasure', she writes (Willig 2008: 698). Indeed, it appears that they undertook the activity in direct defiance of pleasure: 'the possibility of suffering is a necessary dimension of the experience' (Willig 2008: 700). Yet in suffering, they achieve something of greater satisfaction: a sense of being alive, of being fully present. By exploring, testing and 'possibly transcend[ing] the confines of the "self"', these practitioners of the sublime find an effective way of managing existence tensions in a creative and purposeful way', Willig concludes (2008: 700). More importantly, they create happiness for themselves – the specific happiness of exercising free will.

It is this last point – free will encountering the sublime – that warrants further study. In describing the intense pleasures of participating in, and even watching, extreme sports such a skydiving or surfing, Jesus Ilundáin-Agurruza (2007) and Carl Thomen (2010) also situate their analysis in pre-Romantic European thinking on the sublime, particularly Kant's *Critique of Judgment*. As they point out, physical danger can create the same curious combination of joy and fear that the awesome power of nature thrills in us. It has the power to overwhelm the will – unless, that is, it is free will that has brought us to this moment, unless we have *chosen* to run with the bulls of Pamplona or paddle out to meet the terrifying waves of Ohua's North Shore. Sublime experiences with fear and danger trigger a double movement: submitting to something greater than one's will paradoxically activates and enlarges the sense of free will, manifesting a more profound sense of self than a life given to practical concerns can afford. They reveal, however transiently, a higher order of living, of being.

Of course, not everyone has the derring-do to hurl herself out of a perfectly good aeroplane. For that matter, few possess the creative gifts of the poet, the concert pianist, the prima ballerina. No matter, Burke, Tillich and May would say. One can still surmount difficulties, challenge fear, sacrifice security, take risks, and move *through* the anxieties of being and freedom by *choosing* to face challenges. Choice is the essential element. 'A man or woman becomes fully human by his or her choices', May writes (1975: 14). No aspect of life presents us with such self-actualizing occasions of free will as does play. In choosing to play, in whatever way, we necessarily choose difficulty, injury, failure and fear. It may not come off. We may get hurt. We may be defeated. We may be embarrassed. We may suffer. But in affirming our free will through play we will have affirmed ourselves. It is '[b]y moving through anxiety-creating experiences [that] one achieves self-realization, i.e., one enlarges the scope of his activity and, at the same time, increases his freedom', May writes. '[G]oing to school of anxiety enables one to move through the finite and petty constrictions and to be freed to actualize the infinite possibilities of personality' (May 1950: 232, 44). Play provides that education. In play, we face and accept the risks of the human situation directly, and in doing so we realize the satisfactions and joys of our essential selves.

Notes

1 'All art is quite useless': Oscar Wilde, *The Picture of Dorian Gray* (Oxford: Oxford University Press, 2006), p. 4. 'Poetry makes nothing happen': W.H. Auden, 'In Memory of W.B. Yeats', *Another Time: Poems* (New York: Random House, 1940). The artist Richard Serra has outraged many with a similar observation about architects: that they are not, properly speaking, artists. For a thing to be art it must be useless. That is art's very essence. And however spectacularly inventive a building's design may be, it, unlike Serra's own sculptures, must nevertheless serve a useful function.
2 The cultural anthropologist Clifford Geertz eloquently expresses this principle in 'Deep Play: Notes on the Balinese Cockfight'. *Interpretation of Cultures*, 443, 453.
3 'Happy loves has no history', writes Denis De Rougement in *Love in the Western World* (1939), a study of this perplexing feature of literature (p. 15). Stephen Davies addresses this paradox in 'Why Listen to Sad Music if it Makes One Feel Sad', in *Aesthetics in Perspective*, ed. K.M. Higgins (New York: Harcourt Brace & Co, 1996).
4 Jacques Lacan's concept of *jouissance* inverts that formulation. The term means enjoyment – an orgasmic enjoyment – but it implies pleasure in extremis, felt partly as suffering. We may say that it is the pleasure beyond pleasure, and as such presents a challenge to the theory of the 'pleasure principle', which Freud himself would later revise.
5 '[A]nxiety is the dizziness of freedom'; it is 'the alarming possibility of *being able*' writes Søren Kierkegaard (his italics) in *The Concept of Dread* (1844: 40).

Bibliography

Burke, E. (1757) *A Philosophical Enquiry into the Origin of the Sublime and Beautiful*, ed. David Womersley (1998). London: Penguin.
Caillois, R. (1961) *Man, Play and Games*; trans. Meyer Barash (2001). Urbana, IL: University of Illinois Press.
De Rougemont, D. (1939) *Love in the Western World*, trans. Montgomery Belgion (1956). Princeton, NJ: Princeton University Press (revised edition 1983).
Eliot, T.S. (1919) 'Hamlet and His Problems', in *Selected Essays* (1964). New York: Harcourt, Brace & World.
Freud, S. (1907) 'Creative Writers and Day Dreaming', in *The Freud Reader*, ed. Peter Gay (1989). New York: W.W. Norton.
Freud, S. (1920) 'Beyond the Pleasure Principle', in *The Freud Reader*, ed. Peter Gay (1989). New York: W.W. Norton.
Geertz, C. (1973) 'Deep Play: Notes on the Balinese Cockfight', in *The Interpretation of Cultures*. New York: Basic Books.
Groos, K. (1899) *The Play of Man*, trans. Elizabeth L. Baldwin (1901). New York: D. Appleton.

Huizinga, J. (1938) *Homo Ludens: A Study of the Play Element in Culture*, trans. R.F.C. Hull (1955). Boston, MA: Beacon Press.

Ilundáin-Agurruza, J. (2007) 'Kant Goes Skydiving: Understanding the Extreme by Way of the Sublime', in *Philosophy, Risk and Adventure Sports*, ed. Mike McNamee (2007). London: Routledge.

Kant, I. (1790) *Critique of Judgment*, trans. James Creed Meredith (2007). New York: Oxford University Press.

Kierkegaard, S. (1844) *The Concept of Dread*, trans. Walter Lowrie (1968 reprint). Princeton, NJ: Princeton University Press.

May, R. (1950) *The Meaning of Anxiety*. New York: W.W. Norton.

May, R. (1975) *The Courage to Create*. New York: W.W. Norton.

Plato. *Laws*, trans. Trevor J. Saunders (1970). London: Penguin.

Tillich, P. (1952) *The Courage to Be*. New Haven, CT: Yale University Press (reprinted 2000).

Thomen, C. (2010) 'Sublime Kinetic Melody: Kelly Slater and the Extreme Spectator'. *Sports, Ethics and Philosophy*, 4(3): 319–332.

Willig, C. (2008) 'A Phenomenological Investigation of the Experience of Taking Part in "Extreme Sports"'. *Journal of Health Psychology*, 690(13): 691–702.

11 Playing in a Deleuzian playground

Stuart Lester

The aim of this chapter is to bring a Deleuzian gaze to play, and by doing so unsettle dominant accounts of this form of behaviour. It will set to work some key concepts from Deleuzian philosophy to reveal play as an affirmation of creativity, opening 'ourselves to the experimentation that the future offers rather than clinging to the illusory identity that the present places before us' (May 2005: 68). Playing from this perspective reminds us that the future is not given, but always contains the potential for novelty and the unexpected. It asks 'what if' the world is thought, felt and acted on differently and by doing so brings about different becomings, new trajectories, new responses, unheard-of futures (Massumi 1992).

The discussion opens by bringing Deleuzian concepts into play, proceeds to situate them in an experimental space of Jack and the Beanstalk before moving into the Deleuzian playground itself. But it should be made clear at the outset that this is not a definitive reading, or an act of precision. Many have commented on the nonsense and impenetrability of Gilles Deleuze's writings; his thoughts are among the most esoteric and even obscure of recent thinkers (May 2005), producing an eclectic fusion of 'misbehaving concepts' (McGowan 2007). For anyone who is accustomed to conventional ways of writing and language use, reading the work of Deleuze, and his collaborations with Felix Guattari, can be confusing, unsettling and infuriating. An extreme viewpoint from Wheen (2004) refers to Deleuze's writings as gibberish which in itself presents a significant lure to someone who has spent much of their life studying and working with play.

There are many existing objections to Deleuzian concepts, and this piece will no doubt give rise to further questions. So be it: the task at hand here is not about veracity but rather an attempt to elucidate how certain refrains make possible a different and difference reading of play. The appeal of Deleuzian philosophy lies with its capability to be 'used in many different ways and in direct relation to practices and events in everyday life' (Olsson 2009: 24–25). The question from a Deleuzian standpoint is not 'what does it mean' but 'how does it work'?

Deleuze was prolific in designing and involving his philosophy and used philosophers, scientists, artists, musicians and writers as resource kits for his own musings (Buchanan 2000) to produce a political philosophy concerned with the complex and ever-changing practicalities of the everyday that reveal it to be anything but everyday. The collection of single and co-produced work invites the reader into a space that lies beneath habitual ways of seeing the world, and by doing so reveals a realm of ever-present virtualities, the not yet known, waiting to be released. Above all it is a philosophy of movement and experimentation.

The main force of the argument presented here is that children's play marks a time/space in which ever-present virtualities are actualised, producing moments in which children are *becoming-different*; that is, following their own desires rather than following adult determined pathways. But it is perhaps more than this; thinking differently about play inevitably disturbs the foundations upon which dominant understandings of the nature of children's play, and by inference childhood and adulthood, are constructed and reveals a different way of attuning to and caring for multiple and lively ways of being together.

Deleuzian philosophy

Deleuze and Guattari (1994: 2) consider philosophy to be 'the art of forming, inventing and fabricating concepts'. But as they elaborate, forming, inventing or fabricating concepts doesn't quite fit: concepts are not forms, discoveries or products, but more rigorously are *created*; a concept is something that is always new. Concepts are not waiting to be discovered, already formed, but are always in the process of creating themselves. Concepts are not valued for revealing 'truths', but for what they can do and the affect they create – it is a matter of production rather than reflection (Zayani 2000).

For Deleuze and Guattari the history and task of classical philosophy has been to form stable sites for thinking, where thought is subject to logic systems and rational analysis. It manifests and maintains itself through resemblance, analogy, identity and opposition. But theirs is a philosophy that is nomadic, constantly and restlessly wandering, encountering other concepts to assemble novel connections. The process of producing concepts brings about an act of deterritorialisation, injecting disturbance into the system of orthodox thought and habits of mind. Just as with children's play, the creation of concepts is an opportunity to invent, create and experiment. Deleuze and Guattari (1994: 33) explain that the philosophical purpose is to 'extract an event from things and beings, to set up the new event from things and beings, always to give them a new event: space, time, matter, thought, the possible as events'. The actualisation of different conceptual possibilities produces an approach to life itself that is affirmative and constantly disturbing; who knows what concepts are yet to be formed and what universes await discovery? This starts to explain the intellectually mobile concepts which lead into new landscapes littered with the stuff of geophilosophy.

Whatever its nomadic wanderings, playful inversion of language and reworking of ideas, there is a central point that poses the question 'How might one live' (May 2005)? At the heart of Deleuze (and Guattari) lies an exploration of the possibilities of human relations, a challenge to worn-out binary relationships between individual and society, freedom and control, and so on. But it is not a complete revolution or overthrow of what exists; to do so would lead to despair and paralysis (Deleuze and Guattari 1988). Rather, the mobile concepts enable a reworking of power, interrupt common-sense and escape the constraints of order to discover new ideas and movements.

Where does one begin?

As intimated in the introduction, this is not an attempt to present, interpret or produce an authoritative reading of Deleuze's philosophy. Neither does it seek to explain play by a simple application of Deleuzian concepts. Rather it releases these into action; it is an intuitive response or a creative process that emerges by negating the old and resisting the temptation to understand the new by using old concepts (Grosz 2005). It necessitates affirming odd connections to create new affects. The approach is 'playful' through injecting disturbance into habits of thought and common sense to produce new and (potentially?) exciting possibilities. It thrives on the belief that the world is indeterminate and contains far more than can be ever accounted for, which suggests that meanings are always open to further inventions, experimentations and possibilities.

Deleuze dares us to think differently by using conceptual tools that unsettle and penetrate a universal and dominant way of seeing and explaining the world. It carries a critique of 'state philosophy' for its tree-like, or *arborescent*, production of thought in which everything can be traced back to a single point of origin (the fixed root of thought). While the root may divide, everything is derived and situated in a hierarchical relationship to the main root, or 'deeply rooted' (Markula 2006). It relies on binary logic of dichotomy which makes it impossible to consider multiplicity. It has come to mould and dominate our ways of thinking (Zayani 2000). Countering this, Deleuze and Guattari (1988) introduce the concept of *rhizomatic* thought as a network or decentred multiplicity; there is no central point which holds things together (Bonta and Protevi 2004). A rhizome is marked by connectivity and heterogeneity; it 'has neither subject nor object, only determinations, magnitudes, and dimensions which cannot increase in number without the multiplicity changing in nature' (Deleuze and Guattari 1988: 9). It may be broken, but it will start up again on one of its old lines or start a new line. It contains lines of segmentarity that seek to order, stratify and territorialise, and also lines of deterritorialisation; 'there is a rupture in the rhizome whenever segmentary lines explode into a line of flight, but the line of flight is part of the rhizome' (Deleuze and Guattari 1988: 10). Each rhizome has multiple entry ways and lines of escape; 'thought is not arborescent but rhizomatic, the production of the unconscious, and with it new statements, different desires' (Deleuze and Guattari 1988: 20).

So who is the 'hero'?

A simple experiment is introduced here to elaborate on rhizomatic thinking by posing a question: 'In the story of Jack and the Beanstalk, who is the hero'? The question itself raises some fundamental issues: it assumes that there is a heroic figure, and that this is a 'subject'. Traditional accounts clearly present an anthropocentric perspective; the world revolves around Jack and serves to meet his transcendence from simpleton to hero.

Now imagine we are asked to present a case for the primacy of mother, cow, beans, soil, giant, axe or any other material/character assembled in the story as the 'hero' (which immediately takes us into a landscape of highly complex and layered historical, spatial and cultural forces and formations). The question disorders or deterritorialises dominant accounts and replaces them with another way of reading the story. At this point, while Jack's position has been disturbed and Jack's identity as hero displaced, the thinking that has positioned Jack remains the same, i.e. we have transposed one central character with another, with competing claims for supremacy and through the application of common sense seek some 'truth' and make judgements of value. It marks the application of arborescent (or possibly beanstalk) thinking.

Deleuze and Guattari's philosophy invites a further deterritorialisation with the concept of assemblage *(agencement)*. In the context of this experiment, the juxtaposed materials which make up the story congregate to form an intense relationship of Jack, soil, beans, cow, mother and so on. The fabric of the story is revealed through the conjunction 'and' (soil *and* beans *and* cow *and* mother *and* ...), which then does away with the imposition of foundational roots and negates the power of fixed endings and beginnings. The constitutive assemblage of all the parts of the story cannot be reduced to a binary relationship and cannot be organised in terms of identity. No longer can the story be seen as discrete components, with their manyness reduced to one fixed relationship organised by rank; rhizomatic thought 'synthesises a multiplicity of elements without effacing their heterogeneity or hindering their potential for future arranging' (Massumi 1988: xiii). In this sense, assemblage refers to an 'ad hoc grouping of diverse elements, of vibrant materials of all sorts' (Bennett 2010: 23). It does not privilege human action with 'passive' things or situate a subject as the 'root cause of an effect' (Bennett 2010: 31). It also suggests that a human-non-human assemblage has a collective force or power to act that cannot be attributed to a single determining substance. In simple terms, rhizomatic thinking disassembles bordered and fixed concepts about space, materials, bodies and movement (Legg 2011).

The assemblage of materials in Jack and the Beanstalk operates across physico-chemical, organic and social registers, each with their own speeds and flows but which opportunistically combine and interpenetrate for a period before falling apart or becoming something else. The story arises from a collection of singularities each with their own becomings or immanent relations that involve nothing outside of the territory, and each with their own impulses or force, a 'swarm of vitalities at play' (Bennett 2010: 32). The story of Jack, recounted through the fairy-tale, becomes the actuality of what happens. It represents the ways in which heterogeneous materials and forces are assembled in a certain milieu and proceed to order themselves into a pattern. By doing so they *assume* a law-like relationship of independent and dependent variables; they appear in actuality as stratified and fixed substances in relationships that become settled over time. This, through common-sense reading, becomes the focus of attention through subject–object analysis, seeking to draw some causal laws within this actual realm to fix identities in time and space.

But Deleuze/Guattarian philosophy introduces another critical dimension to this dominant account: there exists in the story of Jack a *virtuality* which consists of a multiplicity of forces that play beneath the surface. The use of virtual here is an attempt to see what escapes cognition by paying attention to the incorporeal, inorganic and the possibilities that pass between them rather than being derived from a single root (Markula 2006). The virtual field is actualised by a process of differentiation which brings about exclusions, i.e. it prohibits the actualisation of other virtualities. But the virtual world remains as an ever-present force from which many possible actualities can be created; they are planes of difference or '*consistency*'. From a Deleuzian perspective, the world is a possibility before a reality, 'there are a crowd of pretenders to actualisation that never get actualised' (Dewsbury 2009: 150). Actualisation brings forth specific forms and modes, but does not freeze them; the 'present always holds more than it seems' (May 2005: 70). The body moves as it feels and feels itself moving, it is in a process of constant change, never present in a position but always passing through, it is always being-becoming (Massumi 2002).

It is this relationship between the virtual and the actual, and the intense affects that surface differences that are of central concern in this chapter. It shows us that the present is never complete and 'acknowledges the real's capacity to be otherwise, its ability to become more and other' (Grosz 2005: 9). The idea that what is actualised represents the limit of what a body can become negates the existence of a multiplicity of virtualities and seeks to plot a specific trajectory to the future; looking for signs of what to expect and designing minds and bodies to steer towards a knowable destiny. By doing so, creative possibilities are stifled and intensities of desire to become different are restricted and subsumed into a plan(e) of organisation. Playing reveals novelty, remarkability and vitality that temporarily sets to one side the illusion of truth.

Playing in the deleuzian playground

This brief introduction to these mobile concepts establishes the foundations of the *Deleuzian playground*, a space for thinking creatively and differently about the scientific classifications and categorisations that account for the identity of play. In the spirit of Deleuze, the conceptual construction of this playground defies the 'fixed equipment' of common sense which determines actions and orders bodies. The study of play is marked by attempts to define and distinguish this form of behaviour in order to better understand its utility. Play is framed in terms of self-identity, a 'special mental set toward the world and one's action in it ... [the rhetoric of] progress, the imaginary and the self are relatively Western, relatively modern, and relatively utopian discourses about individualized forms of play' (Sutton-Smith 1997: 174). Modern accounts fix specific meanings to play, pinned like a butterfly for observation and categorisation. By doing so it isolates children's play from the heterogeneous materials, flows and forces which surround them. Arborescent thought establishes oppositions between play and other ways of being, marking the modern segmentation of human life into discrete parts in which play and childhood are separated from the rest of human life. It reflects binary thinking that involves dualisms of work/play, control/ freedom, seriousness/frivolity, reality/fantasy, adult/child and so on. Play, through resemblance and opposition, is represented as an object that distinguishes childhood and positions children as lacking in relation to their oppositions. Common sense declares that children need to develop the requisite skills and qualities to become independent, autonomous citizens, 'programmed in the present as a prescription for the future' (Massumi 2010: 3). This is a legacy of an 'ideological fiction' (Lee 2005: 157) established by the dominant paradigm of a particular reading of developmental psychology and neoliberal economics. Dominance is erected and maintained through the construction of *molar assemblages* (Deleuze and Guattari 1988), a particular configuration of language, institutions, materials and space that shapes understandings of child, adult and play. The use of *molar* in this context is not an expression of scale but an account of modes of organisation and accountability (Bonta and Protevi 2004). A molar assemblage is founded upon norms of behaviour, used as a descriptor of the whole assemblage and employed as a form of measurement of its components to ascertain any deviation from this norm. It establishes standards based on the presupposition of some ideal or perfect development.

Molar accounts of play produce segregated time/space (playtime and playground) and provision of 'playthings' that serve to meet children's desires/needs. Desire, in this sense, is a negative condition; an object that is desired implies a current lack. This lack is not pre-existing in children; binary thinking produces this understanding and by doing so positions the child within the world as 'needy'. Thus, 'children need to play' becomes a slogan for adults by which they assume control over the conditions under which playing is provided and tolerated. This plane of organisation seeks to feed off play for its own purpose. For example, children's creative expressions are desirable and encouraged as long as they are not disturbing ('play nicely'). Play becomes a medium for fixing a child's identity as a future adult, the child required to become that which it is currently not (from lacking to possessing); children need to grow up and out of play. Any attempt to break away from this trajectory is seen as untimely and out of place. Forms of playing that appear to be irrational and irresponsible are repressed by powerful assemblages that claim moral authority and superiority: 'institutions working with the logic of desire as lack do all they can to tame children's desires; to predict, control, supervise and evaluate them to predefined standards' (Olsson 2009: 141). Adults too are caught up in this process, their identity as adult in relation to child assumes an order of maturity, rationality and fixity.

Playing differently

Robert Fagen (2011: 92), the distinguished scholar of animal play, claims that 'a place remains for novel perspectives on play, imaginative and bold as play itself'. Deleuzian anti-arborescent concepts offer such a bold perspective by moving beyond molar accounts 'towards new more agile thoughts that palpates what it cannot perceive and gestures at what it cannot grasp' (May 2005: 115). Central to the discussion here is Deleuze's (1992) reading of Spinoza's *conatus*, or the desire of bodies to enhance their capabilities to joyfully exist and to avoid relationships that reduce this capacity. This is not the body of science as a self-contained organism, rather a *body assemblage*, a dynamic, ever-changing ensemble of connections between human and non-human bodies and materials (Duff 2010). Desire is immanent to the productive process, always striving to become more, but is actualised in concrete relations within the assemblages it co-produces. It thrives on the potential for configuring new and extensive assemblages with the widest possible materials at hand to increase the body's force of existence or power of acting. Significantly, desire is distributed; we do not desire alone or in relationship to a single object but in a complex network of relations (Olsson 2009).

Molar assemblages may express patterns that seek to establish equilibrium, exercise power over other affects and subjugate bodies to their will, but they are always open to other interpretations, moments and movements of *deterritorialisation* (Deleuze and Guattari 1988). Deterritorialisation holds the most promise for self-ordering and 'joy'; it is a desire to seek out leakages in the constraining molar system and establish molecular *lines of flight* away from the plane of organisation. The contention here is that playing may be seen as such a movement away from order, stability and predictability. It is the process of being a child becoming different and open to what it not yet is.

So let us return to our experiment: the molar unity represented by the common-sense rendition of Jack and the Beanstalk attempts to form and stabilise an identity, seal in its energies and intensities, and fix relationships into a certain stable pattern. But playing traverses such a system, creates a path, destabilises, and exposes leakages in molar unities. Children's playful desire may produce a different assemblage of materials from traditional accounts:

FIRST CHILD: Let's pretend we sold the cow for some beans but on the way home we get hungry so we have to eat the beans (with sharing of beans and swallowing).
SECOND CHILD: Yes, and then we do enormous farts (shared laughter).
FIRST CHILD: And then a giant beanstalk grows out of our arses, all the way up to the sky (more laughter).

This experimental moment of playing is a desiring assemblage engaging with the world with a particular force instigated by problematising what is presented as reality. It marks a unique configuration of materials that create a time/space for new relational capacities and affective sensitivities (Duff 2010). Rather than the binary representation of fantasy/real, it becomes the interplay between potentiality and actuality (Olsson 2009). Children's restless bodies encounter other bodies and materials to produce intense moments when other versions of reality appear. Intensive in this context implies a *molecular* collective force that overflows from dominant structures. It is not apart from the actual; indeed it draws on the real to release other virtualities, just as the 'actual' seeks to over-code these leakages and reassign them to molar structures. The important point here is not to see molar and molecular as oppositions; they are indivisible from one another (Buchanan 2000). Playing may be seen as desiring to affect and be affected by creating uncertainty and disturbance, and to play with the relationship between disequilibrium and balance (Spinka *et al.* 2001). An assemblage can maintain its joyful urges by collectively being in control of being out of control, spinning centrifugally away from order, 'always swinging between the surfaces that stratify it and the plane that sets it free' (Deleuze and Guattari 1988: 178). Regaining equilibrium is not a return to the same. The act of disturbance redistributes bodies, time and space, allowing for an intensity of becoming different while creating the extensive possibility that things can go on becoming different. But equally, and pushing this experiment to breaking-point, the playful assemblage can be constrained and over-coded; molar forces (e.g. adult) may see such behaviour as deviant, dysfunctional, and re-establish order by various means of control and coercion.

Thinking and developing differently

While Deleuze and Guattari present becoming as openness and possibilities, it is not the case that anything can happen; rather, anything can happen given, or by creating, the right conditions. The dynamic capacities of human and non-human bodies are actualised in encounters (Deleuze 1992): some assemblages increase a body's power to act (becoming beanstalk), while others may lead to a loss in capacity (becoming proper). The thing that we identify as play is one way in which humans compose themselves in encounters with other bodies and materials to produce a more powerful body by asking the question 'what if …' to create more joyous states. It presents a totally different reading of children growing out of play. Rather than abandoning this desire as one achieves adulthood, playing becomes a driving force for a lifetime of change and creativity.

Thinking differently shifts focus from what is happening inside individual minds to what is produced within and between bodies and materials that constitute the spaces of encounter. Lines of flight are produced by wandering from the segmented lines of 'development' and composing paths that actualise other contemporaneous possibilities; beanstalks can grow out of backsides, and by doing so momentarily make the world a more vibrant place.

Following Deleuze/Spinoza, development may be seen as the discontinuous process of restless bodies and affects, relations and encounters (Duff 2010), transformed through the formation of myriad assemblages, suggesting that the body holds no advance notice or blueprint of what it can become. Developmental capabilities are affectively and relationally produced and reproduced. Agency can no longer be seen as individual freedom to make choices and act on these, but rather the space of encounter is always a human–non-human assemblage (Bennett 2010). There is no stable human experience because bodies are constantly reinvented as things happen, always in a state of being and becoming: 'we know nothing about a body until we know what it can do, in other words, what its affects are, how they can or cannot enter into composition with other affects' (Deleuze and Guattari 1988: 294).

Representations of play, in molar accounts, miss this very point and continue to inscribe a certain identity to both play and players that sets them apart and fixes them to the tracing of teleological normative development. But there are always opportunities for molecular activity; indeed, one might suggest that the position of children in adult-designed institutions is 'built on a massive molecular movement' (Olsson 2009: 76). Increasingly Deleuzian concepts are being set to work to reveal the ways in which children and adults may deterritorialise the rigid structures of institutional space and resist the constraining forces of power through everyday performative practices (see e.g. Harker 2005; Leafgren 2009; Mozere 2007; Olsson 2009). Other studies of institutional adult–child relationships, while not specifically 'Deleuzian', reveal the many ways in which adults and children can co-create lines of flight that delimit molar demands, wonderfully illustrated by Hannikainen's (2001) study of kindergarten circle time in which children disturb the routine by injecting 'rude-nonsense' into the roll-call, with the support from the teacher who shares this line of flight to establish a temporary unity across differences. What these studies suggest is that adults attentive to the process of children becoming different will try to favour this movement, to experiment with it, to be alert to potential moments and movements of deterritorialisation (Deleuze and Guattari 1988). The playing child becoming different is, for both children and adults alike, a line of flight from molar identities of 'adult' and 'child', breaking apart the binary opposition that sees adults as complete and children as lacking and needy (Tarulli and Skott-Myhre 2006). Such occasions question dominant and illusionary accounts of development and the 'normalization system is forced to give way to emancipatory forces of desire' (Mozere 2007: 295). Perhaps, as Sutton-Smith (1997) asserts, playing's utility may simply be to increase the desire for more playful assemblages, and by doing so continue to reveal the world as a source of joy, to have greater satisfaction in being and becoming alive.

Problems and questions

This brief foray into a Deleuzian *difference* playground disrupts molar space by creating disturbing concepts that resonate with understanding the complexity of the real (Grosz 2005). Playing is not something apart from reality, not a lesser state, or a rehearsal for becoming adult, and not an individualised deliberative choice as fixed molar structures of childhood, adulthood and development would have us believe. It problematises the taken-for-granted by drawing upon the qualities of playing itself, as a restless desire to release new virtualities into the world through novel assemblages. By doing so it reveals development and growth to be a multitude of singular events, moments which escape representation and categorisation. Assemblage thinking is an affirmation of the vitality of life through understanding the make-up and organisation of the social in more inventive and experimental ways (Dewsbury 2011).

'Being' in this playground foregrounds an ethos of experimental relationship with the world that attends to its eventful liveliness. It poses an ethical question, 'how can we come to experience a maximum of joyful passions' (Deleuze 1988)? For adults, this suggests witnessing everyday playful moments, not to colonise and over-code children's desires, but to open ourselves to a 'generous sensibility, one that might be capable of re-enlivening our affective engagements with others and fostering a heightened sense for what might be possible' (Popke 2009: 84). It marks a greater affective capacity, to affect and be affected by the possibility of becoming other than adult and by doing so bring about new forms of engagement and response-ability, caring for playful being-becoming in common with others rather than apart.

Bibliography

Bennett, J. (2010) *Vibrant Matter. A Political Ecology of Things*. Durham, NC: Duke University Press.

Bonta, M. and Protevi, J. (2004) *Deleuze and Geophilosophy.A Guide and Glossary*. Edinburgh: Edinburgh University Press.

Buchanan, I. (2000) *Deleuzism. A Metacommentary*. Durham, NC: Duke University Press.

Deleuze, G. (1988) *Spinoza: Practical Philosophy*. San Francisco, CA: City Lights.

Deleuze, G. (1992) 'Mediators', in J. Crary and S. Kwinter (eds) *Incorporations*. New York: Zone Books, pp. 281–294.

Deleuze, G. and Guattari, F. (1984) *Anti-Oedipus: Capitalism and Schizophrenia*. London: The Athlone Press.

Deleuze, G. and Guattari, F. (1988) *A Thousand Plateaus*. London: The Athlone Press.

Deleuze, G. and Guattari, F. (1994) *What is Philosophy?* London: Verso.

Dewsbury, J.D. (2009) 'Language and the Event: The Unthought of Appearing Worlds', in B. Anderson and P. Harrison (eds) *Taking Place: Non-representational Theories and Geography*. Farnham: Ashgate, pp. 147–160.

Dewsbury, J.D. (2011) 'The Deleuze–Guattarian Assemblage: Plastic Habits'. *Area*, 43(2): 148–153.

Duff, C. (2010) 'Towards a Developmental Ethology: Exploring Deleuze's Contribution to the Study of Health and Human Development'. *Health*, 14(6): 619–634.

Fagen, R. (2011) 'Play and Development', in A. Pellegrini (ed.) *The Oxford Handbook of the Development of Play*. Oxford: Oxford University Press, pp. 83–100.

Grosz, E. (2005) 'Bergson, Deleuze and the Becoming of Unbecoming'. *Parallax*, 11(2): 4–13.

Hannikainen, M. (2001) 'Playful Actions as a Sign of Togetherness in Day Care Centres'. *International Journal of Early Years Education*, 9(2): 125–134.

Harker, C. (2005) 'Playing and Affective Time-spaces'. *Children's Geographies*, 3(1): 47–62.

Leafgren, S. (2009) *Reuben's Fall: A Rhizomatic Analysis of Disobedience in Kindergarten.* Walnut Creek, CA: West Coast Press.

Lee, N. (2005) *Childhood and Human Value.* Maidenhead: Open University Press.

Legg, S. (2011) 'Assemblage/Apparatus: Using Deleuze and Foucault'. *Area*, 43(2): 128–133.

Markula, P. (2006) 'Deleuze and the Body Without Organs: Disreading the Fit Feminine Identity'. *Journal of Sport and Social Issues*, 40(1): 29–44.

Massumi, B. (1988) Translators' Foreword: 'Pleasures of Philosophy', in G. Deleuze and F. Guattari *A Thousand Plateaus*. London: The Athlone Press, pp. ix–xvi.

Massumi, B. (1992) *A User's Guide to Capitalism and Schizophrenia: Deviations from Deleuze and Guattari.* Cambridge, MA: MIT Press.

Massumi, B. (2002) *Parables for the Virtual: Movement, Affect, Sensations.* Durham, NC: Duke University Press.

Massumi, B. (2010) 'What Concepts Do: Preface to the Chinese Translation of a Thousand Plateaus'. *Deleuze Studies*, 4(1): 1–15.

May, T. (2005) *Gilles Deleuze: An Introduction.* New York: Cambridge University Press.

McGowan, K. (2007) *Key Issues in Critical and Cultural Theory.* Maidenhead: Open University Press.

Mozere, L. (2007) 'In Early Childhood: What's Language About?' *Educational Philosophy and Theory*, 39(3): 291–299.

Olsson, L. (2009) *Movement and Experimentation in Young Children's Learning.* London: Routledge.

Popke, J. (2009) 'Geography and Ethics: Non-representational Encounters, Collective Responsibility and Economic Difference'. *Progress in Human Geography*, 33(1): 81–90.

Spinka, M., Newberry, R. and Bekoff, M. (2001) 'Mammalian Play: Training for the Unexpected'. *The Quarterly Review of Biology*, 76(2): 141–168.

Sutton-Smith, B. (1997) *The Ambiguity of Play.* Cambridge, MA: Harvard University Press.

Tarulli, D. and Skott-Myhre, H. (2006) 'The Immanent Rights of the Multitude: An Ontological Framework for Conceptualizing the Issue of Child and Youth Rights'. *International Journal of Children's Rights*, 14: 187–201.

Wheen, F. (2004) *How Mumbo-Jumbo Conquered the World: A Short History of Modern Delusions.* London: Perennial.

Zayani, M. (2000)'Gilles Deleuze, Felix Guattari and the Total System'. *Philosophy and Social Criticism*, 26(1): 93–114.

12 'We sneak off to play what we want!'

Bakhtin's carnival and children's play[1]

Maria Øksnes

Traditionally, children's play has been explored through the views and understandings of adults who claim to speak for children. Hence, the practice has been to study children on the outside of the life they lead through a language that may primarily be connected to an objective scientific discourse between adults, which precludes specific ways of regarding play. According to Brian Sutton-Smith (1997, 2004), this discourse has described play as being primarily about learning and development rather than enjoyment and fun, and has been identified as the rhetoric of play as progress. Because of the freedom associated with play, it is said to be the best way to learn and develop. He writes: 'play effectively becomes privileged over work both as a learning or arousal-seeking activity and as a major factor in the individual's mental and emotional development' (Sutton-Smith 1997: 203). This play-as-progress rhetoric seems to constitute how children should play and may be viewed as an exercise of power. We see in our culture that children's play is subjected to institutional guidelines. Adults attempt to regulate and control play, suppressing activities they deem inappropriate, aggressive or dangerous, and encouraging activities they consider productive, beneficial or therapeutic (Ailwood 2003; Cannella 1997). This attempt to govern play implies that play is something that can be subordinated to both adult and children's own intentions. It follows an idea that an outcome of play can be predicted.

The idealized play relating to children's progress is only part of the picture. Gail Cannella (1997) stresses the importance of acknowledging the full range of children's play behaviour. As children spend increasing amounts of time in educational situations, including preschools, kindergartens and after-school programmes, and have less time to themselves, it has become increasingly important to understand the relationship between 'schooling' and children's play (cf. Sutton-Smith 1987). Sutton-Smith writes: 'Paradoxically, children, who are supposed to be the players among us, are allowed much less freedom for irrational, wild, dark, or deep play in Western culture than are adults, who are thought not to play at all' (Sutton-Smith 1997: 152). I fear that despite ideological statements about the value of play, the world is becoming a tougher place for children to find room for their own play.

It is important to question the ideology with which the study of children's play has often been approached. Play researchers critical towards the dominant play discourse agree that children's voices and ideas should be involved in the construction of new understandings about children's play. I have therefore conducted an empirical study of children's play within preschools, kindergartens and after-school programmes in Norway. The aim of my study has been to explore children's own thoughts and perceptions of play. In this chapter I will argue that children can offer us a more balanced understanding that challenges the prevailing instrumental view of what play is. The Russian philosopher and literary theorist Mikhail Bakhtin's (1895–1975) concepts of the unofficial carnival life and revelations of a side of life that cannot be shown through the use of the official language may provide us with new perspectives on play in certain educational settings. Based on Bakhtin's description of carnival I discuss to what extent children find room for their own play and what seem to characterize this play. I start with a more detailed description of what I consider to be the dominant perspective on children's play.

Competing play discourses

In his book *Dionysus Reborn* (1989), Mihai Spariosu shows that there has always been disagreement among Western philosophers over whether play should basically be understood as an orderly and rule-governed affair, or a chaotic, violent and indeterminate interaction of forces. Spariosu claims that most Western philosophers have attempted to rationalize play, pointing to children supposedly learning from their play. He puts this in the category of order and civilization and it is similar to the declaration of play as progress. We can talk about a play that is stripped of every irrational, violent and arbitrary connotation and is subordinated to morality, seriousness and reason. Due to this aesthetization, play is valued as a useful and speculative instrument in the service of fulfilling certain functions in Western civilization (Spariosu 1989).

Concurring with Spariosu, Sutton-Smith (1997) proposes a fluctuation between various rational and pre-rational sets of values, but he explains that educators and parents seem to favour the rhetoric of progress. 'Play as progress', he claims, 'is an ideology for the conquest of children's play behaviour through organizing their play' (Sutton-Smith 1997: 205). To paraphrase Sutton-Smith we thus forget, neglect or deny the ways in which children play by themselves or together with other children; the play of disorder, carnival (cf. Bakhtin), deep play and play-fighting, which can be associated with disorder and chaos and irrationality. From my point of view, there seems to have been a trend away from the consideration of *what* and *how* children play to the instrumental investigation of *why* children play. The question of why children play indicates that the focus is on educational aims that adults often connect to children's play and might privilege what we want children to play and where we want them to be rather than what they are actually playing. Words, cognition, imagination and so on seem to be the central focal points of this way of understanding children's play, while the physical, bodily aspects of play are often ignored. As a critic of this approach, Sutton-Smith observes that this rhetoric serves adults' needs more than the needs of children.

According to Sutton-Smith, educational scholars have been perhaps the principal champions of this 'play as progress' ideology. They have tended to see play from a functionalistic perspective where the focus is on the benefits and positive outcomes of play. These viewpoints have been buttressed, for the most part, by studies from cognitive and developmental psychology (cf. Piaget, Erikson, Vygotsky). Play here is understood as a civilizing activity that helps children to become adults. This implies that play may be guided in correct, future-oriented directions. We could say that the idealizing tendency goes hand in hand with what Spariosu (1989) calls a 'rationalizing tendency'.

Douglas Kleiber (1999) writes that there is a tendency for children's play to be instrumentalized and reduced to an education tool for something else that is not play. Playful situations are produced in educational settings primarily to lure children to acquire knowledge, competence and defined skills. The educational interests connected to children's play thus have a paradoxical tendency to always be referred back to an educational mindset that play and learning are two sides of the same coin. Bearing this in mind, the idea has been to raise children according to 'good' and 'correct' play, believing that this would enable them to develop in a direction that is important for school work, and would also prepare children for 'real' life as adults.

Sutton-Smith (1997), however, states that if play is to be understood, we need to know that play is sometimes about risk-taking, sometimes nonsense and sometimes festive. He celebrates the ambiguity of play and is critical of scholars who seem to be trapped in their own narrow conceptions of play. He writes that we need to transcend our limited mindsets. Whereas the narrow instrumental approach to play has been well established for quite some time, its interpretive counterpart has only recently come more into focus (Meire 2007). This interpretive approach builds on philosophical appraisals of play inspired by hermeneutic and phenomenological theories, and might broaden our ideas on children's play. These philosophers often have different basic concepts about play, an approach that heralds play's indeterminism, chaos and irrationality, and they are not particularly concerned with child growth, writes Sutton-Smith (1997), who then lists the names they give play: anarchic power (Spariosu), deep play (Geertz), dark play (Schechner), nonsense (Stewart), wilfulness (Nietzsche) and grotesque realism (Bakhtin). This type of play behaviour is not goal-directed and does not point to any instrumental purposive context. From this philosophical approach, play is not valued for its 'usefulness' but for exactly the opposite: for moving beyond instrumentality. I will expand on this approach by turning to Bakhtin and my own empirical material.

Bakhtin, carnival and children's play

I have used Bakhtin's model of a carnival life to analyse children's play in my empirical study. Even though Bakhtin does not write directly about educational settings, he furnishes an ideal type, a philosophical and cultural ideal that enables his concepts to be used in new contexts. As I will show, the unofficial carnival life Bakhtin describes is relevant in the process of understanding children's play. I have both conducted conversations with children (aged 4 to 9) and observed their play (aged 1 to 9) for several years. Using Bakhtin's concept of carnival problematizes uncritical and naively empiricist interpretations of children's play. Bakhtin disrupted my habitual viewpoints and made me aware of the carnivalesque overtone that remains in children's play that I did not notice before.

Living two lives?

In his book *Rabelais and His World* Bakhtin (1984) studies the folk culture of laughter and shows how people in the Middle Ages lived dual lives, an official life and an unofficial life, the latter called carnival life. Official life was related to work, seriousness, traditions, an established hierarchic closed system and ideology, and was built on a truth delivered by centripetal powers striving to make things cohere. Unofficial life, on the other hand, was tied to centrifugal forces aimed at promoting ambivalence and special ideas of freedom allowing dialogical openness and transgression. Carnival was a feast celebrating renewal, being critical and derisive of anything that was presented as completed and concluded. It was a feast with great importance for human culture because it was symbolically destructive: various authorities and official culture became the target, and bore the brunt of jest and ridicule during the carnival. A joyous carnival atmosphere with much laughter dominated the unofficial sphere and continued to be present in everyday life when the carnival season was over.

Bakhtin sees a close connection between carnival and play. According to Bakhtin, carnival makes us discover that truths are relative and that the world is open and free in a manner reminiscent of how children play with and have fun with the order of things, turning things inside out and upside down. With the increased institutionalization of children's play one might get the impression that children are subordinate to official institutional regimes. A closer look reveals, however, that everything cannot be captured by what Bakhtin calls centripetal forces. I was frequently able to observe and hear children who resisted such forces in their own ways. They cause trouble and generate disorder and surprise. Children are able to find the opportunity to play in strictly structured teaching and work situations in spite of bans and hierarchic barriers (King 1987). They defy precise definitions and concluding schemata that adults might have for their play and thus we may say that they live a carnival life.

In the book *Play World*, James E. Combs (2000) writes that children learn from a very young age what play means. His point is that since there is an official social world related to seriousness, institutional duties and social responsibility, children will learn what it means when they ask: 'Do you want to play?' or that what they are doing is 'just play'. The children I talked to seemed to prefer some play activities to others, and when asked they would reel off typical activities. However, as our conversation continued, the children started to challenge the authoritative official voices that prescribe 'correct' play activities for children. They laughed and talked loudly as they told stories about activities that were not so popular with adults, containing the darker, grotesque and carnivalesque sides of play. The children told me stories from situations where they turned things upside down and had fun.

'If we can't play we get bored!'

The instrumental view of children's play that I have described above may be compared with what Bakhtin called the official feast where the state intervened in the festive life and made it into a parade. People became spectators of and not participants in the feast, and the feast became an individual carnival confirming what was already there: the existing hierarchy, the religious, political and moral values, norms and prohibitions. Laughter was controlled and people were bound by choreographic rules. This might be similar to how some view play as something we can teach children to do correctly, to laugh in the right places or to play silently. I noticed that children are sometimes instructed to use toys in correct ways. Gun play and playing cops are sometimes banned from pre-school, kindergarten and after-school programmes. Children who try to use any toy as a gun are put in their place with a reminder: *That is not a gun – it's a spade!*

Bakhtin argues that the unofficial carnival life was people's 'other life'. In this life the normal rules of social conduct were temporarily suspended. People could be liberated from the roles played on the public stage and devote themselves to another side of themselves. Such a carnival life created a radical break with the official life, where formalities of hierarchies and inherited differences were broken down with a 'free and familiar' mode of social interaction. Bearing Bakhtin's ideas in mind, the unofficial carnival life must be understood as a fundamentally important aspect of human life, a perfect complement to official life. The children in my study spoke of play as something very important and essential for their idea of institutionalized life. One girl exclaimed: 'If we can't play we get bored!'

Most of the descriptions of play given by children generally centre on having fun, being with friends, choosing freely, not working. This might illustrate that children understand play as a complement to their official institutional life. We may say that the children emphasize three Fs (Fun, Friends and Freedom) and that this could probably not be reduced to the three Rs that are the foundations of a basic skills-orientated education programme within schools (Reading, wRiting and aRithmetic), as there seems to be little emphasis on the kind of growth that adults have in mind with their progress rhetoric.

One of my concerns about children's play was that children were given too much structure in the above-mentioned educational settings, allowing school pedagogy to gain too strong a hold. The children I spoke to seemed to think of their lives in institutions as something far more ambivalent. It appears as if they have a full overview of the rules and norms of conduct that apply within the official life they generally live, and that unaided they maintain a balance between the official and unofficial life. On the one hand, children perceive their institutional life as 'only' playing games and having fun, but on the other hand, they also have to comply with orders and scolding from adults. When I asked the children what adults think about children playing, Eva responded: 'They think it's nice … if we don't play loud.' Guro continued: 'We have to play nice. Playing nice means that you have to play quietly.' One of my observations might illustrate that children sense that there is a notion of 'correct play':

> Frode is lying in the sandpit by himself. The other children he was playing with suddenly disappeared on their bikes. Now Frode is lying fully dressed on his back, a spade in his hand and looking up at the sky. He stretches his body and sighs. After a little while one of the instructors walks in Frode's direction. Frode probably catches a glimpse of her out of the corner of his eye and immediately sits up and starts shovelling sand in his bucket. The instructor stops and looks at Frode before she turns and walks in another direction. When the instructor is out of sight Frode stops shovelling and lies down in the sand again. I see a smile on his lips.

It might be 'the normalizing gaze' (cf. Foucault 1977) that Frode feels when he changes behaviour according to whether adults can see him or not. Frode seems to know that some kinds of play or activities are preferred to others.

'We just play!'

Bakhtin develops the idea of carnival as a special creative form of life based on the grotesque spirit and laughter. Such laughter does not come out of an individual sense of humour; rather it stems from a deep sense of social community. This ambivalent laughter both denies and confirms, doing away with what is old to make room for new opportunities. The carnival was simply the celebration of *what was to come*: a celebration of what is dialogic, unfinished, open, transcending time and the future.

According to Bakhtin it was precisely such a 'festive life' that could be understood according to the principle of play, a principle where we melted together with particular events. This is not surprising. A number of theorists in Nietzsche's tradition have used the idea of feast to express what happens when we lose ourselves through carnival, and play and surrender to and allow ourselves to be carried away by the events. Many have actually gone so far as to assign the feast central importance in our aesthetic life and as an example of how we experience meaning in the world surrounding us. One of the reasons for this is that the feast has a special time horizon which we are lured into. Everyone who participates is enthusiastic and may develop it into what Bakhtin calls a person's second life. Through the feast we will adopt a special rhythm or mood whether we are aware of it or not, and those who participate actively will be included in a kind of play which occurs independently of their choice and the wishes they may have. Who would actually wish to 'objectivize' a festive mood? It is simply there and we 'share' it. Any carnival, any feast and play, it appears, is performed and celebrated in an uninhibited togetherness.

The children in my study seem to reflect the difficulty of 'objectivizing' play. They could not give me a clear answer to what play is; instead, they responded: 'Playing is just something you do' or: 'We just play!'

I ask: 'What do you do when you play?' Nora says: 'I just feel like playing – I just do it!' Martine: 'I just play'. Tuva: 'We just do fun things'. Martine: 'You know something, we like to play fun games; look!' Martine grabs Nora's hands and they whirl each other round and round and suddenly they let go and fall on the floor. Both laugh loudly. They repeat the same routine over and over again, screaming and laughing. Then suddenly they run after each other. After a while they return to me: 'Do you know what this game is called?' 'No', I answer. 'It's called *tullbaill* (nonsense)', they both exclaim.

Play turns out to be a diffuse concept that is difficult to describe with certainty. Perhaps this could be told with Hans-Georg Gadamer's words: 'the player knows very well what play is, and that what he is doing is "only a game"; but he does not know what exactly he "knows" in knowing that' (Gadamer 1989: 102). The children appeared to be open to the idea that play might mean many things. Content that is found to be meaningful play for one child may appear meaningless to another and caused productive disagreement where the understanding of play was not concluded once and for all. To illustrate this point I present part of our conversation:

MARIA: How do you know that you are playing?
THEA: We try as hard as we can and in the end we make it work.
NORA: No, in the beginning we make it work and in the end we don't.

Grotesque realism

Bakhtin relates carnival to the grotesque in contrast to the classical aesthetic. The latter fashions perfectly rounded-off form in which the apertures are sealed and the protuberances flattened. A *grotesque aesthetic* emphasizes orifices and bulges in larger-than-life forms that make them ecstatic. Manifestations of this life, according to Bakhtin, refer not to the isolated private individual, but to the collective ancestral body of all the people. For Bakhtin we cannot ignore the body as part of the social dialogue. Bakhtin describes the grotesque realism of Rabelais' serfs in their carnivals, with their laughter, blasphemy, cunning, coarseness, farting, nose picking, dirtiness, scatology, gross gluttony and sexuality. Bakhtin says these are their ways of coming back to life and rising above their most oppressed circumstances (Sutton-Smith 1997). He maintains that the carnival festivity is associated with a special view on life, where laughter loosens the grip of various types of coercion linked to authoritative or one-dimensional perceptions. In play, children catch a glimpse of a possible world they do not already know.

For Bakhtin, carnival appears as a feast for the sake of the feast or for laughter, not because it has a function to some other end, and he emphasizes that there is room for both seriousness and humour. Bakhtin rejects the idea that popular (children's) humour is naive, and frequently emphasizes children's way of thinking because it distorts all fixated and logo-centric thinking. Instead of following already established lines, children challenge these and playfully gambol into unknown and risky terrain. Laughter for Bakhtin is the sole force in life that cannot be entirely co-opted by powers and made hypocritical. As such, the carnivals are a commentary, a transcript from the bottom up, on the domination of the masters whom the serfs despise, and in some cases their wild play is the seedbed of revolution. Bakhtin does not just provide yet one more variant of an aesthetic play. For him, carnival is a crucial dimension of life that must coexist and interact with other dimensions.

Wild play

The children notice that they are not allowed to play anything they want, but they do not blindly obey the play instructions they encounter.

Thea tells me that sometimes when adults tell them what to play, 'they tell us to sit quiet and that is boring'. What happens then? I ask. Thea looks at me with a smile: 'We sneak off to play what we want'. I ask her if there is something adults want her to play prior to other things: 'Do they want you to play in certain ways?' 'Yes, they don't like that we shoot other children and we're not allowed to sit on each other's backs, but we've done that a lot!'

During our conversations many of the boys identified rough-and-tumble play and especially play fighting as a popular activity. Adults do not like this game and the children know this perfectly well.

'What kinds of play do adults want you to play?' Eskil answers: 'We're allowed to play everything except in wild and bad ways.' 'What kinds of games are those?' I wonder. Eskil explains: 'It's when we run after each other, shoot or when we play rough on the slide.'

My further explorations of what children prefer to play indicate that the content of play can be less innocent than adults might want – it can be dark and wild. The children often pointed out episodes where they have done something they are not allowed to or broken socially accepted norms. I regularly observed that the children have been involved in a kind of play many educators have not seemed to appreciate. I have also seen children making fabulous snowmen in the winter, only to cut their heads off or destroy them in other creative ways, and I have seen them having a lot of fun torturing dolls.

This kind of illicit play (King 1987) or carnival play (Bakhtin 1984) that I have observed is characterized by clowning, laughter and spontaneous breaking of the rules; it is a kind of play children try to hide from adults. The glorification of play as functional, voluntary and cooperative ignores the coercive, cruel and dangerous aspect of many forms of play. Play, however, is not always fun. It also has the potential for pain and distress (Ailwood 2003). Ivy Schousboe (1993) made several observations of what she calls evil play, and argues that if our premise is that play is a socio-cultural phenomenon, it should not be a surprise that it could also be evil. Even though children are completely aware of the rules of official life in the institution and that what they are doing may have consequences, such as a scolding from adults and other children, breaking rules and conventions appears to be a popular activity in preschool, kindergarten and after-school programmes.

Carnival play

My study has shown that children seem to challenge the authoritative official voices describing 'good' play and that their play may be understood in terms of Bakhtin's concept of carnival. In play, children seem to lose themselves and to allow themselves to be carried away by events. This is something all of us experience from time to time when we read, exercise, write or are in love; a time where we forget ordinary clock time. This may be characterized as a condition of flow. It is however important to be aware that it is not to be compared to the kind of flow Csikszentmihalyi (1997) has promoted that has been associated with educational 'use of play'. His flow concept is grounded on a logic that we are in control of what we are doing. For him flow is the point where participants live out their optimal abilities. This means that we reach an ever higher level for excitement that will increase our experience of competence. Such a flow demands certain abilities in which we need to be competent in order to experience it.

For Bakhtin, the experience of flow that play offers has nothing to do with subjective freedom, but is being a part of carnival play itself, and it is exactly when they are caught up in the playful movement of carnival play that children experience play as their own. Implicit within it lies a critique of the overestimation of the individual freedom often associated to play. As a matter of fact, I have noticed that it is sometimes not easy for children to stop the laughter or what they are doing when they are having fun, even if strictly put in their place by the adults. When I ask children why they run around in the cloakroom even though they are scolded, or why they continue rolling on the floor laughing out loud, they tell me: 'We can't help it because it's so much fun!' This might indicate that children are not able to make a rational decision to play but that they are 'swallowed up' by play.

The problem of play pedagogy has been the wish to predict what should be the result of children's play. According to Bakhtin, carnival play does not provide any instrumental bonus. Play is oriented towards neither children's nor adults' intentions. Children's seemingly purposeless play is meaningful and fun because of the simple pleasure of doing precisely what one is doing. This is about collective laughter where children forget themselves and become part of a living 'we' (cf. Bakhtin 1984). Thus the value of play for children seems to lie in 'the in-between', the here-and-now – and not in any positive outcomes in the future.

The children turn towards each other in dialogic interplay, where being open to each other's unpredictability, or what remains to be said, may allow for the unexpected. Children create a culture of laughter, a second carnival life, where control of space and disciplining of time do not find acceptance at all times and in every little nook and cranny. Laughter and carnival play as Bakhtin asserts do not allow them to be controlled and may therefore not be understood by reason that aims to find causes and seek defined goals. Thus play is not something we can plan or restrict to certain rooms or hours; we cannot force children to play. This also means that we cannot prohibit play; children can find room for play also in strictly structured and regulated official educational situations.

For Bakhtin, all socio-cultural phenomena (including play) are maintained by the ongoing dialogic relation. Bearing this in mind, I have argued that play appears to be a dialogue where children may be children, a place where they can interpret meaning into new events without being strapped to unnecessary conventions from previous generations. Such play is not something we use, it is rather a relation we enter into, where the activity is an end unto itself. This carnival life in the sense that Bakhtin meant it is not something adults can plan for children; it is something children must give themselves.

Note

1 Some of the paragraphs in this chapter are taken from my article Øksnes, M. (2008) 'The Carnival Goes On and On! Children's Perceptions of their Leisure Time and Play in SFO'. *Leisure Studies*, 27: 149–164.

Bibliography

Ailwood, J. (2003) 'Governing Early Childhood Education through Play'. *Contemporary Issues in Early Childhood*, 4: 286–299.
Bakhtin, M. (1984) *Rabelais and His World*. Bloomington: Indiana University Press.
Cannella, G.S (1997) *Deconstructing Early Childhood Education*. New York: Peter Lang.
Combs, J.E. (2000) *Play World. The Emergence of the New Ludenic Age*. Westport, CT: Praeger.
Csikszentmihalyi, M. (1997) *Finding Flow: The Psychology of Engagement with Everyday Life*. New York: Basic Books.
Foucault, M. (1977) *Discipline and Punishment: The Birth of the Prison*. London: Allen Lane.
Gadamer, H.-G. (1989) *Truth and Method*. London: Sheed & Ward.
King, N. (1987) 'Elementary School Play: Theory and Research', in J.H. Block and N. King *School Play: A Source Book*. London: Garland Publishing, pp. 143–165.
Kleiber, D.A. (1999) *Play, Experience and Human Development*. New York: Basic Books.
Meire, J. (2007) 'Qualitative Research on Children's Play: A Review of Recent Literature', in J. van Gils and T. Jambor (eds) *Several Perspectives on Children's Play*. Antwerpen-Appeldoorn: Garant, pp. 29–77.
Schousboe, I. (1993) 'Den onde leg: en udvidet synsvinkel på legen og dens funktioner' ['The Evil Play: An Expanded View on Play and its Functions']. *Nordisk psykologi*, 2: 97–119.
Spariosu, M.I. (1989) *Dionysus Reborn*. Ithaca, NY: Cornell University Press.

Sutton-Smith, B. (1987) 'School Play: A Commentary', in J. Block and N. King (eds) *School Play*. New York: Garland, pp. 277–290.

Sutton-Smith, B. (1997) *The Ambiguity of Play*. London: Harvard University Press.

Sutton-Smith, B. (2004) Foreword, in J. Goldstein, D. Buckingham and G. Brougère (eds) *Toys, Games and Media*. London: Lawrence Erlbaum, pp. vii–x.

13 What's play got to do with the information age?

Kevin Flint

> Breakfast: on the TV news is breaking from around the world. Travelling to my office in the city I am presented with other versions of the same stories on the radio and in newspapers. Featured centre-stage among the presentations are members of the public who have particular stories to tell. The backdrop is created by news-readers, politicians, leaders ... and so on. With digital technologies our 24/7 news coverage would appear to give every impression that, given time and sufficient information, it is quite possible for us all to get a complete story of events unfolding in our world.

This citation is taken from Ash's diary. Ash is a manager in a multinational company and is currently completing research for a Doctor of Education. The news items are grounded in substantial evidence. This excerpt of information forms part of my research concerned with the significance of play in language. Drawing on Heidegger's philosophy, one aim of this chapter is to consider our relationship with such digital information, as one essential form of technology, in which all unfolding events and issues in our world are regarded as being in danger of being reduced down to bivalent programmable information.

The growth of digital technologies and of information dissemination is now so deeply inscribed in many of our ways of doing things that it is difficult to grasp what it all means or how it may affect our humanity. Heidegger's (1977) sobering analysis of the essence of such technologies, he identified by the neologism, *das Gestell*, translated as 'enframing' (or 'framing'). From Heidegger's perspective in our relationship with technology there is always a danger that counter-intuitively rather than using and being in control of our technologies we are always in danger of being controlled by them – his word for this complex relationship.[1] He sees this as an essential ordering of our world through our relationship with being, in which everyone is always in danger of being constituted as its puppets (Heidegger 1977: 36–49). The subject of this chapter is the challenge posed by play when faced with the possible danger of enframing and a thesis concerning the significance of play in opening up ways of thinking in which enframing and its very structuring no longer have any grounds.

The generation of theses concerning how humanity may be saved from enframing is not a new phenomenon, and in his typically cryptic style

Heidegger suggests how this may happen by reference to words from the poet Hölderlin:

> But where the danger is, grows
> The saving power also
> (cited in Heidegger 1977: 28)

For Heidegger, the saving power is already revealed in enframing, but how this might arise and what exactly is meant by these lines is never fully explained. Heidegger's writings suggest that he thought what may be needed is an education in ontology, and for this he takes his readers back to Plato's (1993: 241–245) 'cave allegory' in *The Republic*. Let us keep this idea in play.

For some readers this may be seen as being inflected towards nostalgia for a European tradition that is far removed from our multicultural globalised world. My own thesis concerned with practice in *any* culture is directed towards opening space for our humanity:

> *Thesis:* In looking to the future, what is at play opens up possibilities and so generates space in language where humanity is no longer conceivable as programmable information and is thus given back its freedom to be: in so doing play also opens up possibilities for confounding and resisting the structured drives in enframing – drives that in their appeal to our subliminal desires would otherwise continue to build bridges over the flux of time. We already have philosophies opening us up to ways of thinking; what we need is education. But not education as currently conceived, rather education as the practice of critical bricolage: being situated in any practice it is always in play and opens us up to the possibilities at play in humanity. Such education carries with it the prospect of liberation from circumstances of enslavement.

Thus a significant possible challenge to enframing arises without any fanfare of a possible challenge at all; it is a matter of keeping play alive in our language, of keeping alive the difference in any identity.

In order to illuminate what is meant by the play of difference and its significance for the information age, this chapter opens with a Derridean reading of the anthropologist Huizinga's (2008 [1938]) *Homo Ludens* ('Man the Player'), which seeks to draw out the radical elements of his work. Huizinga's intention had been to characterise the nature and significance of play in a variety of cultural contexts – civilisation, law, war, poetry and so on. He viewed play as a necessary precondition for the generation of new cultures. What becomes evident from this deconstruction is that despite Huizinga's own suggestions to the contrary, his reading of play is largely structured to favour what Derrida (2001a: 360) suggests may be identified as an engineer's vision of play; one which brings play into the present with a sense of plenitude and control over what play *is*, in terms of how it is characterised and functions. The structuring of this engineered understanding of play is entirely consonant with enframing, which is shown to be derived from metaphysical principles that have unfolded from the philosophical tradition running from Plato through to Husserl. These continue to be directed towards generating truth claims about play and, indeed, any other identity.

In reading Huizinga it will be evident that there is another side to his understanding of play, which accords with the work of the bricoleur. In contrast to the character of the engineer, the bricoleur, in working with what is at hand in the world is always open to keeping in play possibilities. In drawing on Derrida, and deconstructing Huizinga's (2008[1938]) sense that in play there is something 'at play' (ibid: 1$_e$),[2] it will be shown that there are many different ways in which the identity of 'play' may be at play in language. To see how this may happen we return to consider humanity's relationship with the philosophical tradition.

The question remains of how one might educate others about issues that arise from the engineer's and the bricoleur's contrasting understandings of play. At this point a critical examination of Thomson's reading of Heidegger will be undertaken, which favours a return to ontological education in its rereading of Plato's cave allegory. However, paradoxically, Thomson fails to see how his approach remains imprisoned within its own specialist discourse, which is another marker of enframing (Heidegger 1977: 126–128).

Viewing education as critical bricolage, this Derridean reading favours deconstruction as a way of liberating possibilities unfolding from the play of difference – for Derrida (1988: 7) this is a matter of reiteration, repeating again, but differently, so transforming contemporary discourses and practices in any area of professional activity.

In play in the throw of enframing

Huizinga's (2008[1938]) Foreword contains a warning that readers should not come too easily to a metaphysical conclusion that all human activity might be called play; but metaphysics is not the problem. Although Huizinga makes no explicit reference to the principle of being, his writings hold on to the guardrails of the classical metaphysical principle of 'being as presence': 'something is repeatable to the extent that it is' (Caputo 1987: 123). In the ancient tradition of philosophy stemming from Plato it is this principle that is most valued. For Huizinga as a historian at that time, 'the play-concept as expressed in language' 'is' projected as an object; the identity of 'play' for him 'is' already present (Huizinga, 2008[1938]: 1).

But Derrida (2001a) suggests that in the dominant vein of argument in his book, Huizinga tacitly holds on to the 'myth' of the engineer who, as a 'subject, would supposedly be the origin of his own discourse, and would allegedly construct it out of nothing' (ibid.: 360). A subject, in fact, that in being the mythological origin of ideas about, in this case play, has already supposedly removed her/himself from the drift of signs and the play of *différance*.

It may be helpful at this point to uncover what is meant by *différance* before returning to the engineer. An understanding of what is signified by the play of *différance* may be gained by considering what unfolds in the space revealed to us as readers in reading these words. It opens us up to various signifiers – the words, phrases, pictures, etc. that fill up our mass media – and thus alerts us to what is possibly signified, so that there is always a difference between the signifier and what is signified. It is also apparent that many signifiers, which have their origin in the ancient tradition of philosophy, in literature and other forms of writing published earlier, have been, in effect, deferred to what is now signified to us. Derrida coined the neologism *différance*, to express both a difference and a deferral in what is happening here. *Différance* is not a distinction, 'an essence, an opposition, but a movement of spacing, a becoming space of time, and a becoming time of space: hence, a certain inscription of the same' (Derrida 2004: 21). It has a temporal structure, which is also always already in play in all that we do and say.

In Huizinga's discourse, therefore, in which he sought to gain mastery and control of understandings of play as grounds for the cultivation of cultures, he did so tacitly by means of the classical metaphysical principle of being. In this deconstructive reading, such deferral of the 'is' can be traced back to the philosophical tradition running from Plato to Husserl. In modern thought the intention of using this principle is always directed towards generating truth claims to knowledge. This metaphysical principle, therefore, appears to block any possibility of being already unfolding in play. In addition, any conceivable play in language tends to be reduced down to the work of signs connecting subject with object in accord with enframing.

Paradoxically, enframing always directs us towards mastery and control while constituting humanity as its puppets: self-directed objects and subjects in what may be seen as moves towards a Matrix-like world[3] (Flint 2012a). Metaphysics, then, as ontotheological structuring (Heidegger 1998: 340), is considered to be a pivotal locus of enframing (Heidegger 1977, 1991): it 'grounds an age' (Heidegger 1977: 115).

It should be no surprise that Huizinga held on to the classical principle of being. Both Heidegger (1977: 115; 1998) and, more recently, Thomson (2000, 2005) recognised that metaphysics provides a double grounding of being. Being is 'simultaneously giving the ground ontologically' and creating a theological 'founding' for entities in the world, in the sense of establishing the source from which beings issue and by which they are 'justified' (Thomson 2000: 303–304). For example, the locus of such foundations includes the 'principle of reason' (Heidegger 1991), the 'principle of assessment' (Flint and Peim 2012), the 'substance' of the news, and the 'subject', including the engineer identified above (Thomson 2000: 303).

Thomson (2005) also provides an incisive response to many of Heidegger's critics (ibid.: 47–52), who have variously charged him with being a 'philosophical redneck' (Rorty's colourful sobriquet), a 'Luddite' imbued with the spirit of 'technophobia' (in Feenberg's terms) and as a 'reactionary anti-modern' (as alleged by Marcuse, Habermas, Feenberg and Pippin) (Thomson 2005: 45–46). Thomson's argument underlines what he sees as Heidegger's 'profound and far-reaching critique of technology' (ibid.: 45), which, it is suggested, 'forfeits much of its philosophical force' in being 'detached from the background of ontotheology that motivates it' (ibid.: 45).

Thomson (2000, 2005) makes good this detachment by showing how the double grounding of ontotheological structuring constitutes a strong motivational force for the unfolding essence of technology, which as Heidegger (1977) remarked, 'is nothing technological' (ibid.: 4). The double structuring of enframing generates only one way of revealing the world. It heralds Heidegger's dystopian vision of the nihilistic cybernetic epoch of what is now called the 'information age'.[4] It is an age in which, in the extreme, only 'what is calculable in advance counts' (Heidegger 1998b: 136; Thomson 2005: 56) as an entity, and in which 'all intelligibility can be reduced to bivalent programmable information' (Thomson 2005: 25), of the type used to open this chapter, for example.

Play may be seen as a locus of creativity, and the grounds for exploration of new ideas – 'mind games', 'thought experiments' and so on – supposedly a necessary precursor to matters of hard economic decision making, and also as grounds for the production of new technologies so attempting to overcome the current limits of enframing. However, in each of these cases its ontotheological structuring has already rendered it as grounds for an optimal ordering in enframing. It is indicative of the legacy of enframing, which in the extreme renders all entities, including people, as raw material – 'standing reserve' (*Bestand*, Heidegger 1977: 17) – that societies are always in danger of being reduced to great lakes of energy and so are available for use in a constant process of overcoming. Overcoming enframing in those many moves towards greater mastery and control of the world serves only to reduce down the scope for play and to reproduce enframing; it is a repetition of the same.

At play in language

A clue to one locus of Heidegger's (1977: 28) 'saving power', identified earlier, may be gained from deconstructing Huizinga's (2008[1938]) more radical side, made obvious in the introduction to his book where he recognised that in play there is something always beyond our control 'at play' (ibid.: 1$_e$). What exactly does it mean to be 'at play' in language? Derrida's (1973) deconstructive reading of Husserl shows formally that 'the presence of the present is derived from repetition and not the reverse' (ibid.: 140). For Derrida the signified concept 'play' is never present in itself. Something 'is' according to the unity of an object (or subject) that is brought forth and sustained by repetition; being and identity in this rereading of Huizinga's discourse 'are proportionate to repetition' (ibid.: 140).

In Derrida's (1981) deconstruction, therefore, many of us in the Western world are caught up in the endless play of signs disseminated from what he calls 'Plato's Pharmacy' (ibid.: 120–171). For the most part, however, and in the extreme, in accord with enframing, any play tends to be reduced down to the work of signs, in moves towards the objectifying of knowledge, which are all brought into the present in accord with the ontotheological structuring in our modern world. In fact, in Heidegger's (1962) earlier analysis, enframing contrasts radically with the space for play opened up by the many possibilities of being unfolding in our lived time. Recent studies of the workplace have shown that in entering this digital age much of our discourse can still be understood from the basic structures of being and lived time or 'temporality' that shapes our lives (Heidegger 1962; Flint 2011, 2012a, 2012b).

Experientially, of course, our recollections of what comes into being with information presented to us tend to be fragmentary, contingent and almost invariably incomplete. Huizinga's (2008[1938]) discourse, in contrast, is predicated upon a tacit understanding of the identity of 'play', and of identities more generally, in terms of determinate ends. Ironically, it contains an assumed *telos* of memory, deferred from earlier writings in the philosophical tradition (*vide*, Plato 2002), in which any space for play is closed down.

However, the teleology of enframing, the endless moves towards the supposed fulfilment and totalisation of identity, is confronted by Derrida. What particularly interests him is that Husserl, Freud and Heidegger 'challenge our conception of identity in terms of a teleology of memory' (Dooley and Kavanagh 2007: 67; emphasis in original). What remain for Derrida are the cinders of identity from the lives we variously live.

Although Husserl had positioned himself as the culmination of the ancient tradition of philosophy, in opening questions about our relationship with signs he was already heralding many different readings of the so-called 'linguistic turn' in social theory. Strictly speaking 'being as presence' is only ever a trace, the a priori that shapes beings, and we are left with fragments or cinders of those beings that testify to the work of mourning in attempts to keep memory concerning play safe. As Derrida himself recollected, 'the thought of incineration ... of cinders runs through my texts' (Rand 1992: 210). Dooley and Kavanagh (2007) explain that for Derrida, 'to burn something is the desire *both* to keep it *and* to let it go' (ibid.: 15; emphasis in original), which again amounts to the possibility of keeping things in play. Derrida continually worked to breathe life into the ancient tradition of philosophy, which, in its alignment with enframing in modern education, continually closes down on play (Flint and Peim 2012).

In deconstruction, too, signs remain at play in language. In an interview in 1993 Derrida (2001b) remarked:

> Deconstruction moves, or makes its gestures....It is a sort of great earthquake, a general tremor, which nothing can calm. I cannot treat a corpus, or a book as a whole, and even the simple statement is subject to fission.
>
> (ibid.: 9)

Everything for Derrida is divisible. The plenitude and unity of an identity, for example, 'are produced out of division and divisibility' (Royle 2003: 26). It is important, too, to keep in mind the forces at work in enframing. Its structures are there to create order from such play of differences, as seen in the continual drives in the late modern world towards the 'improvement' of education (Flint and Peim 2012). Signs at play in language do not of necessity, therefore, somehow dissolve away any enframing.

One way forward suggested by Heidegger (2002) and Thomson (2000, 2005) is a form of ontological education, in which they take us back to what they see as the origins of enframing located in one part of 'Plato's Pharmacy', which for Heidegger had occupied a key position in his philosophy, namely 'the cave allegory'.

Ontological education through Plato's cave allegory

Heidegger's (2002) 'The Essence of Truth' sets out to educate readers about the follies of ontotheological structuring (although he does not use these terms) as double grounds for enframing in our modern world. More recently, Thomson (2000, 2005), too, has engaged with this same project of ontological education as a way of challenging enframing. However, this is seen to have limited possible application because enframing, in constituting grounds for their specialist philosophical discourse, is already at work within institutions of reason, and of education. Specialisation is a necessary precondition for gathering being into the present and so generating truth claims that may be understood and shared within a community (Heidegger 1977: 123–127). It does, however, bring us back to the heart of what was identified earlier as 'Plato's Pharmacy'.

Heidegger's exposition in 'Plato's Doctrine of Truth' is complicated by the fact that he is both narrating and developing his own critical understanding of education, and simultaneously providing a critique of a pivotal transformation in the history of truth inaugurated by Plato (Thomson 2005: 141–154). At issue in the allegory is how Plato moves from the language of *aletheia* – unconcealment and concealment – to the language of correctness – *orthotes* used to describe the disposition of the prisoner who has escapes the cave.

Plato's allegory of the cave moves through four stages, which keep in play the various contested understandings and emphases placed by Plato, Heidegger and Thomson.

(1) 'The prisoner' (Thomson 2005: 162) or the human condition of being shackled begins in captivity in the cave; this is reality 'unhidden' (*alethes*) (Heidegger 2002: 22) before 'the prisoner' found in our everyday world. In this dwelling place it is the unhiddenness of something to which 'man' comports himself (ibid.: 22). At this stage there is no distinction made between 'hidden and unhidden, shadows and real things, light and dark' (ibid.: 22). Recent studies of late modern systems of education indicate that this remains a dominant position adopted and driven in enframing (Flint and Peim 2012).

(2) 'A 'liberation' of man within the cave' (Heidegger 2002: 23): the prisoner escapes the chains and 'turns to discover the fire and objects responsible for what are now seen as shadows on the wall that were previously taken to be reality' (Thomson 2005: 162). The play in Heidegger's writings remains

palpable: 'What *is* admits of *degrees*'! But the freeing from chains is short lived; emancipation does not come to fulfilment' (Heidegger 2002: 27). What is shown to the prisoner is not seen with any clarity. The ones freed do not understand their freedom. Plato had seen the prisoners being unshackled as a counter to *phronesis* (Plato's word for knowledge in general). In Heidegger's reading, Plato here holds that the 'prisoner sees genuine beings *more correctly*' (ibid.: 26). Heidegger's own position, in contrast, places emphasis on 'the essence of truth (*aletheia*) as unhiddenness', which he situates in the precise context of 'being-free of man, the looking into the light, and the comportment to beings' (ibid.: 29). Heidegger's reading emphasises that 'truth as correctness is grounded in truth as unhiddenness' (ibid.: 26).

Herein lies the historical foundation for the 'principle of reason' connecting the mythical subject with what is supposed to be a correctly identified object. The Enlightenment project of the assumed *telos* of the object as a focus for the epistemological subject, for Heidegger, begins with too little.

(3) 'the Genuine Liberation of Man to the Primordial Light' (ibid.: 29) where the prisoner is coming to understand 'what is seen there as made possible by the light of the sun'. This is a stage of genuine liberation. Heidegger uses the language of the open, which is one of his names for 'being as such'; that is, for 'what appears antecendently in everything that appears and … makes what appears be accessible' (Heidegger 1998: 170; Stambaugh 1992: 35–41). 'Dwelling' is the identity given by him to the attainment of – or better the comportmental attunement to – this 'open' (Thomson 2005: 164). For Heidegger (1998), when such positive ontological freedom is achieved, 'what things are … no longer appear in the man-made and confusing glow of the fire within the cave … things themselves stand there in the binding force and validity of their own visible form' (ibid.: 169).

It is also important to recognise that Heidegger (1991) does not fall down on keeping in play Heraclitus' great child of world-play (ibid.: 113) in his detailed, multi-layered deconstruction of the 'levels of unhiddenness outside the cave' (Heidegger 2002: 32). Heidegger reveals the ongoing play in terms of unconcealment or unhiddenness. He points out that for 'genuine liberation' the violence of escaping the foregoing shackles requires 'persistence' and 'strident courage' that is 'not deterred by reversals' and endures through 'the individual stages of adaptation to the light' (ibid.: 32–58).

Emerging out of the cave may be seen as a movement into liminal space: what has been called a 'no-man's land betwixt and between' (Turner 1990: 11–12) and 'a threshold between two worlds at the limits of culture' (Wright 2000: 6). Liminality constitutes an embodied space involving all the emotions of endeavouring to unshackle one's body from a previously established regime of practice, and an attempt to explore some new ways of understanding the world. It is a space fraught with risk, uncertainty and anxiety, which sometimes proves to be a 'fructile chaos' – a locus of something new unfolding.

In Kincheloe's (2004: 98) view the bricoleur needs to be continually vigilant and alert to the invisible artefacts of power. However, given that the powers at work in enframing are generally the subject of deep-seated, sometimes brilliant disguises, and that even advocates may not be fully aware of (Flint 2012a: 22–23), it is considered important to foreground any examination of hidden powers by reference to critical bricolage. Critical bricolage indicates that the intentionality of the researcher so engaged is directed towards liberating 'human beings from the circumstances that enslave them' (Horkheimer 1982: 244), including enframing.

In their own different forms of the critical bricolage, Heidegger's play of *aletheia* and Derrida's play of *différance* are never specifically directed; they remain forever in play and are always open to being channelled in particular directions. In contesting that the complex play of Heidegger's discourse is directed towards a form of ontological education, Thomson (2005), for example, draws upon enframing to argue that:

> Ontological freedom is achieved ... when entities show themselves in their full phenomenological richness and complexity, overflowing and so exceeding the conceptual boundaries our normally unnoticed ontotheological enframing places on them.
>
> (ibid.: 164)

For Thomson, therefore, the goal of 'ontological education' (ibid.: 162) is to 'help students attune to the being of entities, and thus to teach them to see the being of an entity – be it a book ... a rose ... or themselves – cannot be fully understood in the ontologically reductive terms of enframing' (ibid.: 164). Yet this approach is always in danger of building bridges over the ongoing movement of Heraclitus' play and attempting to channel it in different ways. Although play is mentioned, it is not thematised as such in Thomson's (2005) account of 'ontotheology' and with it the possibility of mystery, of some necessary remainder beyond what can be known, of the play of *différance* in which we are all variously caught up. Perhaps this provides some explanation as to what confronts the prisoner on return into the cave.

(4) 'The Freed Prisoner's Return to the Cave' (Plato 1993: 243–245): On returning to take up the struggle in freeing other prisoners, the would-be liberator meets only violent resistance. As Heidegger (2002) illuminates, one of the essential features of this stage is that it ends with the fateful prospect of being killed, 'the most radical ejection from the human historical community' (ibid: 59). Heidegger argues that the would-be liberator is the 'philosopher who exposes himself to the fate of death in the cave' (ibid.: 61); the fate that famously awaited Socrates.

What matters from the phenomenological perspective, in Richardson's (2012: 152) reading of Heidegger, is *not* when and how death happens, but 'how I am towards the possibility, how I cope with it, and how I shape and mean it by coping' (ibid.: 152). It is an intentional standpoint that comes to see the play of possibilities as possibilities, rather than resulting in the projections of facts.

One possibility is always the status quo – looking back at Huizinga's thesis it may simply be accepted that play creates grounds for the cultivation of cultures. But, the earlier promise of the radicalisation of Huizinga's thesis concerned with play may open up as yet unforeseen possibilities for information cultures. At issue remains our relationship with enframing that is currently structuring much of our use of information.

The supplement at play

Play in language creates resources that can both generate grounds for, and at very least resist, enframing. In writing these concluding words there is a supplement on my desk. More broadly, of course, a supplement could be a word, phrase, idea or interpretation that is added on to something to give it a new identity, so in some way making up for what is missing and enriching it. Thomson's critical reading of Heidegger is a case in point.

The supplement may be seen everywhere, in the sense that it *is nothing* (Derrida 1976: 244); space or spacing always supplements signs. Heidegger (2000) featured this same point in his 'Introduction to Metaphysics', where beings are understood in relation to 'nothing'. However, what is added on in each case is merely an 'extra', meaning outside.In addition, we can now see what Derrida meant when in considering the 'supplement' he notes that 'it is not simply added to the positivity of presence ... its place is assigned in the structure by the mark of emptiness' (Derrida 1976: 144–145).

On returning to the diary excerpt from Ash which opens this chapter, it is clear that it could be read as presenting the facts of various cases from news desks around the world. Indeed, whether we read the original news items as facts or in terms of the play of *différance* is, for Derrida, 'undecidable', which he sees as a 'ghostliness that renders all totalisation, fulfilment, plenitude impossible' (Derrida 1998: 116). In the play of *différance* the ontotheological grounds, like the character of the engineer at the heart of enframing, are simply mythologies.

In the play of *différance* critical bricolage keeps in play both outside and inside, and the supplement is invested with what Royle (2003) calls a 'crazy logic – it is neither inside or outside the presence of whatever is being referred to in the supplement, and/or both inside and outside at the same time' (ibid.: 49). It is this logic of keeping in play the critical bricolage that opens up possibilities of profoundly disturbing both the 'principle of reason' and 'enframing' more generally – as Derrida puts it: 'it is almost inconceivable to reason' (Derrida 1976: 149). Even from the one example taken from Derrida's work, *play*, therefore, may be seen as grounds for critical bricolage; it opens up the possibility of the desire to make strange, to disturb and to destabilise everyday familiar ideas that are always at risk of being caught up in enframing.

In returning to digitalisation, the 24/7 news coverage, and in looking to the future, one might ask: What does this thesis on play mean? Straightforwardly, in response there is a need to distinguish between the unfolding of what is predicted, calculated or engineered for tomorrow, and the future. 'The future is what is to come, it is unknowable' (Royle 2003: 110). Whether the play of critical bricolage comes to shore in the mass media, in education, or in other domains cannot be anticipated: what identities it may assume have yet to be invented. It is a matter of hospitality as to whether the argument concerned with play and with critical bricolage presented in this chapter does generate a space in which humanity is no longer conceivable as bivalent programmable information. This is a matter of liberating new thinking and education about the play of difference that is located in practice (rather than any specialist discipline), as a way of confounding the logic of enframing and of continuing to infuse humanity with much-needed oxygen for the play of *différance*.

Notes

1 Lovitt translates *das Gestell* with 'enframing' (Heidegger 1977: 1–35) and Stambaugh (1992: 31–35) with 'framing'.
2 The subscript, $_e$, indicates that the page number refers only to the English edition of the book, published in 2008.
3 The dramatic production of 'The Matrix' has generated considerable interest in opening up a space for the general public to explore issues of philosophy. See, for example, Irwin (2002) and also 'an interpretation of the Matrix Trilogy at www.the-matrix101.com/contrib/myoung_aitptm.php (accessed 20 May 2012).
4 Randy Kluver, 'Globalization, Informatization, and Intercultural Communication'. Sydney Observatory. Available at www.acjournal.org/holdings/vol.3/Iss3/spec1/kluver.htm (accessed 18 August 2010).

Bibliography

Caputo, J.D. (1987) *Radical Hermeneutics: Repetition, Deconstruction, and the Hermeneutic Project*. Bloomington: Indiana University Press.
Derrida, J. (1973) *Speech and Phenomena and Other Essays on Husserl's Theory of Signs*, trans. D.B. Allison. Evanston, IL: Northwestern University Press.
Derrida, J. (1976) *Of Grammatology*, trans. G.C. Spivak. Baltimore, MD: Johns Hopkins University Press.
Derrida, J. (1981) *Dissemination*, trans. B. Johnson. London: Athlone Press.
Derrida, J. (1988) 'Signature, Event, Context', trans. S. Weber and J. Mehlman, in *Limited Inc*. Evanston, IL: Northwestern University Press, pp. 1–24.
Derrida, J. (1998) 'Afterword: Toward an Ethic of Discussion', trans. S. Weber, in *Limited Inc*. Evanston, IL: Northwestern University Press, pp. 111–160.
Derrida, J. (2001a) 'Structure, Sign, and Play', in *Writing and Difference*, trans. A. Bass. London and New York: Routledge, pp. 351–370.
Derrida, J. (2001b) 'I Have a Taste for a Secret', Jacques Derrida in conversation with Maurizio Ferraris and Giorgio Vattimo, in J. Derrida and M. Ferarris, *A Taste for a Secret*, trans. G. Donis. Cambridge: Polity Press, pp. 3–92.
Derrida, J. (2004) *For What Tomorrow . . . A Dialogue with Elisabeth Roudinesco*, trans. J. Fort. Stanford, CA: Stanford University Press.
Dooley, M. and Kavanagh, L. (2007) *The Philosophy of Derrida*. Stocksfield, Northumberland: Acumen.
Flint, K.J. (2011) 'Deconstructing Workplace "Know How" and "Tacit Knowledge":

Exploring the Temporal Play of Being within Professional Practice'. *Higher Education, Skills and Work-based Learning*, 1(2): 128–146.

Flint, K.J. (2012a) 'The Importance of *Place* in the Improvement Agenda', keynote lecture presented at the Postgraduate Conference on *Using Philosophy in Research*. University of Brighton, 23 June.

Flint, K.J. (2012b) 'What Does Using a Heideggerian Analysis as an Analytic Tool Give You that other Analytic Approaches do not?', guest lecture given at the School of Education, University of Durham, 17 July.

Flint, K.J. and Peim, N.A. (2012) *Rethinking the Education Improvement Agenda: A Critical Philosophical Approach*. London and New York: Continuum.

Heidegger, M. (1962) *Being and Time*, trans. J. Macquarrie and E. Robinson. Oxford: Blackwell.

Heidegger, M. (1977) *The Question Concerning Technology and Other Essays*, trans. W. Lovitt. New York: Harper & Row.

Heidegger, M. (1991) *The Principle of Reason*, trans. R. Lilly. Bloomington and Indianapolis: Indiana University Press.

Heidegger, M. (1998) *Pathmarks*, ed. W. McNeill. Cambridge: Cambridge University Press.

Heidegger, M. (2000) *Introduction to Metaphysics*, trans. G. Fried and R. Polt. New Haven, CT: Yale University Press.

Heidegger, M. (2002) *The Essence of Truth: On Plato's Cave Allegory and Theaetetus*, trans. T. Sadler. London: Continuum.

Horkheimer, M. (1982) *Critical Theory*. New York: Seabury Press.

Huizinga, J. (2008[1938]) *Homo Ludens: A Study of the Play-Element in Culture*. Abingdon, Oxon: Routledge.

Kincheloe, J. (2004) 'Redefining and Interpreting the Object of Study', in J.L. Kincheloe and K. Berry, *Rigour and Complexity in Educational Research: Conceptualizing the Bricolage*. Maidenhead, Berkshire: Open University Press, pp. 82–102.

Plato (1993) *Republic*, trans. R. Waterfield. New York: Oxford University Press.

Plato (2002) *Five Dialogues: Euthyphro, Apology, Crito, Meno, Phaedo* (2nd revised edn), trans. G.M.A. Grube. Indianapolis, IND: Hackett.

Rand, R. (1992) 'Canons and Metonymies: An Interview with Jacques Derrida', in R. Rand (ed.) *Logomachia: The Conflict of the Faculties*. Lincoln, NE: University of Nebraska Press, pp. 197–218.

Royle, N. (2003) *Jacques Derrida*. London: Routledge.

Richardson, J. (2012) *Heidegger*. London and New York: Routledge Philosophers.

Stambaugh, J. (1992) *The Finitude of Being*. New York: State University of New York Press.

Thomson, I. (2000) 'Ontotheology? Understanding Heidegger's *Destruktion* of Metaphysics'. *International Journal of Philosophical Studies*, 8(3): 297–327.

Thomson, I. (2005) *Heidegger on Ontotheology: Technology and the Politics of Education*. New York: Cambridge University Press.

Turner, V. (1990) 'Are there Universals of Performance in Myth, Ritual, and Drama?', in R. Schnecher and W. Appel, (eds) *By Means of Performance*. Cambridge: Cambridge University Press, pp. 1–18.

Wright, S. (2000) *The Trickster Function in the Theatre of García Lorca*. London: Tamesis.

14 Towards a spatial theory of playwork

What can Lefebvre offer as a response to playwork's inherent contradictions?

Wendy Russell

Introduction

In the UK, playworkers work in a range of settings with children across the 4 to 16 years age range. These settings include adventure playgrounds, play centres, out-of-school care schemes, play buses, holiday play schemes, play ranger projects (streets, parks and open spaces), schools, hospitals, refuges and prisons (Russell 2010). The official articulation of the role of the playworker within the Playwork Principles (PPSG 2005) is 'to support all children and young people in the creation of a space in which they can play'. Such a definition has the potential to open the way for a spatial turn in playwork theorising, offering an alternative to the dominant temporal focus on professional interventions in the lives of children in order to help children develop into productive future citizens. This chapter draws on the work of French Marxist philosopher Henri Lefebvre (1991), and in particular his triadic conceptualisation of the social production of space (perceived, conceived and lived spaces), to develop an analysis that acknowledges the contradictions which playworkers navigate in their day-to-day experiences of working with children at play. The conceptual, theoretical design of designated 'play spaces', with named zones, material content and daily routines, is based on the assumption that this will give rise to particular practices (play forms) leading to particular instrumental outcomes (the development of specific skills). From this position in the triad, playwork may be seen as a form of labour that produces the next generation of producers and consumers. Children's own bodily and emotional engagement with spaces gives rise to a wide range of playful disturbances of adult order; when conditions allow, children appropriate their own 'lived' space which incorporates the real and the imagined, often in ways that adults deem unsafe or offensive. Playworkers can find themselves promoting some forms of playing over others (through their spatial practices) while espousing notions of children's agency and freedom to play (ideals belonging to conceived spaces). Lefebvre's threefold dialectical formulation of the production of space offers the possibility of seeing beyond the dualisms of order and chaos, certainty and uncertainty, repetition and difference, structure and agency. These binaries emerge from the dialectic between abstract, theoretical space and the material spatial practices; Lefebvre maintains that there is always a third. For playworkers, this is the 'lived' space of children's playfulness and also of their own moments of playfulness and imagination.

The dialectics of playwork

The analysis in this chapter is drawn from a broader study that seeks to interrogate the contradictions inherent in the playworker's role and to explore how playworkers navigate these contradictions in their day-to-day work. The study focuses on playwork within what is termed an 'open access' setting. The term is employed to differentiate out-of-school care schemes (where parents pay for childcare and children stay within the setting until collected) and settings where children are free to come and go. Playwork in open access settings has developed largely from the tradition of the adventure playground movement imported from Denmark in the mid-twentieth century. Adventure playgrounds grew up mostly on bomb-sites following the Second World War. They were rough-and-ready affairs where, under the permissive and supportive eye of a playworker who supplied materials and tools, children built and destroyed, made dens and fires, and generally played in any number of ways. Advocates saw them as places where children could be free to experiment and to create their own bottom-up democratic worlds (Allen 1968; Kozlovsky 2008).

Official definitions of playwork espouse the principle of play as 'a process that is freely chosen, personally directed and intrinsically motivated' (PPSG 2005), but this is fraught with tensions and contradictions, not least because of contested notions about the nature, value and purpose of both childhood and children's play. Perhaps the broadest and simplest statement is from Newstead (2004: 17), who describes playwork as 'the art and science of facilitating children's play'. That it might be seen as an art and a science allows for a multiplicity of understandings and practices, of epistemologies and paradigms. Such a statement also invites the question of whether children's play needs adult facilitation, or whether such facilitation may indeed turn play, understood as inherently non-productive, into something productive and rationalised and therefore not-play.

There has long been a school of thought that has questioned both the need for and the benefit of adults' involvement in children's play (see e.g. Douglas 1931; Opie and Opie 1969). Arguments for the involvement of adults in children's play rest on two assumptions: that today's children have forgotten how to play and that modern life somehow prevents children from playing. These ideas are not new (see e.g. Allen 1968; Opie and Opie 1959; Stallibrass 1977). In 1985, Play Board (the Association for Children's Play and Recreation, the then national body for children's play) stated in its discussion document on play policy for the future:

> We have built ourselves a hazardous, alien, materialistic and uninteresting environment for our children to grow up in, and we expect them to be unaffected by it. We are surprised when they show signs of looking for

challenge and stimulation in ways unacceptable to us; we are surprised to see them become disaffected, sullen, unco-operative and aggressive; we were surprised by the riots of 1981.

(Play Board 1985: 2)

A contemporary justification for the existence of playworkers is the notion of *compensation* for what Sturrock *et al.* (2004: 29) term 'chronic pollution of the child's ludic habitat' across spatial, temporal and psychic domains.

The spatial metaphors in these two examples evoke ideas of a once-existing Rousseauesque natural childhood when children were free to play untainted by the effects of modern progress. Children do not feature much in Lefebvre's political and spatial analysis, but he was equally concerned with the impact on everyday life of the modern neoliberal state. Writing in 1974 (but not published in English until 1991), he states:

The state is consolidating on a world scale. It weighs down on society ... in full force; it plans and organizes society rationally, with the help and knowledge of technology.

(Lefebvre 1991: 23)

The fundamental contradiction for playworkers within this discourse, however, is how playworkers can avoid a *colonisation* of children's play in a microcosm of state rational, technological and homogenising power described by Lefebvre (1991) and in the way suggested by Opie and Opie (1969: 10):

In the long run, nothing extinguishes self-organised play more effectively that does action to promote it. It is not only natural but beneficial that there should be a gulf between the generations in their choice of recreation ... If children's games are tamed and made part of school curricula, if wastelands are turned into playing-fields for the benefits of those who conform and ape their elders, if children are given the idea that they cannot enjoy themselves without being provided with the 'proper' equipment, we need blame only ourselves when we produce a generation who have lost their dignity, who are ever dissatisfied, and who descend for their sport to the easy excitement of rioting, or pilfering, or vandalism.

There has not, to date, been a comprehensive examination of how this fundamental contradiction might be theorised, and the interpretative application proposed here of the dialectical and political analysis of the production of space suggested by Lefebvre (1991) may offer some steps towards this.

The production of space

For Lefebvre, all human activity is situated in space. However, space 'is not a mere thing but rather a set of relations between things' (Lefebvre 1991: 83); as such it is *produced*. This idea forms a basic premise from which Lefebvre's ana-lysis is built. Key to this fundamental concept is the relation of space to power, and particularly to the power of the state, in thrall to the global economy and its processes of production, exchange, distribution and consumption. Any ana-lysis of children's play and of playwork that does not take this into account is less than complete. Playwork operates within a landscape dominated both by social policy initiatives and the actions of a neoliberal state operating within a global capitalist economy. The two are related.

In Lefebvre's conceptualisation of a unitary spatial theory, space is produced through the dialectical relationship among and between three dimensions or processes. Each embodies contradictions of dominance and agency, power and resistance, alienation and authenticity. These three dimensions/processes are:

1   Spatial practice (perceived space: *l'espace perçu*).
2   Representations of space (conceived space: *l'espace conçu*).
3   Representational spaces, sometimes translated as spaces of representa-tion (lived space: *l'espace vecu*).

Given the dialectic and interrelated nature of each dimension and Lefebvre's meandering and continually developing pronouncements on them, interpreta-tions of what each dimension entails vary considerably. Such ambiguity is entirely in line with Lefebvre's approach to epistemology, and it also confers licence upon the current study; that is, to see how the dimensions and their interrelationship might throw light upon the dialectics of playwork. Given that the production of space emerges from the dialectical and interdependent rela-tionship between all three dimensions, a brief introduction is given on each dimension, with the ensuing application to playwork encompassing their inter-relation, finally illustrating this through an extract from the field notes.

Spatial practice/perceived space refers to the materiality of everyday life, the embodied experiences of social activity and interaction, and to the way in which elements of everyday life are connected. Daily routines are carried out in fragmented, separate spaces designated for specific use (work, home, leisure), and much of spatial practice is concerned with the routes and networks that connect these separate spaces. A paradox arises because the connections high-light the separateness, fragmentation and atomisation of daily life. Spatial prac-tice also 'ensures continuity and some degree of cohesion' (Lefebvre 1991: 33).

Spatial practice is concerned with the relations between production, con-sumption, distribution and exchange. These determine daily routines and the separateness of activities. The drudgery of the daily grind of work (encapsulated in the French phrase *metro-boulot-dodo*) can lead to a sense of emptiness, a sense of disconnection between everyday life and the meaning of life, with escape often being sought in material consumption (shopping, entertainment and other leisure pastimes).

Lefebvre offers an extension of Marx's concept of *alienation*, seeing it as 'a fundamental structure of human practice' (Kelly 1992); this may be understood also in terms of the interrelationship between his three dimensions of the production of space. Kelly (1992) describes the three-staged evolution of human activity where spontaneous responses (in the case of this study, children's play) become rationalised and organised (through the provision of separate adult-designed and controlled spaces) and eventually fetishised. Abstract ideas emerge (for example, adult representations of children's play or the nature and value of playwork), and become reified within a capitalist framework of production, exchange and consumption. This materialised abstraction then takes on a life of its own and ends by dominating (Charnock 2008).

Representations of space/conceived space refers to the mental space of cartographers, planners and architects. For Lefebvre, this is the dominant space of state/capitalist power and discipline; experts and professionals impose ideologies and logic on to space through both design and discourse. *Representations*, within such hegemonic epistemologies, mediate between presence and absence (Shields 1999). The authoritative statements of experts both mask the absence of meaning and turn abstract ideology into a felt reality. The power of representation may be seen in adult rational representations of childhood and play, and through play's reduction to a thing that then takes on a powerful life and logic of its own, masking the absence of children's subjective experiences while rendering them fixed and knowable and open to adult manipulation.

While conceived space does not determine spatial practice (the two are in a dialectical relationship with each other in the production of space, as design is often a response to, and effort to control, particular forms of spatial practice), the power of the experts is evident. Rationality and efficiency tend towards the planning of separate spaces for specific functions: the industrial quarter, the shopping centre, the university campus, residential suburbs and, of course, the playground. Such rationality also leads to a homogenisation of space, evident in town and city centres, the branding and signage of multinational corporations, in housing estates, and in the design of what has been termed the KFC playground (Kit, Fence and Carpet) (Woolley 2008), or in a more contemporary label of 'natural' play areas with ersatz rocks manufactured from fibreglass.

Spaces of representation/lived space: Much theorising on space, including that from childhood studies and playwork, is restricted mostly to these two dimensions of the production of space. Yet, with Lefebvre, there is always a third (Schmid 2008).

If *perceived* space is concrete and material and *conceived* space is abstract and mental, then *lived* space is the space of imagination, emotion and meaning (Harvey 2006). It is the space where people can be whole (*l'homme total*), the space of dis-alienation. Lived space defies attempts to be exhausted through theoretical analysis; there is always a surplus that remains inexpressible through representation and can only be expressed through artistic means (Schmid 2008). This is the space of the *oeuvre*, the authentic work of art, rather than the produced commodity (recognising a dialectical relation between the two); it is the space of emotion, affect, non-representation, the space of resistance to the hegemony of capitalist representations of space and spatial practice. This, in effect, is the space where play resides.

The production of spaces for play

Playworkers' articulations about their work and their understandings of play tend to be couched in a number of discourses and models of practice that are often tacit, borrowed from other work with children and contradictory. They also tend to reside in epistemologies embedded in conceived and perceived space. Sutton-Smith (1995: 283) suggests that 'We treat play too often as a separable text, when in fact it always exists complexly interacting with the various contexts – human and symbolic – of which it is a part'.

In Lefebvre's lived space, playful *moments* are interwoven into the routines of daily life as an antidote to the humdrum and as a way of disordering the expectations of more powerful others. Such moments are seen as 'authentic' and 'break through the dulling monotony of the "taken for granted"' (Shields 1999: 58).

Much play scholarship highlights the paradoxical nature of play, in that it is both a part of the real world and apart from it, that it steers a contradictory path between the rational and the irrational. Sutton-Smith (1999) says that in play children appropriate aspects of their everyday worlds and turn them upside down or rearrange them in ways that render life either less scary or less boring for the time of playing. In a similar vein, Henricks (2006) suggests that play represents a *trans*forming rather than *con*forming stance, giving the player a sense of being able to change external conditions. Adult ordering of time and space is inverted or subverted.

A further paradox to be considered here concerns the value of play. Key characteristics of play (for example, redundancy, spontaneity, emergence, uncertainty, flexibility, unpredictability and self-organisation) point to its non-utility; in this sense its value is intrinsic. Yet, given that play has evolved and persisted across all mammal species, it would seem that it has some instrumental value too (Sutton-Smith 1997). The question of value is further complicated when adults become involved, and further still when those adults are paid through the public purse. Why should children's play be a matter for public policy, and what might the impact be of the involvement of a neoliberal, capitalist state? Such questions require consideration of the place of play within conceived and perceived space epistemologies.

The history of play provision shows that there has always been a link between the concerns of policy makers regarding children and young people and the rationale for spending public money on providing places where they can play (e.g. Brehony 2003; Cranwell 2003, 2007; Hart 2002; Kozlovsky 2008; Woolley 2008). The creeping incursion of New Public Management techniques of measuring effectiveness and quality of service (see e.g. Banks 2007; Dahlberg and Moss 2005; Moss 2007), alongside the dominant developmentalist paradigm for understanding childhood as a period of preparation for adulthood, has fed the growth of universal, standardised and technical interventions into the lives of children. The tools of such practices include National Occupational Standards that underpin vocational qualifications (SkillsActive 2010), quality assurance schemes, registration and inspection forms, initiatives such as the Early Years Foundation Stage, and the many monitoring forms required by funding bodies. Such procedures homogenise relationships and smooth over difference and particularity in favour of universality and standardisation. This has the effect of privileging *conceived* space (evidence-based policy and the justification of adult intervention) and *perceived* space (technical practice aimed at prescribed outcomes), thereby closing down opportunities for moments in *lived* space; although this can never be total, the dialectic arises because these forms of playing may be seen either as undesirable and subject to adult controls or (often at the same time) as authentic moments of playing that cannot be represented in terms of utilitarian value.

An increasing justification for interventions in the lives of children is one of human capital (Woodhead 2006). This economic model assumes that specific inputs (interventions) lead to predictable outcomes that will be of benefit to nations in terms of productivity in the global marketplace. Such a cost-benefit analysis may be seen in contemporary policy documents informing current policy initiatives on child poverty and early intervention in the UK (e.g. Allen 2011), which promote the need to focus on early years and school-readiness, with the purpose of education, outlined in the most recent UK education White Paper, being articulated in no uncertain terms in the Foreword:

> What really matters [in the education debate] is how we're doing compared with our international competitors. That is what will define our economic growth and our country's future.
>
> (Department for Education 2010: 3)

Such a stark statement regarding the purpose of education makes explicit the task of those within the children's workforce, including playwork: it is a form of labour to produce the nation's future workforce. It sets the social relations between adults and children into the broader global economic and political context. To consider the impact of this on playwork and on children's play requires something more than a decontextualised, universal child development theory purporting to be politically neutral.

Within this paradigm, firmly placed within conceived and perceived space, play becomes objectified and commodified, a tool for development in the interests of the capitalist economy. The planners residing in conceived space design spaces for play that are zoned and named (for example, the den-making area, the chill-out zone, the arts and crafts table, the home corner), aimed at encouraging particular forms of playing such as outdoor play, 'natural' play, risky play, social play, locomotor play, creative play, or indeed the full range of play types (Hughes 2002).

Play advocates often build a case for the benefits of play provision by asserting that it can contribute to physical and mental health, community cohesion, crime and antisocial behaviour reduction, and so on (see e.g. Davis 2007; Sutherland 2011). If play is colonised exclusively within this understanding, it becomes objectified and loses its defining characteristics: it is no longer autotelic, nor is it a display of children's power over real-and-imagined worlds. Ultimately, robbed of emotion and meaning, play itself becomes alienating, becoming less like play and more like work. Yet observations of children within playwork settings show that this is not the case: children will find ways to disturb the adult ordering of space and time in order to create spaces for play within lived space.

Vignette: the balustrade

The short vignette below is taken from field notes. It is preceded by a brief explanatory contextualisation and then analysed with reference to Lefebvre's triple dialectic to show how, even in the wake of a major 'kicking off' the previous week at the play centre, when a member of staff had been assaulted and a balustrade fence damaged, moments of shared playfulness still 'take place', but that these moments exist in an interdependent relationship with perceived and conceived space and rarely form part of playwork discourse or official recordings.

The 'kitchen' is an area of the hut separated off by a counter and a low gate. It is out of bounds to children unless a supervised activity is taking place. On the evening in question, some children were performing a play, and tradition says that the lights are out and torches used to light the performance.

> An interesting little episode just as we were closing. Kyle (15) is in the kitchen, having gone in under cover of the darkness during the performance and I follow.... He starts drumming on the paperwork – a pile of membership forms, warning forms, register, etc. I say 'OK, excellent drumming, let's have you out the kitchen now.' He goes to leave and sees the pile of bars from the balustrade [they had been kicked off the previous week] and picks one up. I try and stop him as he goes out, laughing and being jokey. He is very good at letting himself get caught and then just changing hands with the bar, so that each time I think I've got hold of it he swaps hands. It is a real tease. We are both laughing. He breaks loose and runs outside. I chase, but go back in knowing he'll come in the other door. I see his hat which has fallen off in the tussle. I pick it up and he realises I have something he wants. I suggest a simultaneous swap, and we're there, holding our trophies just out of reach of each other. My mind thinks, he won't give up the bar, I'll lose the hat, he's better at this than I am. We are laughing. It's a great game.
>
> (extract from field notes)

What the above vignette illustrates is the difficulty of distinguishing between play and non-play and the subtleties of power and control. It seemed to me that the rules of the centre (ostensibly residing in conceived and perceived space) actually provided a frame for playing with them in lived space. Going into the kitchen would not be so attractive unless there were the risk of being seen and then the power tussle of eviction. Kyle could play at power and control within the dialectic of being seen by peers to challenge authority and still being allowed to play. Kyle was taller than I, considerably more agile, he had a reputation for aggression and I did not have much of a relationship with him. We both knew our respective 'place' in the order of things. The age–power axis was crossed by the gender–power axis and set within the specific space that purported to be one that supported playing while at the same time seeking to normalise the challenging behaviour of lads such as Kyle. He was aware that I had seen him in the kitchen, and his taunting drumming was an invitation for me to try to remove him. I was drawn into the game whether I liked it or not. In conceived space, the kitchen area had a specific name and purpose, which was as an adult-only space occasionally used for supervised activities. Perceived space required that any adult seeing a child alone in the space should try to remove that child, and this was understood. Humour and playfulness were my chosen strategies (where might these have resided at the outset of the encounter?), but as the game progressed I became drawn into the moment and ended up giggling helplessly, partly out of genuine amusement and partly out of anxiety at how the situation might be resolved. The recording of the incident on Kyle's monitoring form for the additional support funding would not have articulated this as playing, and the space that was being produced was one of contestation and power as well as one of play.

Closing thoughts

This brief Lefebvrian analysis of playwork has highlighted the shortcomings of dwelling only in conceived and perceived space, and offered the idea of moments of authenticity in the playing of lived space as both a justification for the existence of playwork that can navigate the contradictions between conceived and perceived space as well as for playworkers' enjoyment of the role. My experience of spending time with the children and playworkers highlighted both the potential that some of these claims may be realised and also the impossibility of predicting this to be so with any accuracy without robbing the space of its authenticity and meaning. It seems to me that the use value of playwork resides in moments of lived space, yet these moments defy representation and therefore commodification. The successful co-production of a space where children can play through the dialectical interrelationship of all three dimensions of space will always be unpredictable, emergent and a site of contest and power.

Bibliography

Allen, G. (2011) *Early Intervention: Next Steps. An Independent Report to HMG.* London: Cabinet Office.

Allen, M. (1968) *Planning for Play.* London: Thames and Hudson.

Banks, S. (2007) 'Between Equity and Empathy: Social Professions and the New Accountability'. *Social Work and Society*, Festschrift for Walter Lorenz: Reframing the Social – Social Work and Social Policy in Europe.

Brehony, K. (2003) 'A "Socially Civilizing Influence"? Play and the Urban "Degenerate"'. *Paedagogica Historia*, 39(1): 87–106.

Charnock, G. (2008) 'Challenging New State Spatialities: The Open Marxism of Henri Lefebvre'. *Manchester Papers in Political Economy, Working Paper 03/08*. Manchester: Manchester University.

Cranwell, K. (2003) 'Towards Playwork: An Historical Introduction to Children's Out-of-school Play Organisations in London (1860–1940)', in F. Brown (ed.) *Playwork Theory and Practice*. Buckingham: Open University Press, pp. 32–47.

Cranwell, K. (2007) 'Adventure Playgrounds and the Community in London (1948–70)', in W. Russell, B. Handscomb and J. Fitzpatrick (eds) *Playwork Voices: In Celebration of Bob Hughes and Gordon Sturrock*. London: London Centre for Playwork Education and Training, pp. 62–73.

Dahlberg, G. and Moss, P. (2005) *Ethics and Politics in Early Childhood Education*. Abingdon: Routledge Falmer.

Davis, L. (2007) *Free Play: Improving Children's Physical Health*. London: Play England.

Department for Education (2010) *The Importance of Teaching – The Schools White Paper 2010*. Norwich: TSO.

Douglas, N. (1916/1931) *London Street Games*. London: Chatto and Windus.

Hart, R. (2002) 'Containing Children: Some Lessons on Planning for Play, from New York City'. *Environment & Urbanization*, 14(2): 135–148.

Harvey, D. (2006) *Spaces of Global Capitalism: Towards a Theory of Uneven Geographical Development*. London: Verso.

Henricks, T.S. (2006) *Play Reconsidered: Sociological Perspectives on Human Expression*. Urbana and Chicago: University of Illinois Press.

Hughes, B. (2002) *A Playworker's Taxonomy of Play Types* (2nd edn). London: Playlink.

Kelly, M. (1992) 'Obituary: Henri Lefebvre, 1901–1991'. *Radical Philosophy*, Spring.

Kozlovsky, R. (2008) 'Adventure Playgrounds and Postwar Reconstruction', in M. Gutman and N. de Coninck-Smith (eds) *Designing Modern Childhoods: History, Space, and the Material Culture of Children; An International Reader*. New Jersey: Rutgers University Press, pp. 171–190.

Lefebvre, H. (1991) *The Production of Space*, trans. D. Nicholson-Smith. London: Blackwell.

Lester, S. and Russell, W. (2008) *Play for a Change: Play, Policy and Practice – A Review of Contemporary Perspectives*. London: National Children's Bureau.

Moss, P. (2007) 'Meetings Across the Paradigmatic Divide'. *Educational Philosophy and Theory*, 39(3): 229–245.

Newstead, S. (2004) *The Busker's Guide to Playwork*. Eastleigh: Common Threads.

Opie, I. and Opie, P. (1959) *The Lore and Language of Schoolchildren*. Oxford: Oxford University Press.

Opie, I. and Opie, P. (1969) *Children's Games in Street and Playground*. Oxford: Oxford University Press.

Play Board (1985) *Make Way for Children's Play: A Discussion Document on a Play Policy for the Future*. Birmingham: ACPR.

Playwork Principles Scrutiny Group (PPSG) (2005) *The Playwork Principles*. Cardiff: Play Wales.

Russell, W. (2010) 'Playwork', in T. Bruce (ed.) *Early Childhood: A Guide for Students*. London: Sage, pp. 312–324.

Schmid, C. (2008) 'Henri Lefebvre's Theory of the Production of Space: Towards a Three-dimensional Dialectic', in K. Goonewardena, S. Kipfer, R. Milgrom and C. Schmid (eds) *Space, Difference and Everyday Life: Reading Henri Lefebvre*. Abingdon: Routledge, pp. 27–45.

Shields, R. (1999) *Lefebvre, Love and Struggle: Spatial Dialectics*. Abingdon: Routledge.

Shields, R. (2011) 'Henri Lefebvre', in P. Hubbard and R. Kitchin (eds) *Key Thinkers on Space and Place* (2nd edn). London: Sage, pp. 279–285.

SkillsActive (2010) *National Occupational Standards for Playwork, Level 3*. London: SkillsActive.

Stallibrass, A. (1977) *The Self-respecting Child: A Study of Children's Play and Development*. Harmondsworth: Penguin.

Sturrock, G., Russell, W. and Else, P. (2004) *Towards Ludogogy Parts I, II and III: The Art of Being and Becoming through Play (The Birmingham Paper)*. Sheffield: Ludemos Associates.

Sutherland, F. (2011) *Childhood Obesity – An Opportunity for Play?* London: London Play.

Sutton-Smith, B. (1995) 'The Persuasive Rhetorics of Play', in A.D. Pellegrini (ed.) *The Future of Play Theory: A Multidisciplinary Inquiry into the Contributions of Brian Sutton-Smith*. Albany: State University of New York Press, pp. 275–295.

Sutton-Smith, B. (1997) *The Ambiguity of Play*. Cambridge, MA: Harvard University Press.

Sutton-Smith, B. (1999) 'Evolving a Consilience of Play Definitions: Playfully', in S. Reifel (ed.) *Play Contexts Revisited, Play and Culture Studies 2*. Stamford, CT: Ablex, pp. 239–256.

Woodhead, M. (2006) *Changing Perspectives on Early Childhood: Theory, Research and Policy*. Paris: UNESCO.

Woolley, H. (2008) 'Watch This Space! Designing for Children's Play in Public Open Spaces'. *Geography Compass*, 2(2): 495–512.

15 To play or to parent?

An analysis of the adult–child interaction in make-believe play

Peter Hopsicker and Chad Carlson

Finding the right recipe: introduction

The universal nature of make-believe games provides a fertile environment for an analysis of childhood playgrounds. For example, the game of House – a role-playing activity that centres on the mimicking of domestic duties – requires one player to portray a role, perhaps that of the 'chef', and another to portray a complementary role, perhaps that of the 'eater'.[1] Constant engagement and communication between these players is necessary for the creation and continuation of the game.

When both players in the game of House are children, the motivations, perspectives and attitudes towards the activity are relatively consistent. Each role-player pretends to be someone else while in some sense executing common domestic practices in an enjoyable fashion. However, the interjection of adult participation into a child's imaginary playground might entail some complexity. The nature of the game may change. While the child may take the lead role in 'cooking' this meal and the parent may support the illusion by 'eating' it, the parent has an obligation that trumps the activity in some notable ways – a parent is always a parent, and certain cultural expectations related to the child's proper growth and development warrant constant consideration in this 'real-life' role. The obligation of the parent as parent is imminent in the activity, since both parent and child recognize that the former has the ability to take control of the game's content and direction – or even end the game – at any time. How does this de facto parental role during participation in children's games affect the play of either the adult or the child? What ethical tensions exist?

What follows is an analysis of the adult–child engagement and interaction in the game of House, specifically related to kitchen and culinary behaviour. We will begin by situating the nature of make-believe play within the literature of well-known play scholars (Johan Huizinga, Roger Caillois and Bernard Suits) and highlight its qualities when the participants are not all children. We will then address ethical considerations for adults as they juggle the play-role of 'eater' and the ever-present responsibilities as 'parent' during the game of House. By doing so, we will show that significant ethical tensions and ambiguities confront the parent who participates in the child's imaginary world.

Setting the table: the nature of play and games

Scholars have described play in many different ways. Some see pure play as a very narrow and relatively rare phenomenon while others have identified it 'under nearly every rock in the social landscape' (Suits 1977: 117). This wide range of descriptions has led Randolph Feezell to develop a pluralistic conception of play, arguing that it may be understood as either behaviour or action; motivation, spirit, or attitude; form or structure; meaningful experience; or an ontologically distinctive phenomenon (Feezell 2010). Within this framework we will focus on the form or structure of House as a play activity in which the participants may or may not be in the play attitude.

Modern philosophical enquiries into ideas of play frequently cite Huizinga's formal characteristics of play. Huizinga suggests that play is a 'free activity' which must be undertaken voluntarily (Huizinga 1950: 13). Generally, those playing House do so of their own volition. A parent can easily refuse a child's invitation to play and do something else, and a child can voluntarily choose to play on a swing set or ride a bike instead. Huizinga further suggests that play must absorb the player 'intensely and utterly', proceeding in its own 'proper boundaries of time and space according to fixed rules in an orderly manner' (Huizinga 1950: 13). Although the demarcation of play space may not have clear lines and the play time may not involve a clock, the game of House clearly has its own space and time. The real time of day and the location of the faux kitchen have relatively little importance.

Huizinga places considerable weight on this 'outside of ordinary life' contingency of play, identifying such activities as being 'not serious' to the daily necessities and duties of survival (Huizinga 1950: 13). While preparing actual meals is an ordinary function of most people's lives and may be viewed as an act of survival, doing so in a play-kitchen with artificial food clearly places this activity in the 'not serious' category, even though 'some play can be very serious indeed' (Huizinga 1950: 5).

Relatedly, Huizinga suggests an intrinsic quality of play connecting it with no 'material interests' or 'profits' and having its aim only 'in itself' (Huizinga 1950: 13). This claim has collected some criticism. While the parent may not come away from playing House with anything tangible (the profit simply being 'parent–child' time), the child may gain skills that may be used later in the ordinary world – as the skills necessary for successful House play and those necessary for success in a real-life kitchen bear stark similarities. Players of all ages continually develop and learn during their play experiences. However, it is an embodied learning of which we are rarely aware while we play.

Skill development of this sort is an extrinsic benefit from the game of House much like cardiovascular health develops from recreational jogging. We can look back on our play experiences to notice the skill development, but that is not why we play. A child may not realize that she or he is acquiring these skills during House, but the appropriate real-world actions at the real-world dinner-table after playtime can arguably be a profit to the child, the parent and society.

Thus, while the child is caught up in the moment with intrinsic motivations during play, he or she often comes out of it having gained something extrinsically valuable. These unintended consequences of play allow us, metaphorically, to have our cake and eat it too.

While it seems self-evident that the child is at play during the game of House, the parent's participation comes with added complexity. While House may be fun, enjoyable 'parent–child' time, the game also presents a strikingly appropriate opportunity for the parent to prepare the child for the real world. Would that prudence preclude the adult from play or lessen the quality of play? A tension may exist here. The adult's dominant motivation for participating in House may be ambiguous. Is the parent playing or teaching real-world preparation? Which motive is driving participation in the game? If the parent comes to the table seeking only to provide the child with this latter profit, then she or he is parenting while the child is playing. The parent is, in Suits' lexicon, failing to play the game and is a 'dramatically enabling device … a non-playing participant intentionally performing the complementary role' simply to develop the child's practical culinary skills and etiquette (Suits 1978: 118–120). However, if the parent enters the miniature kitchen just to participate in the non-serious event, then he or she is more likely to have the play-spirit just like the child. Perhaps the parent has mixed motivations.

Caillois helps us understand the adult's potential perspectives in this scenario. He presents four categories that describe the landscape of play activities – competitive, chance, mimicry and vertigo (Caillois 2001: 12).[2] Mimicry best encompasses the game of House. In this category, the player 'plays at believing, at pretending to himself, or at making others believe that he is someone other than he is' and 'temporarily forgets, disguises, and strips his own personality in order to be another' (Caillois 1988: 11). By mimicking the actions and roles of a chef in a play-kitchen, the child pretends to be a cook.

However, Caillois' definition of mimicry does not appear to clarify the tension created with adult participation. While the child can take on the role of chef and largely forget real-life responsibilities with seemingly few consequences, the adult may find the role of 'eater' competing for priority with the responsibilities (and sensibilities) as 'parent'. The parent may find it difficult or inappropriate to be fully absorbed in this type of mimetic play for any number of reasons (the parent may also find it difficult or inappropriate to be fully absorbed in parenting). If this is the case, how is the adult involved in mimicry?

The appetizer: the experiential landscape

In order to best understand the parent's potential landscape of practical experiences, we offer an explanation of two contrasting attitudes a parent may have while playing House – the 'parent first, player second' adult and the 'player first, parent second' adult. Sometimes the adult prioritizes parenting over playing to the extreme. This ultra-prudent mind-set may lead the parent to take control of the activity, inhibiting play to a large extent. While there may be moments in which the parent is at play, these are only shallow and brief interludes among corrective feedback to the child. This parent might be engaged in a two-person, two-role, one-player game in which the parent is simply a dramatically enabling device perpetuating the child's game (Suits 1978: 111). The adult positively reinforces the child's appropriate actions in the kitchen by enthralling the latter with positive 'yummy' sounds when the parent pretends to eat the food. The child – a success – may feel pride in getting it right. If the child did not act in the appropriate manner when preparing the food, if she or he uses refried beans instead of coffee beans to brew coffee, for example, the adult may respond with a verbal reprimand, displeasure through facial contortions, and body language that exemplifies someone who had just eaten something rotten. The child – a failure – may feel shame that he or she acted inappropriately.[3]

This 'parent first, player second' adult is largely failing at playing the game, but is in many ways succeeding at parenting the child. Early on in the development of the child-player, this may be appropriate at times. The child may have very few skills with which to play the game of House for any substantial period of time. After all, a young child may be new to the game of House and to standard dinner time protocol, generally speaking. However, if the parent continues this type of behaviour, even as the child develops skills in the game of House, the elder may come to be a 'play-inhibitor' (Carlson 2011: v). That is, the adult may, through incessant teaching and correction, drain the fun out of House and discourage the child's interest in the activity. By continually admonishing the child's actions, the parent takes control of the game and encourages the child to be subservient.

In this example, the adult's efforts to play are clearly secondary to parenting. The illusion of using plastic food and miniature dinnerware may mimic the preparation of real food in ordinary life, but the responsibilities of 'father' or 'mother' – the ordinary self in the course of ordinary events – take precedence (Suits 1978: 119). The parent wants the child to learn socially acceptable kitchen behaviour. When the parent relegates playing far below parenting, she or he may not experience much of the play attitude. Consequently, the child may lose the play-spirit in these settings too.

The 'player first, parent second' adult prioritizes playing over parenting to the extreme. This playful mind-set may lead the parent to submit to the child's every whim, allowing the youngster to control the activity. This hedonistic adult as consummate player fully engages in play with disregard for parental responsibility or teachable moments – much like Aesop's 'Grasshopper'. This parent may do whatever it takes to continue playing at all costs. He or she will respond to the child's behaviour – skilful or unskilful in the game of House – in ways that perpetuate the child's play, even if this means turning away from parental responsibility.

In this case, House could turn into a reckless food fight or a destructive game of 'Let's Demolish the Kitchen'. As the parent stays focused on playing, she or he may very easily affirm the child's silliness or inappropriate behaviour in the kitchen as acceptable real-world behaviour, even though this behaviour may not necessarily be harmful in the play kitchen. Without any parental guidance the child might stand on the faux oven, put a stuffed animal in the faux microwave, or throw faux plates around the room. While the parent knows that this type of uncontrolled behaviour could have detrimental real-world consequences, he or she follows the child's lead to ensure the continuation of play. Herein, the child takes control of House, and the parent submits to any of the child's play impulses. Accordingly, the adult is in large part succeeding at playing (regardless of what the particular game may be), but is in some ways failing at parenting because of the unwillingness to honour the socially accepted rules of House that also mimic socially acceptable behaviours in the real kitchen. When the adult relegates parenting far below playing, the child's behaviours may get out of hand.

The previous examples of play that we have seemingly condemned may in fact be healthy play activities in certain instances. The parent and child may both understand that, within the play frame, these activities are 'not real'. However, House is a particular type of play activity that has certain behaviours and meaning structures. Playing the game of House includes abiding by certain broad parameters that help distinguish it from other play activities. Thus, while inappropriate children's behaviour in a faux kitchen may be harmless play at times, the game of House presents a more structured play frame than any spontaneous or frivolous behaviour.

In the end, a blend of the 'parent first, player second' and 'player first, parent second' characterizations may be the healthiest position for 'daddy' or 'mummy'. The parent and child may find optimal experience when the elder maintains a playful attitude without relinquishing parental oversight. Yet how does the parent avoid the pitfalls of unplayfully parenting or playfully forgetting responsibilities? The tension of 'to play or to parent' may be pacified by a creative adult who plays more freely while still honouring parental responsibility. Perhaps we can glean some insight on this balancing act from Suits' arguments.

The entrée: script writing and 'good lines'

Suits identifies four basic features of make-believe games. First, a make-believe game is performed 'for the purpose of evoking a dramatic response, or is such a response, or is both' (Suits 1978: 110). The child's action of serving the parent a 'freshly baked' play cookie is performed to provoke a response from the adult – a happy expression that pretends the cookie tastes good or a sour expression that depicts a bad taste, for example. The adult's responses to the child's actions create the next line in a script that is written while it is enacted. This self-perpetuating script writing constitutes the second basic feature of make-believe games (Suits 1978: 112). The third feature is the willingness by each participant to be duped and to attempt to dupe the other (Suits 1978: 106). The child attempts to dupe the parent into believing that the former actually made a pizza. The parent attempts to dupe the child into thinking that the pizza tastes good. Finally, each make-believe player attempts to continue this role-playing by dispensing 'good lines' and expecting 'good lines' in return. If the daughter serves a make-believe hotdog, and the parent proceeds to clean the floor with it, the adult has not returned a 'good line' for the child's 'good line' in the conventional game of House (Suits 1978: 131). Even though such a response may be playful in a silly or goofy way, it does not perpetuate a realistic chef/eater script. It may, however, be a 'good line' for a different game of House in which the chef is serving a visitor from outer space who knows nothing of Earth.

Suits places games of make-believe and the required exchange of 'good lines' into a larger category he calls 'open games'. In contrast to 'closed games' that have an 'inherent goal whose achievement ends the game', such as crossing a finish line, 'open games' are defined as a 'system of reciprocally enabling moves whose purpose is the continued operation of the system' (Suits 1978: 131, 135). Suits equates 'open games' to ping-pong rallies. The goal is to keep the dramatic action going. Each move is a response to its previous move as well as a stimulus for the next move. The worst kind of move in an open game is the 'unreturnable serve' in ping-pong – the truly 'bad line' that irreconcilably destroys the illusion, such as a parent who throws the kitchen table across the room when served 'unsatisfactory' food (Suits 1978: 135). This 'bad line' temporarily suspends or ends this particular open game.

The reciprocation of 'good lines' in open games implies at least two things. First, the roles in House as a make-believe game are somewhat defined. The chosen roles have an approximate fittingness that separates 'good lines' from 'bad lines' (Suits 1978: 131). Responding with 'good lines' means that one is succeeding at playing the game. 'Good lines' are necessary for the game because 'bad lines' ruin the game. Second, being able to make the role believable is intimately tied to the players' experience and skill in that role. The child's youth and inexperience in real kitchen settings may create uncertainty in the role of chef. The youngster may need gentle suggestions and guidance to define the appropriate actions and responses in the role of chef. A primary challenge for the young child in the make-believe game of House is skill-related – to successfully provide 'good lines' to the parent.

It appears that this is where the proprietary role of parent in these make-believe games becomes significant. While the adult's intention may be to *play* House with the child, the latter may initially need the former's help to *learn* the chef's role. Doing so is, in many ways, similar to teaching a child the 'rules' of a sport or a board game. The parent must guide the child based on real-world criteria and rules. Thus, the parent must also guide the child based on the rules of that particular game of House, which may vary from household to household. The parent may embrace nonsense and turning the kitchen upside down. If this is a response to the child, this is the play attitude and a 'good line' response but the game is no longer House. To continue the game of House, the parent might playfully point out potentially dangerous situations (minding a hot stove), practical applications (carefully handling eggs) or social norms (washing used silverware). The child may have some idea of how to play House, but the adept adult can perpetuate this game with 'good lines' that help keep the child skilfully within the defined boundaries of what Caillois calls the 'institutional existence' of the role (Caillois 1988: 11).

This discussion suggests that, at times, the parent and child may be involved in different levels of play – even if both are giving 'good lines'. Caillois delineates this potential variety in the meaningfulness of games when he applies a sliding scale to his four categories of play. This scale ranges from *paidia* ('low level improvisation and gaiety') to *ludus* ('high level resolution of deliberately created complications'). Applying his scale to House indicates that the child is most likely participating in 'childish imitation; masks; and costumes' – *paidia* – while the adult's participation may be more mature like 'theatre' – *ludus* (Caillois 1988: 11). The parent and child may not be participating in two distinctly different forms of play but they may be doing so at qualitatively different levels.[4]

Interestingly, as the child's skill level increases at House, the child's play may come closer to matching the adult's more refined *ludus*. Accordingly, as an adult becomes more comfortable with mature play forms, she or he may come to better appreciate this deeper interaction. The child will deliver fewer and fewer 'bad lines' and the adult will find a diminishing need to correct 'bad lines'.

The dessert: to play and to parent

Inevitably the child's skill increases with age and experience. Fink, however, has argued that age inherently decreases one's ability to experience the joys of play. For ageing players – especially children becoming adolescents – House often becomes an increasingly unattractive playground. While the child 'shows more freely the characteristics of human play', the adult 'shows less and less of the grace of play'. Ageing discourages play as 'the rude storms of life get the upper hand'. Real life 'uses up the vital energies of the adolescent', Fink explains, and 'as the serious side of life asserts itself, the importance of play diminishes' (Fink 1995: 102).

Thus, House, like certain other children's play activities, provides only a fleeting window of opportunity for a parent and child to share play experiences, since the child's skills and attitudes continually change. How can the adult who is constantly tested to 'keep the game going' by negotiating the tension of 'to play *and* to parent' – to create 'good lines' that help the child play *and* develop as a skilled make-believe player – make the most of this fleeting, unique and special experience, yet remain on solid moral ground?

There is clearly a great deal of middle ground between 'parent first, player second' adult and 'player first, parent second' adult. An adult outside of these two contrasting extremes is able to cultivate the child's play by giving 'good lines' to those received and is also able to cultivate the child's kitchen and culinary skills by giving corrective feedback that is disguised, hidden or blended into those 'good lines'. A creative adult in this middle area may give skill-developing feedback to the child by changing voices to become the cook's boss or a concerned customer instead of stopping the game and giving parental advice. While doing so, the adult may be acting with great moral responsibility.

The parent is developing the child's ability to engage in autotelic experiences – play – and also happens to be enabling the child to develop skills in kitchen and culinary tasks.

But it is not easy to act in this manner, as doing so may require the adult to be a grudging or reluctant parent as well as a cautious but creative player. This 'player *and* parent' adult must extend an arm towards the child's play world while keeping his or her feet firmly trenched in parenting. In fact, in order for the adult to truly succeed at this balance, she or he may have to stretch an arm further towards the tenets of play to compensate for the de facto and obvious parental power over the child. However, this stretch should not pull one's feet from the home base of parenting. We suggest that it may be at this stretched and tenuous point where the highest quality of House – played between child and parent (with consummate play *and* parent attitudes of the latter) – is realized.

We also suggest that creatively navigating this tension may result in a rewarding experience for the parent and the child. House is best when both parent and child feel good about their time together. When these experiences are couched in play, the players may become addicted and crave more. This feeling pulls the parent and child back to the make-believe playground. It may be this unique experience of engagement and communication provided by games such as House that creates such profound memories of childhood. It is therefore ironic that while, at face value, House may not seem like a difficult game to play, it becomes much more complex and potentially overwhelming for the adult if this moral perspective and importance is considered.

Doing the dishes: scrubbing with a morality brush

From this framework, we can identify two challenges the parent faces in securing solid ethical footing when participating in the game of House – one of skill and one of power. First, in addition to the child, the parent must also have particular role-playing skills. The parent must have the skill to disguise or hide the parenting in the 'good lines'. This will, undoubtedly, require the creative adult to negotiate the tendencies to over-parent or over-play. In the end, the parent's lack of skill when invoking theatrical and creative scripts would inhibit the opportunity for playful and practical exchanges while exemplary skill would enhance it.

Second, the creative adult must encourage a healthy balance of power or control in the 'parent–child' activity. The adult takes on too much power by over-parenting, making the child merely an unenthused and subservient pupil. The adult gives up too much power by over-playing, allowing the child to become dictator of the activity without conscientious thoughts or objectives. This tension exists in all play, but becomes more visible when adults enter the fragile play worlds of their children. After all, because of their age, adults often find themselves initially as foreigners, immigrants or expatriates in the play worlds of children.

Yet even an expatriate can learn the customs of long-forgotten worlds. Doing so with moral considerations, however, requires the adult to constantly consider parenting and profit *with* play and pleasure – 'to play *and* to parent'. For the sake of profit, the parent should embrace the direct implications House may have to the child's future well-being. This is succeeding at parenting – being a good father or mother. By succeeding as a parent, the adult is confronting social expectations – the need to produce educated, well-behaved, practically skilled members of society. Parents who would choose to let their children run wild by neglecting to teach social mores may be considered, as Meier suggests, 'irresponsible, foolish and incompetent, if not positively demented'. From this perspective, the playing of House is justified because of its 'utilitarian functions of learning, socialization, and general preparation for later life' (Meier 1988: 191–192). To ignore such benefits can possibly be detrimental to the child's development into adulthood.

In addition, and for the sake of play, the adult should embrace the joy of the intrinsically interesting moments of House with the child. This is succeeding at the game – being a good player. By succeeding at the game or as a player, the parent is encouraging the child to be a part of the play community – and to remain so, in some form, throughout life. 'To play is to play together, to play with others', Fink writes. 'It is a deep manifestation of human community' (Fink 1995: 105). Building community can develop as children work together with peers or parents in make-believe activities such as House or in any other play activity. In order to prolong the exchange of dramatic action in these activities, the players must cooperate to be sure that 'good lines' are consistently being exchanged for 'good lines' or that implicit and explicit rules are followed. Failure of the playmates to cooperate in this manner destroys the game and limits the possibilities for developing community.

Simply, the adult would do well from a moral standpoint to teach profitable skills *while* promoting and maintaining intrinsic interest in the make-believe illusion. The reverse is also true. The adult would be on solid moral ground when attempting to maintain the play-spirit in 'parent–child' interactions while creatively including profitable, teachable concepts that would be valuable in the growth of the child and society. After all, play has been described as among our deepest and therefore most worthwhile experiences, but the adult needs to find the skills to do so quickly. Playtime is fleeting for all the while the child is growing up, learning new skills and gaining other interests while the real world asserts itself.

From the kitchen to the world

In make-believe House, the intentions and desires of the child to have fun and *mimic* the proper roles found in a real-life house meet the intentions and desires of the adult to have fun and *teach* the child the proper roles found in a real-life house. The parent and the child arrive in the play kitchen with the plan of participating in make-believe activity, to take on particular roles, and to work cooperatively to foster a prolonged exchange of dramatic actions and creative lines in a script that is written as it is enacted. It is this mutual desire for the pleasure of quality play that binds the activities of House together, making this game fertile ground for teachable moments, creative expressions and memorable 'parent–child' time.

Perhaps the playing of House, based on its ability to afford these desserts, is one way in which humans of all ages can, as Kretchmar counsels, 'incorporate playful living into our ongoing narrative journeys in life' (Kretchmar 1994: 13). Playful living that will inevitably end when the parent and child playing House are called in for dinner.

Notes

1 While House may be open to the mimicry of a wide variety of household chores, the discussion here will focus on duties usually occurring in the kitchen for consistency.
2 Competitive play (*agon*) is that in which 'the winner appears to be better than the loser in a certain category of exploits'. Chance play (*alea*) is that 'in which winning is the result of fate rather than triumphing over an adversary'. Vertigo play (*ilinx*) is the 'attempt to momentarily destroy the stability of perception and inflict a kind of voluptuous panic upon an otherwise lucid mind' (Caillois 2001: 14, 17, 23).
3 In this discussion and what follows, we focus on a parent's positive or negative reactions to a child's 'cooking'. However, other reactions could exist – namely indifference, apathy, etc.
4 Caillois explains that *ludus* is 'complementary to and a refinement of *paidia*, which it disciplines and enriches. It provides an occasion for training and normally leads to the acquisition of a special skill' (Caillois 1988: 29).

Bibliography

Caillois, R. (1988) 'The Structure and Classification of Games', in W. Morgan and K. Meier (eds) *Philosophic Inquiry in Sport* (1st edn). Champaign, IL: Human Kinetics, pp. 7–16.

Caillois, R. (2001) *Man, Play and Games*, trans. M. Barash. Chicago, IL: University of Illinois Press.

Carlson, C. (2011) 'Agency in Play'. *iP-D!P: academic papers*, 5(22) (July): i–vi.

Feezell, R. (2010) 'A Pluralist Conception of Play'. *Journal of the Philosophy of Sport*, 37(2): 147–165.

Fink, E. (1995) 'The Ontology of Play', in W. Morgan and K. Meier (eds) *Philosophic Inquiry in Sport* (2nd edn). Champaign, IL: Human Kinetics, pp. 100–109.

Huizinga, J. (1950) *Homo Ludens: A Study of the Play-element in Culture*. Boston, MA: The Beacon Press.

Kretchmar, R.S. (1994) 'Qualitative Distinctions in Play', in G. Gebauer (ed.) *Die actualitat der sportphilosophie*. Cologne: Academia Verlag, pp. 3–14.

Meier, K. (1995) 'An Affair of Flutes: An Appreciation of Play', in W. Morgan and K. Meier (eds) *Philosophic Inquiry in Sport* (2nd edn). Champaign, IL: Human Kinetics, pp. 120–136.

Schmitz, K. (1988) 'Sport and Play: Suspension of the Ordinary', in W. Morgan and K. Meier (eds) *Philosophic Inquiry in Sport* (1st edn). Champaign, IL: Human Kinetics, pp. 29–38.

Suits, B. (1977) 'Words on Play'. *Journal of the Philosophy of Sport*, 4: 117–131.

Suits, B. (1978) *The Grasshopper: Games, Life and Utopia*. Toronto: University of Toronto Press.

16 Game over

Calling time on kidult accounts of masculinity[1]

David Webster

Video or computer games[2] are often rated as 18+ – for adults only. We don't blink when we notice that shops selling video games are full of adult men – making purchases for themselves. Extending this type of play into adulthood, most notably for young men, has become rapidly accepted as a cultural norm. While acknowledging that constructions of what it was to be a man in the past also included the idea of certain 'hobbies', the penetration of 'pure play' as represented by video games might be argued to be qualitatively distinct. Might these games construct a myopic account of masculinity in their in-game milieus?

Play as ethically variable

There's play and then there's play. This might sound like a banal commonplace, or a profound response to a Zen *koan*. Nonetheless, what I mean is that we need to be cautious. Too often those associated with the world of play, playwork and the philosophy around sport and games tend to gaze upon the notion of 'play' with, in evaluative or ethical terms, rather a benign and misty eye. While my ultimate concern here is not the ethically variable nature of whatever play is, that must be my first. It should not take too much reflection on the nature of play to establish its ethically variable status. Play can be a means to reconsider the nature and purpose of human existence, it can be fun, and it can lead us to healthier, happier lives. However, play could also exist in a context of bullying, abuse of power and malice. Some play may lead to outcomes we desire and approve, but there is no reason that we might not also see play as potentially leading to a validating of the strong over the weak, the denigration of the losing and the enforcement of pernicious hierarchies. Play is, in a literal sense, what we make of it.

Play and video games

When we think of adults and video games, we may be tempted to call to mind family-friendly TV ads, of tennis and bowling, and groups of friends sat around the console. This is a small[3] portion of the market. A thirteen-year-old boy told me that he saw the Wii as 'for girls and grannies'. 'Serious' gamers will have their Xbox360, PC or PS3 – and online connection. The bestseller on both Xbox360 and PS3 in 2011 was *Call of Duty: Modern Warfare 3*.[4]

In relation to one issue of gender and gaming, there is a small amount of work in this area already – which seems to immediately penetrate the public realm; for example, this piece from December 2008 in the *Daily Telegraph*:

> Playing on computer consoles activates parts of the male brain which are linked to rewarding feelings and addiction, scans have shown. The more opponents they vanquish and points they score, the more stimulated this region becomes. In contrast, these parts of women's brains are much less likely to be triggered by sessions on the Sony PlayStation, Nintendo Wii or Xbox. Professor Allan Reiss of the Centre for Interdisciplinary Brain Sciences Research at Stanford University, California, who led the research, said that women understood computer games just as well as men but did not have the same neurological drive to win.
>
> (Moore 2008)

The original piece (Hoeft *et al.* 2008) looks at brain chemistry, and uses MRI scans of gamers. Brains and wires may tell us something – but do they tell us whether this alleged gender difference has its roots in biology or culture? Even if we accept these studies whether the brain chemistry they reveal is causal, or a consequence, is not made clear at all. That is, one can read about cortexes, and MRI data – and still be left asking 'so what?' I am more interested in the cultural consequences, most notably political-cultural ones, of seeing a particular model of play embedded into our idea of what an adult male *is*, and how video games relate to this. What is worth noting, though, is the extent to which many video games *are* aimed at an adult male audience. While many under-18s do play them, a look at bestseller charts for games shows many as 18+ rated, very expensive (on expensive hardware), and with explicitly adult themes. Spend some time in a large high-street games retailer, and you will often find it full of young adult men, buying their own games. There will be women in the shop – and there is a female gaming subcultural grouping – but many of the women may also be purchasing 18+ games for their under-18 sons.

What I want to do initially is offer a blatantly provisional typology – and then look at what the phenomena at hand do to that typology. How do *I* see play? These seem to be ways in which we might read it:

- As relaxation – a gentle and temporary retreat. We might suggest that these games are merely fun. The violence is cartoon, the player wise enough to know the difference between games and reality, and no harm is done. Why are those outside the phenomena so judgemental about that which they understand in such a limited way?
- While I will return to the classic text *Escape Attempts* in this context later, I also want to think about how we might see games as a *line of flight* away from a life we find overbearing, absurd or intolerable. Deleuze and Guttari

have a short passage which, for me, typifies how we might conceive of these games in particular, and human endeavours in general:

> This is how it should be done: lodge yourself on a stratum, experiment with the opportunities it offers, find an advantageous place on it, find potential movements of deterritorialization, possible lines of flight, experience them, produce flow conjunctions here and there, try out continuums of intensities segment by segment, have a small plot of new land at all times.
>
> (Deleuze and Guttari 2004: 178)

- As socially constructed, permitted and authorised ways of 'letting off steam' that do not endanger structures of power and control. This moves beyond the idea of the first point: they seems harmless, and are *exactly* that. They have become the way in which many burn off their excess aggression and anger. You could read this in a number of ways. First, we could take a view echoing evolutionary psychology. We are violent species, which evolved in an environment of risk, where we needed to be on guard, react fast and often with violence. Now we live lives which are soft and cushioned, where we value 'soft skills', leaving us with an excess of aggression. These games do us a service by ridding us, without there being victims, of this excess. This overlaps with the notion of these games as the re-emergence of a sub-verted self – normally kept at bay by social pressures and norms.
- As existential self-expression/definition, being a means whereby we cannot find an inner self that already exists, there not being such a thing, but can begin to construct one. Of course, what type of self we might construct from the current gamut of available games might turn out to be rather a disturbing question.
- Before we plunge into the everyday I have another qualification to make: that we should not see the video game as too closely allied to all practices of play in hobbies, pastimes and enthusiasms. Video games are an element of the mass market entertainment industry. While the interactivity they embody allows us to see them as 'games' we 'play', we should note that they are perhaps often closer to watching television, or films, than they actually are to many other forms of play and gaming. We tend to think of them as being played, but they play us just as thoroughly.

Men of ages

A term which in a male context may seem a little dated in the twenty-first century is that of the 'hobby'. But for many in the past, the idea of a hobby cut across (to an extent) class barriers and was a relatively normalised aspect of our model of what it was to be a man. I have argued elsewhere (Webster 2012) that often hobbies can become an obsession, which tips over into mortality denial. But here I want to consider the second of these ideas of play: using Stanley Cohen and Laurie Taylor's 1976 book *Escape Attempts: The Theory and Practice of Resistance to Everyday Life*.

Reading this book now, there is the temptation of nostalgia. The sections on hobbies have a real feel of a male world which is gradually slipping away.[5]

> Hobbies are sometimes conceived of as sacrosanct escapes from the daily round – the spatial location in the garden, the games room, the cellar or attic reinforces this – and also as ways of dislodging the weight of everyday routine. But they remain, behaviourally and subjectively 'at home' for most people. The gardener, philatelist, pigeon breeder, trout fisher, model train enthusiast, is not pitting himself against a hostile and alien world. He is carving out some free areas within that world.
>
> (Cohen and Taylor 1976: 98)

Hobbies are notable for their gendered nature in our culture. To be a 'hobbyist' was almost always to be male.[6] A feature of this type of activity is how much it looks like work, but has no economic or practical benefit. Hobbies are not play in an obvious sense: when a man 'plays' with his model trains he does it seriously, with regard for 'realism'; when a philatelist arranges his collection it is ordered, neat and categorised. I have a theory about hobbies – which I have philosophical intuition rather than evidence for – so will outline it only briefly. In middle age, death hovers ever closer and less obscurely on the horizon, its breath is felt in the night, close at hand. Where do we find the middle-aged in their leisure time? Lost in a golf catalogue; deep down the hobbyist's rabbit hole of the mind: lost in the sweet bliss of mind-filling detail. Among the minutiae there is no room for other thoughts, of mortal decline, to intrude. So while we may be partly convinced by the *Escape Attempts* account of hobbies, I would supplement it with an account that attributed to hobbies the status of an alternative, less authentic response to the finitude of human life. A half-recognition of Heidegger's *Being towards Death*, that brings us not to face it full on, but to flee into a forest of details, reference numbers, charts or league tables. Heidegger, in *Being and Time*, refers to 'the evasion of death which covers over, dominates everydayness so stubbornly' (Heidegger 1996: 234). He talks of a 'constant tranquilization about death' (ibid.: 235), of how in our normal relation to death 'everyday being-toward-death is a constant *flight from death*' (ibid.: 235). William Large characterises Heidegger's insights as follows:

> Whenever I am occupied with something it fills my attention. I lose myself when I am involved and absorbed in the world. When, however, I am anxious of my death, then my whole life is visible to me in a moment. I ask myself, 'Why am I doing this?', 'How did I get into this situation?' I am not asking about this or that activity or occupation, but the significance of my life as a whole.
>
> (Large 2008: 93)

One might suggest that to demonstrate a mastery of these details – of this mass of data – stands in the place of a self-realisation, where the garden shed functions as a refuge from the real.

Nonetheless, while we may see an existential inauthenticity to hobbies, there are components of them that we might consider laudable. There may be craft skills (feasibly transferable); there is often care and attention to detail. They may inculcate modes of quiet reflection and contemplative stillness (like the fisherman in Zen-like repose[7]). While hobbies may be obsessive and a flight from life, it is clear that they also have the scope to be other, more benign, aspects of a rounded and well-lived human life.

Pure play

In terms of what we find in video games, they seem stripped back. Despite the graphics, the game play and labyrinthine plots, they are not a craft practice. You need to play with care, and indeed much skill, but it seems as though the action – the playing – is what there is. It is something akin to a pure form of a certain type of play. Thus we have this large constituency of young men engaging in a substantial amount of 'play': but what type of play might it be? How does it engage with my aforementioned provisional typology?

Relaxation

There is no doubt that video games can be relaxing and soothing. To play them is distracting and entrancing; we can forget time and our worries. However, when my idea of relaxing after a hard day is to sit in a dark room and simulate acts of murder and violence, further things are at work. 'All a bit of fun' seems to be inadequate as a means of capturing what is going on here.

An escape attempt

Returning to my concern with hobbies and our escape: Might video games be a form of more substantive escapism? Is the play of video games a *line of flight*, like a leap *over the wall* from our prison? We flee the drabness of our dirty, shabby, broken and obviously futile lives into a world where everything relies on us. Only *I* can save the hostages, kill the Nazi zombies or take command of the fleet. But where is the escape *to*? We could ask: Can any play act as a line of flight if it only takes us on a circular excursion, depositing us back in the same old life? Can a video game, like some other types of play,[8] leave us transformed? Have we successfully escaped our previous self?

Socially safe pressure release

Rather than allow the frustration I feel at inequality, social injustice, the stupidity of power, my own failed ambitions and the preposterous lives we lead to cause a rising pressure, leading to an explosion – a great rebelling and cleansing destruction – we manage to maintain the illusion that the world today is normal, and we can accept it. Is the violence and extreme nature of many games the very form of this practice? It is notable that the same games often appeal across national, political and class (if not always gender) boundaries. Might something about the appeal or function of these games go beyond the social context and relate to some kind of metaphysical underpinning? Perhaps they reveal something *inner* of us?

The real self

Under the surface, compressed and controlled by socialisation might lie the real me. This could be the self we suppress – and freed from responsibility, and encouraged by the content, in video games it bursts forth. We might be tempted by this kind of discourse. I would caution against such temptation, as it seems overegged. Perhaps it reveals an alternative self, but I am not sure I even understand what 'real self' means. Do we really believe in such essentialist accounts of personhood? I doubt many of us do, though we may imply as much in our use of language. I would argue that human personalities are subtle and we have many accounts and models of who we are, which we blend and present. Video games *may* allow the venting of some rage (if they don't make it worse[9]), the emergence of a version of us – but the discourse of 'real selves' is as hollow as it is tempting.

I would balk at the idea that for many people their real self is the ranting lunatic (troll) of the chat forum; the reloading and re-firing into a crowded room. Can we even argue that the game-emergent self in a video game is ours – and not a negotiated construction between game author, form of the medium and our subconscious?

Positive oblivion of mind/existential self-expression

This is all the rage for some kinds of embodied play be it via the faux-Buddhist dogma of 'flow', the discourse (so often in martial arts) of 'no-thought', of a qualitative opposition between thinking and being. This can even be represented such that play is a manifestation of 'being' in some philosophical sense. I find this hard enough to be persuaded by for embodied play, where we are things of sweat, pain and exhaustion. In playing a video game there *is* flow and self-forgetting – but the void is for a reason, often to allow a new filling – even in an explicit meditative context. The still calm of Buddhist *Samatha* meditation is to allow space for the mind to fill with a value-based suite of virtues. The stilled, in-the-zone mind of the gamer is open; but to what? A cynical answer might be that the mind of a gamer is open like the gaping jaw of a zombie – slack and without content. Perhaps we should see the self-forgetting and oblivion as negative, as total nihilism. In many video games the violence has no meaning other than as power and competence. Players skip cut-scenes, disregard plots – they want to get to the 'action', like a would-be masturbator fast-forwarding the porn film past the plot/set-up. 'Action' here is de-contextualised. Of course there are exceptions – and I want to hold in the end to a notion that video games have no intrinsic negative (or positive) features: the fears I have regarding the way they impact on masculinity and our broader culture are as a result of the specific construction of the models within current versions/games/gaming culture.

As a minor additional point in this context, we might indeed note that video games bring no health benefits, no useful skill, no embodied experience; so much of this is true that we might feel that they see the body as an obstacle and a retreat into a mind-only being. Nonetheless, there *is* a link to a key idea in sporting terms – to a sense of mastery and competence. In the light of the paragraph above, though, we might worry that it is a nihilistic mastery. Once the game is played, completed and resold it means nothing – barely even to the player. This echoes what I said earlier about the game experience leaving us unchanged. While some games, in theory, have the imaginative scope to do so, the majority seem a world away from even such an aspiration.

Beyond the game: a contrast to the hobby?

Is there not a case for arguing that video games as play fit into a model of neo-masculinity that is not a childlike wonder, or sense of self-ownership, or as existential psychic-reorientation, but as child-ish? Is there a repugnant phenomenon of self-inflicted arrested development being validated in young men by notions of play? Play is a healthy and important component of the human condition. As a metaphor for life, it offers cause for potentially instructive reflection. Nonetheless, it can overwhelm our broader character when it malfunctions. Obviously there are issues with the misogyny, violence, and the presentation of sex, race and culture in many video games. But this is not the primary issue here. My concern is to ask if video games validate, most notably among adult men, disengagement with social realities, responsibility and socio-political activity in the broadest sense. In a world where many view their socio-political duties as having been fulfilled by clicking a 'like' button on a Facebook campaign, these are serious matters.

So how do we address this?

What might change in men, as they become adults, that would take us away from this flight into perpetual youth, and therefore from adult reality? First, we need to admit who 'we' are. We are adults – not teens, tweens or kidults. The first thing to jettison is the temptation to remain in a teenage-like orbit of 'cool'. Many UK adults have been locked into the idea that the priorities of a 16-year-old are the full range of available options. That the greatest fear is not of ageing, sickness and death, but of being naff, uncool or out of touch. This carries out the existential function of shielding from view our ever-approaching death. We see the widespread fetishisation of youth culture all around us. Men in their thirties riding mini-scooters on the pavement; urban mothers pushing über-rugged three-wheel pushchairs with decals denoting association with snow-boarding clothes manufacturers; and adults walking around under the impression that a corporate anagram of a swear word is witty.[10] When adults 'consume' the products of youth culture, we must do so with a mix of humility and distance.

Humility first: we can appreciate youth culture, but we cannot *be* it. We will never know again what it is to look out of young eyes at an old world. This is someone else's party – we can enjoy it, but it's not being thrown for us. The second is the matter of 'distance' or even, perhaps, superiority. What do I mean by recognition of our distance from youth culture? I definitely do not mean an attitude of ironic detachment – the view that allows one to enjoy it and mock it at the same time. Surely people have got beyond the postmodern, faux-wry, kitsch-loving nostalgia-fest of the last decade by now? We may ♥1982, but we should not mistake the ability to name the Trumpton firecrew[11] as equivalent to scholarship. The 'distance' I mean is both born of the humility above, but also of a need to make critical judgements. So, I clearly do not mean that distance allows us to disengage our critical faculties; we should resist the temptation of a knowing-slacker smile at the nu-rebelliousness. That kind of approach is a betrayal of youth culture, but also of our own abilities as fully grown autonomous and discriminating subjects. Rather, we need to both acknowledge our experiential, existential distance from the products of youth culture, while not seeking a patronising assimilation of it via eclectic acquisitiveness. We might just about be able be participant-observers in youth culture, and perhaps it is best to view it through the lens of critical anthropology rather than as the gateway to any kind of cool/eternal youth/credibility. Once we have jettisoned the notion that authenticity and credibility are linked to some kind of pure essence of youth culture, we can come closer to seeing how an adult, contemporary masculinity might be considered.

Gaming at the end of history

We live in a period of Fukuyama-esque, post-ideological consumer choice. This is the view that the only choices are between second-order goods ('would you like fries with that?'; 'what do you buy?'). The possibility of choosing different first-order goods ('who should own the means of production?') is eclipsed by the ideology of post-ideology. We receive, culturally, the impression that only second-order choices exist so strongly, so resolutely and in such a non-problematised manner that we forget that there was ever a choice of primary values. Second-order, cultural and retail, choices – the minutiae of existence – come to be seen as the way we define ourselves. Life becomes Lifestyle, politics is instrumentalised, and self-identification is transformed into a process of label-affiliation and self-as-brand solipsism rather than personal and communal ideological commitments. So, what do we do about it? Is, as the Daleks would have it, resistance useless, or, as the Borg say, is it futile? The old tools seem blunted from too long striking brick walls. To put it another way: the assimilatory nature of capitalist cultural strategy is subtle and canny. When the images of resistance, the old heroes, are seen now the gun is gone from their hand and their face is on a T-shirt. In a system that claims not to be a system, can philosophising with a hammer still smash the state? In a culture where explicit ideological (or religious) commitment is often seen as naff, humorously nostalgic or as the vanguard of dangerous fundamentalist absolutism, the answer must be 'no'. The hammer will bounce off a system that has become flexible and pliant. So where does this leave our consideration of video games and (especially male) maturity?

Am I arguing here for all video-game play as a form of futile gesticulation, and the wasting of a valuable human life, often one with the potential and resources to do good in the world? Partly – but not entirely. Video games are amazing – people become so drawn in because they are fantastic – compare them to the games of twenty years ago. There is great potential to draw us beyond ourselves and offer the things we value in that medium that class and intellectual snobbery would place at the opposite end of a qualitative spectrum: books. Books are immersive, narrative, non-physical (weakly, bookish children were often told to get more fresh air – but reading books is now an activity children are encouraged to engage in), and somewhere we lose ourselves, in imagined worlds, but also a place where we are challenged by new and uncomfortable (sometimes big) ideas. There is no intrinsic reason that video games cannot offer this too, but this potential is a long way from being realised.

A paradox of imagination

Play can be a route to *establish* meaning by stripping away artifice – not as a means to construct artifice. If we can be anything (like a Second Life body designer), what a chance to rehearse worlds, means of interaction, social ideals and more.[12] At the moment, perhaps too much of this is bogged down in buying a larger penis for your purple dragon – but there could be more. The slogan of so many on the left: *another world is possible* – might not games be the place to work out where and how? However, I am sure that if we want a world populated by emotionally stunted, solipsistic, apolitical men, then video games are more than capable of assisting in delivering it. The open question is: Can they be an ally in delivering another kind of man, for another kind of world?

Beyond doom

Video games can be part of nihilistic flight from death; a buried flight into detail. They can be progenitors of a fierce new masculinity of aggression and violence. They can turn us into perpetual children: not childlike with wonder, but childish: spoilt, whining about our lot as we sit in comfort deriving entertainment from the extremes of war and violence that many have to endure as reality. But we should also remember that they can be whatever we choose – but choosing to disengage from them would be to cede the ground to what is already there. If we are to take this seriously – I would suggest that while some will no doubt re-invent the video game in better, creative and exciting ways – the real issue is twofold. First, what might a better, more challenging video game culture

look like? Second, we may decide that before such questions can be answered
our contemporary and ongoing reconstructions of what it means to be a man in
the twenty-first century need attention. Rather than the indulged and pam-
pered, faux-tough buffness of Men's Health, or the retreat behind the screen,
what we surely need is the idea of men (and women) as agents in a shared world,
where video games retain their absorbing pleasure and thrill, but somehow are
reimagined as a conversation with our external reality, rather than acting as a
mere, and possibly inauthentic, flight from it.

Notes

1 This is not an engagement with the extant literature on this topic, but the reflections
and concerns of an outsider who is very much 'looking in through the window' to the
world of play. It represents an exercise in philosophy, rather than being an academic
critique of what others have said on this topic.

2 I will treat them as the same thing for this piece. I am sure purists will be outraged.

3 Nonetheless, it is growing. *Zumba Fitness* was a surprise entry in the 2011 bestsellers
across all formats at number four: www.eurogamer.net/articles/2012–01–11-the-best-
selling-uk-video-games-of-2011 (accessed 2 October 2012).

4 Other top-grossing titles were similar war-fests such as *Battlefield 3* and *Gears of War
3*.

5 We can see a hint of the nostalgia for this in the picture/gift books of 'men and
sheds'.

6 Many of those things we now see as identified as 'women's' hobbies were once just
actual, real, necessary work. Baking, needlework, soap-making, crafting/quilting and
the like may now be seen as pastimes, but were once chores. There are some potentially interesting lines of sociological enquiry here.

7 I am conscious of a danger here of being overly sentimental or nostalgic about these
practices too. Many have also been a flight from wives, families and responsibility –
but I think the truth of this does not negate their positive potential.

8 I would argue this for some embodied activities, and perhaps for others. The person
completing a long run, or even a game of cricket, is not the same person who began
it: we are changed by it.

9 This is a debate I am now going to step away from – as even those *with* some empirical evidence seem unable to decide.

10 One is tempted to blame much of this on Madonna – her endless 're-invention' is a
tedious, tired trope of the press – but her leech-like clinging ('Hey Britney') is a
symptom, not a cause. She has fallen into the trap – she is both a victim and per-
petrator of the conflation of contemporary and youth culture. Many seem to forget
that youth is a transitional phase – between being an infant-child and a proper,
mature adult.

11 A 1970s UK children's TV show.

12 A tiny minority of games do seem to be trying to move towards some kind of social
action. www.urgentevoke.com/ seeks to be a 'ten-week crash course in changing the
world'. And despite appearing to be a little short on substantial politics (seemingly to
only imply micro-solutions), and being a little worthy, it has much of interest to
recommend it.

Bibliography

Cohen, S. and Taylor, L. (1976) *Escape Attempts: The Theory and Practice of Resistance to Everyday Life*. London: Routledge.

Deleuze, G. and Guttari, F. (2004) *A Thousand Plateaus*. London: Continuum.

Evoke. Available at www.urgentevoke.com/ (accessed 2 October 2012).

Heidegger, M. (1996) *Being and Time*, trans. J. Stambaugh. New York: SUNY.

Hoeft, F., Watson, C.L., Kesler, S.R., Bettinger, K.E. and Reiss, A.L. (2008) 'Gender Differences in the Mesocorticolimbic System during Computer Game-play'. *Journal of Psychiatric Research*, 42(4): 253–258.

Large, W. (2008) *Heidegger's Being and Time*. Edinburgh: Edinburgh University Press.

Moore, M. (2008) 'Men Enjoy Computer Games 'Because of Basic Urge to Conquer'. *Daily Telegraph* [online]. Available at www.telegraph.co.uk/science/science-news/3965269/Men-enjoy-computer-games-because-of-basic-urge-to-conquer.html (accessed 2 October 2012).

Webster, D. (2012) *Dispirited*. Alresford: Zero Books.

Index

procrastination 124
the project of 'trying-to-be-God' 110–15
Prout, A. 33
PS3 186
pure reflection 111–12, 117

Rabelais and His World (Bakhtin) 144
rationality 3–4, 21, 34, 41, 72, 122, 125, 136, 168
reason 1, 3–4, 15, 17, 35, 39, 49, 60, 72, 110, 114, 116, 122–4, 142, 150, 155, 158–9, 161, 185, 190, 193
reflection: impure 110; pure 111–12, 117
regulative rules 54–7, 62
repetition 24, 26, 91, 156, 164
representation 26, 100, 137, 139, 168
The Republic (Plato) 59
resistance 54, 105, 160, 167–8, 187, 192
resources, reallocation of 45–7
The Revolution Will Be Televised (BBC Three) 7
Rhees, R. 54, 58–9, 60, 62
rhetoric 59, 67, 71, 92, 135, 141–2, 145
rhizomatic thought 132–3
Rilke, R. M. 94, 105
role-play 175, 178
rough-and-tumble play 148
Rousseau, J.-J. 36, 166
Royce, R. 44, 46–8, 50
Royle, N. 161
rule-governed play 22, 24, 28, 54–7, 62, 142
rules, breaking 149

Sartre, J.-P. 2, 109; *see also Being and Nothingness*
saving power 153, 156
Schechner, R. 143
Schiller, J.C.F. von 3–4, 113, 122
Schleiermacher, F. 36
Schmid, S.E. 46, 48–50
Schmitz, K. 21, 28
Schulz, W. 94
scolding 146, 149
Searle, J. R. 54
Self Determination Theory (SDT) 49–50
Seneca, L. A. 120, 126
seriousness 3, 14, 20, 45, 47, 51, 60, 64–5, 77, 100, 103–4, 106, 109, 113–14, 117, 122, 135, 142, 144, 148; necessity of in playing 77; spirit of 114
Shakespeare, W. 32, 123, 126
significance of play 11, 152–3
skills development, play and 50, 176–8, 182
skydiving 127
Social Contract (Rousseau) 36
socio-cultural phenomena 150
Socrates 59, 61, 64–72, 82, 160

Some Thoughts Concerning Education (Locke) 37
sophisticated play 50, 52
sophistry 54, 59–61, 71
Sophocles 40
space: conceived 167–8, 170–2; lived 167–9, 171–2; perceived 167, 169–72; playwork and the production of 166–9; transcultural 8
Spariosu, M. I. 2–3, 142–3
spatial practice 167–9
spectator/spectators 19, 25–6, 65–7, 77–8, 98–106, 124, 145
Spielraum (play space) 100
Spinoza, B. 120, 126, 136, 138
spirit of seriousness 114
spoilsports 59–61, 77, 80
spontaneity 22–3, 27, 35, 40, 76, 169
sport: and the desire to win 28; Olympic athletics 18–19, 28; as play 18–19, 27–8; as source of attitudinal pleasure 20
state philosophy 132
Stewart, S. A. 143
story 4, 34–5, 38, 55, 89, 133–4, 152
subject 23, 25–6, 68–71, 75–6, 78–9, 81–3, 94, 132–4, 154–6, 159
subjectivity 21, 25–6, 39, 111, 113–16
the sublime 120, 124, 126–7
suffering 69, 106, 120, 122, 124, 127
Suits, B. (*see also* Suits' definition of play) 12–14, 17–19, 21–2, 26–9, 54–5, 60, 175, 177, 179–80
Suits' definition of play: Bäck's criticisms 50–1; direction of criticisms 48; and game-playing 44–7; Morgan's criticisms 47; persuasiveness of criticisms 46; as response to Wittgenstein 44, 52; Royce's criticisms 47–8, 50; Schmid's criticisms 48–9; types of play 50
surfing 127
Sutton-Smith, B. 15, 37, 138, 141–3, 169

Taylor, L. 187
technology 152, 156, 166
teleology 157
telos 157, 159
tennis 13, 18, 24, 27, 185
theology 35–7, 121, 155
theoros 66
Thomen, C. 127
Thomson, I. 154–6, 158, 160–1
Tillich, P. 121–2, 125–7
time 1, 13–15, 17–18, 20, 22–5, 34, 36–9, 41, 45–6, 48–9, 51, 56, 59–60, 66, 69, 76, 79, 89–92, 101, 104, 122–4, 128, 131, 134–5, 137–8, 141, 143, 146, 149–50, 152–5, 157, 161, 169–72, 175–8, 182, 184, 186–9, 191–3

31972430R00120

Printed in Great Britain
by Amazon